A Foreigner
Carrying in the
Crook of His Arm
a Tiny Bomb

✳

AMITAVA
KUMAR

A Foreigner
Carrying
in the Crook
of His Arm
a Tiny Bomb

Duke University Press
Durham and London
2010

© 2010 Duke University Press
All rights reserved
Printed in the United States of
America on acid-free paper ∞
Designed by Cherie Westmoreland
Typeset in Carter and Cone Galliard
with Sumner Stone's Magma Com-
pact display by Tseng Information
Systems, Inc.

Library of Congress Cataloging-in-
Publication Data appear on the last
printed page of this book

For Rob Nixon

||||||||||||||||||||||||||||||||||||||||||||||||||||||||||||||||||||||||||||||||||||||||||||||

Some years ago, I had written
that the West's political paradigm was no
longer the city state, but the concentration
camp, and that we had passed from Athens to
Auschwitz. It was obviously a philosophical
thesis, and not historic recital. . . .

GIORGIO AGAMBEN,
"No to Bio-Political Tattooing"

What is a foreigner?
A man who makes you think you are at home.

EDMOND JABÈS,
A Foreigner Carrying in the Crook of
His Arm a Tiny Book

||||||||||||||||||||||||||||||||||||||||||||||||||||||||||||||||||||||||||||||||||||||||||||||

 Contents

✳ Acknowledgments

First, the non-experts

In February 2009, a U.S. judge denied an injunction against force-feeding of detainees at Guantánamo by asserting that her court lacked the necessary competency to administer justice. The matter was best left, the honorable judge wrote, "to the discretion of those who do possess such expertise."

I am grateful to the lawyers, journalists, teachers, writers, activists, and artists, who have been undaunted by questions about expertise. These are the people who have tried to understand and explain to us how, after the attacks of September 11, the world changed, and then changed again. Joseph Margulies, Jane Mayer, Philip Gourevitch, John Sifton, and Jonathan Raban, are a few of those from whose work, and in a couple of cases from whose guidance, I have benefited a great deal.

The expert's assumption of omniscience is matched by the terrorist's illusions of omnipotence; unlike them, and more self-consciously, the nonexpert maps the limits of our knowledge as well as our existential comfort. In the middle chapters of this book, I present the work of writers and artists who have adopted, sometimes with relish, the tools of the surveillance state; in those chapters and elsewhere, I also engage with lawyers and journalists working on issues of detention, torture, and human rights. My thanks to these individuals, many of whom I also interviewed for this book; their collective work is not a matter of expertise, but, instead, an act of troubled witness.

Second, the losers

If the concerned citizen is a kind of an amateur seeking to learn more about a new world, then what are we to do with that other sort of amateur, the one who can best be described as a bungler? For example, the type I have come to think of as the accidental terrorist. I thank Hemant Lakhani and Matin Siraj, along with their families and their lawyers, for sharing their experiences with me. The two long chapters in this book about Lakhani and Siraj are, I admit, unflattering portraits of the two men convicted of terrorism, but much of my reportage here is in the service of presenting the anti-terrorism state as the biggest bungler. But how to thank the state for its tender mercies?

I have also written in this book about my experiences in the classroom, teaching the literature that deals with Guantánamo and Abu Ghraib; I'm indebted to my students, some of whom I've quoted, and hope that they will find of interest the report from the academic trenches. The same applies to my report on Steve Kurtz, the theorist who was suspected of being a terrorist. My greater debt is to those who, particularly near Mumbai and in Kashmir, spoke to me about their wrongful arrests and abuse; in particular, S.A.R. Geelani, who despite severe torture and long incarceration has kept whole his sense of humanity. He is an example of what it means to remain human despite inhuman violence.

Third, the small people

This book was in its final stages when, on November 26, 2008, ten men arrived by sea from Karachi and launched their spectacularly devastating attack on various locations in Mumbai.

The attacks went on for more than sixty hours; partly because of the intense coverage, the trauma felt further prolonged and magnified. During that time, I despised much of the media for its overexcited babble and the ugly jingoism that easily overwhelmed any decent concern for human lives. I hated the obscene display of privilege by those who reminisced fondly about their dining experiences in exclusive restaurants now under siege, as if the ordinary people killed in the crowded train-terminus and elsewhere had no worth even in death. And as if all that wasn't enough, in the cretinous blogosphere, the night-sky was lit up by the flak of a thousand denunciations of religious tolerance. More bizarrely, a string of comments were fired at those Indians in the United States who had voted for Barack Obama in the alleged hope of appeasing jihadists in the mid-east.

I should clarify that my own response was not very composed. In fact, the sorrow and rage I had felt at that time returns when I watch footage of the events in Mumbai. In a recent Channel Four documentary about the attacks, I heard the voice of one of the handlers in Pakistan directing the terrorists by phone, helping them maximize the mayhem. The Indian authorities had been able to intercept the calls, and as I listened to the taped conversations it was clear to me that the handler's voice was the voice of pure evil.

And yet, what saves me from the annihilating hatred, if only for a moment, is the voice of the terrorist at the other end. When being urged to quickly set fire to the curtains and carpets in the opulent Taj Hotel, he is more interested in describing to his superior the rooms that he says are large and lavish. It's amazing, he says, the windows are huge here. There are two kitchens, a bath, and a little shop. The handler reminds him to start the fire. In the footage recorded by the CCTV inside the hotel, you can see the terrorist taking in the sight of the tiled corridors, the intricate wood-work, and the lush plants. An hour earlier, the same terrorist, or another one at the same hotel, had said on the phone that he couldn't find out where the cameras were or even the switches for the lights. It was difficult to know what the numerous switches were for, he said; and then, unable to recognize the flat-screen plasma television screens, he reported that there were huge computers on the walls. The handler urged him to set it all on fire. But, rightly or wrongly, I'm caught by the drama of the displaced provincial, the impoverished youth finding himself in the house of wealth. He is using terrible violence to set fire to this palace of dreams but he is in a daze: a murderous thug who is a figure in the invisible machinations of people and plans that are larger than anything he can imagine. This moment brings the terrorist an inch closer to the near-nameless people he and his cohort have killed—the men and women and children lying dead on the floor of the city's biggest train station. They are all small people. They have lasted so long in a world that grants them visibility only as killers or as corpses. I can't thank them for anything but this would be the right place to acknowledge that they exist and, in fact, represent the starting point for this book.

Finally, my friends

When I began this work, Ian Jack at *Granta* and Mukund Padmanabhan at the *Hindu* wrote the necessary letters of introduction that opened the heavy prison doors. Sree Sreenivasan, Naresh Fernandes, and Lucia Sommer provided vital help with names and advice. I benefited from Ayesha Karim's suggestions on an early draft, and I remain grateful for the comforting presence and support of my unflappable agent, Gillon Aitken. The Office of the Dean of Faculty at Vassar College and the Susan Jane Turner Fund bestowed monies for research and travel. My sincere thanks to Ken Wissoker at Duke University Press who asked me to write this book and sent my draft to readers who contributed to this project. As always, Picador India's Shruti Debi has been in addition to a superb editor a wise and loyal friend.

✳ A Missile in the Living Room

The explosive RDX used in the Bombay blasts in 1993 had come to India on boats that had dropped their cargos on the Konkan coast. (Bombay was given the Marathi name Mumbai in 1996.) In that stretch of white sand fringed by coconut groves is a village named Walavati, and I was going there to meet Iqbal Haspatel. He had been arrested on charges of terrorism a month after the bombings. When I went to Walavati, the specially designated anti-terrorism court was about to deliver its judgment in the Bombay blasts trial. This had been India's biggest criminal case and the court had taken thirteen years to reach a verdict.

On March 12, 1993, there had been a series of bombings—one bomb in the Stock Exchange, another in the offices of Air India, still others, placed in scooters and cars, in crowded areas outside a temple and elsewhere. These had resulted in the deaths of 257 people. The bombings were to avenge the deaths of Muslims in riots just a few months before. All this was unleashed by the destruction, at the hands of a Hindu mob, of a sixteenth-century mosque in northern India. In those riots, according to a report by a government commission, thirty-one police officers had killed innocent Muslims and, sometimes, had participated in the riots themselves.

It rained for nearly all of the five hours it took me by car from Mumbai to Walavati. The driver's name was Sharda Prasad Pandey, but he was called Doctor because he had been frequently ill as a child. Every few miles, to my great dismay, Doctor would press the brakes, and make the car skitter like water on a hot pan. The painted blue-and-white boards on the Sion-Panvel highway, offering clichés like "Time is Money, but Life is Precious," suddenly appeared full of wisdom to me. Because of the rain, the hills around us overflowed with water. Small waterfalls dotted the hillsides. An elderly Muslim couple, hiding from the rain under a tree, stood so close to each other that they appeared to be embracing.

Then, when we were about a half hour short of Walavati, the rain stopped. We passed the Little Engels Children's School, and Doctor expertly splashed a line of school kids with water from a roadside puddle. The traffic had slowed down on the winding road and I watched the cattle, tiny and lithe, grazing on the rain-washed blades of grass.

Walavati appeared—small, neat houses dwarfed by coconut trees, and, stretching around them, fields of paddy and Alphonso mangoes. At the Haspatel home, tea was served and a bed laid out for Doctor in a tiny room toward the front because he wanted to sleep. On the desk in the living room was a file of yellowing newspaper cuttings. I was looking at a smiling policeman, displaying for the press a cache of captured goods. The photograph had appeared in the national newspapers on April 14, 1993, and the smiling man was Tikaram S. Bhal, who was at that time the superintendent of police in Alibaug. The *Times of India* had stated that an "arms haul was reported from Walavati area of Srivardhan late yesterday evening. Twenty-five projectiles and seventeen pipe bombs and ammunition were recovered from the creek. Combing operations were going on. . . ." A missile had been found in the Haspatel living room. In its greater zeal, a right-wing newspaper had claimed that the materials recovered by the police were to be used to demolish the home of the leader of the Shiv Sena, a neo-nationalist Hindu party. It took four days for the police to realize that the "projectiles" they had found were actually parts of textile machinery and were called "bobbins" or "twist-blockers."

About eight years before this episode, a truck had overturned thirty miles away, depositing its cargo into the river that runs past Walavati. Children had dived in the water and come up with armloads of the bobbins that the truck had been taking to a textile plant in Ahmedabad. That is how one of those plastic objects had found a place in the glass cupboard of the front room in the modest home owned by Iqbal Haspatel.

Haspatel is a retired working-class man. He had worked as a gas-pump attendant for seventeen years in Muscat, in the Sultanate of Oman, before returning to his family home in Walavati. Three months after his return, upon the discovery of the mysterious projectile in his house, and after every piece of furniture had been ransacked, he suddenly found himself being paraded in the village. Bhal, the police officer, slapped him in front of other worshippers at the mosque and called him a traitor to his country.

Over the next four days, Iqbal Haspatel was interrogated and beaten. He wasn't alone. His wife, his daughter-in-law, and a six-month-old granddaughter, along with two of his three sons, were also taken into custody. Ten to fifteen people were crammed into a small room in the Srivardhan police station that wouldn't comfortably house five persons. Sometimes, there were at least twenty-five. The stench of urine alone was a torture.

Even after all these years, the Haspatels have received no apology from the police, nor have they been compensated for the damage done to their house. The valuables taken from their home, including gold jewelry, were never returned. What the family talks of most about their experience during their detention is the extraordinary presumption of guilt on the basis of their faith. This presumption was shared by all ranks. One of the interrogators hit Iqbal Haspatel and said, "Kidhar hai tumhara Allah? Bulao tumhare Allah ko." (Where is your Allah? Call your Allah.) His family recalls a constable named Lohare who would, after each beating, inquire what their God had done to protect them against the police. The villagers were so scared that they threw away even their kitchen knives.

Mubeen Haspatel is the second of Iqbal's three sons. He speaks slowly, and with some difficulty. On the evening of April 13, 1993, when he was taken to the police station with the rest of his family, he was allowed to keep his underwear on, but after that day he remained there without a shred of clothing on him. The policemen beating Mubeen used a strip of rubber, cut from the belt in a flour-grinding machine, on which with chalk they had written "Satya Katha" (Truth Tale). They trussed him on a pole—as one might tie together on a wire the wings of a bird being roasted over a fire—and hit him until he flipped over. Mubeen's hands were held on a table and they were ground under wooden staves; the knuckles are now misshapen and one of them has disappeared. So many years later, his back still has black scars. After each bout of torture, the young man would collapse. It was during those days that Mubeen started having fits, and they continue to attack him today, particularly when he finds himself in any situation of stress. There were times during those days when his torturers would bring him, bruised and naked, to stand in front of his female relatives. His groin had been burned black. His elder brother told me that each policeman would put out his cigarette on Mubeen's private parts. He said, "They wanted to make him useless for a woman."

Iqbal Haspatel would come back from his own session with the interrogators and find his son lying unconscious on the floor of the cell. After telling me this Haspatel fell quiet and then Mubeen stuttered and tried to finish his story. When I was listening to Mubeen, a man leaned closer to me and, speaking in a confidential tone, said, "What the Americans were doing in Abu Ghraib, they learned from our policemen here." The man's name was Abul Jalal. He owned a poultry business and was the only one in the room with a little education. It was he who had told the police that the object they had mistaken for a projectile was only a piece of a textile machine. When I heard his remark about Abu Ghraib, I thought that he was telling me that even in this tragedy there was glory. It was we who had taught the Americans, we had given knowledge to the dominating West, to the West that usurps for itself the role of the provider. But I then realized that Jalal, the poultry farmer, was only trying to link what had happened in Walavati to the wider world. Abu Ghraib was a name that people all over recognized. The torture practiced there had attracted universal condemnation. Could Walavati, too, please get its fair share of outrage if not justice?

I'm telling you this here so that you can see how ordinary men and women whose lives are entangled in the war on terror tell stories about themselves and their place in the world. Theirs are stories that bring together, whether as acts of fancy or as pictures of grim reality, different parts of our divided world. Of course, as any writer knows, a story might begin at one place and then through an extraordinary, unexpected turn end up somewhere else entirely. Abul Jalal was undeniably a minor fabulist, spinning a striking tale that tied his village to a distant prison where a people, and arguably, a faith, were being treated as the enemy to be broken and humiliated. I think of him as a humble participant in the struggle over the meaning of September 11 and its global aftermath.

Every time we watch the news these days we are reminded that an authoritative, influential story told about the reasons behind what occurred on a Tuesday morning in September has resulted in an array of far-reaching and devastating consequences. The disaster in Iraq is perhaps the most visible effect of the powerful story that began to be told soon after the attacks. We were told that the war on terror was being fought against an enemy that was at once more singular and shadowy. This war attested to the arrival of a murkier world, where not only morality but even identity got blurred. In this realm of fictions, the wizards of truth were adept at practicing magical acts of deception. In February 2002, here is how Donald Rumsfeld offered in his smirking, didactic way the map of the new world: "As we know, there are known knowns. We also know there are known unknowns. But there are also unknown unknowns, the ones we don't know we don't know." The individual vanishes in a dark place of secrets. Or we watch him disappear on the brazen stage of propaganda. The particulars of an individual life are sometimes all that we have as a precious lifeline to firm reality: this is where he was born, this is his father in the mosque, this is when he was taken away, and if you find him this is what he can tell you about those he left behind. And even then, the spectral space that is the individual's is haunted by still more stories, as stark as questions. What is of interest then is how the stories are being meticulously put together, the uncanny purpose that they serve, and the ways in which they link with other stories and other silences.

When I had come out of the Haspatel home after our conversation, I was taken by Abul Jalal to the place on the coast where the smugglers had brought in the RDX from Pakistan. The road was on the side of a hill and the water below us stretched out as far as the distant, pencil-thin line of the horizon. A cooling breeze was coming in from the sea and, standing under the open sky, I felt my spirits lifting. We remained quiet for several minutes. Then Jalal cleared his throat. He wanted me to know that one of the policemen who had tortured the Haspatels and mocked their religion had later met with an accident. A truck had hit his motorcycle and broken his back. He was paralyzed. Jalal said, "By the time he died, there were insects crawling out of his body." I nodded. Then, Jalal asked me a rhetorical question, "What could Iqbal Haspatel or his boy have said when they were being beaten so badly?" I kept looking at the small white waves crashing on the beach a hundred feet beneath us. Jalal asked, "In America, they have a machine that tells you if a person is lying?" He was saying that the existence of this machine, a lie-detector, must make torture unnecessary.

We got back in the car. The arrival of avian flu earlier in the year had made it necessary for Jalal to kill all the chickens on his farm. That was the subject that he began to speak about next, and I never got a chance to talk to him about how torture might be used to elicit not truth but lies. In November 2005, a report in *Newsweek* on the use of torture by the United States mentioned Ibn al-Shaykh al-Libi, the Libyan paramilitary trainer for al Qaeda whom the Americans had interrogated at the Bagram Air Base in Afghanistan and then renditioned to Egypt: "The CIA took al-Libi, strapped some duct tape over his mouth and put him on a plane to Egypt, where the interrogators are a little rougher than down at FBI headquarters. At the airport, according to Jack Cloonan, a retired FBI officer who handled al-Libi, a CIA case officer went to the suspected terrorist and said, 'You're going to Cairo, you know. Before you get there I'm going to find your mother and I'm going to f—— her.'"

As Stephen Grey writes in his important book *Ghost Plane*, "In the world of renditions, Egypt has been torture central." When interrogated by the Egyptians, al-Libi "confessed that Al Qaeda terrorists, beginning in December 2000, had gone to Iraq to learn about chemical and biological weapons." This piece of information, extracted under torture, and recanted later by al-Libi, provided the foundation that the Bush administration needed to invade Iraq. More recently, the *Washington Post* carried a report about al-Libi's alleged suicide in a Libyan prison in May 2009; it also mentioned that al-Libi had suffered a "mock burial" under the hands of his Egyptian interrogators who "put him in a cramped box for 17 hours." His confession had come after such treatment. The *Post* cited Tom Malinowski from Human Rights Watch who said that al-Libi was "Exhibit A in the narrative that tortured confessions contributed to the massive intelligence failure that preceded the Iraq war."

Al-Libi's statement to his interrogators was used by President Bush in a speech in Cincinnati in October 2002, and it was repeated by Colin Powell to the U.N. Security Council in February 2003. However, as the *New York Times* later reported, at least a year before Powell's speech the Defense Intelligence Agency had already called into question the reliability of al-Libi's claims. The intelligence report had said that it was probable that the prisoner was "intentionally misleading the debriefers" in making claims that Iraq was training members of al Qaeda in the use of chemical and biological weapons. These warnings were ignored.

The war machine had the capacity to manufacture its own truths. In his address to the U.N., which he would later call a permanent "blot" on his record, General Powell held up a model vial of anthrax and warned about Iraq, "They can produce enough dry biological agent in a single month to kill thousands and thousands of people." The evidence bolstering that claim was quickly shown to be inaccurate. The U.K. intelligence dossier that Powell had invoked, for instance, was actually based on material twelve years out of date and had plagiarized an essay by an American graduate student. That didn't stop the drumbeat toward war. The torture of al-Libi had given reason for an invasion that, soon thereafter, in places across Iraq, led to more acts of torture. In a way, Abul Jalal, a poultry farmer plus harmless fabricator of history, turned out to be right. Pre-empting later celebrated testimonies about the war on terror—for example, the Academy Award-winning documentary *Taxi to the Dark Side*, about an Afghani taxi-driver named Dilawar who was murdered in custody by American soldiers at the Bagram Air Base—Jalal had spoken to me about the global migration of torture. His judgment had certainly come to pass.

Undeniably, al-Libi was a terrorist, and he was a trainer of terrorists, but he ought to have been tried in a court of law. He should have been brought to justice for his crimes, just like all of those other "high-value detainees" that President Bush later ordered sent to Guantánamo. When those men were moved from overseas black sites to Guantánamo, President Bush announced that the International Committee of the Red Cross would have the chance to meet with them. The Red Cross team-members interviewed the prisoners over several days in October and in December 2006. The journalist Mark Danner got access to the records of those confidential interviews and, in March 2009, noted that the Red Cross document had chapter headings like "suffocation by water," "prolonged stress standing," "beatings by use of a collar," and "confinement in a box." The legal implication of this is that these detainees will probably not be tried anytime soon because both military and civilian judges have been throwing out of court the cases of prisoners who have been tortured. These include men like Abu Zubaydah, Walid bin Attash, Khalid Sheikh Mohammmed, terrorists who are linked to lethal operations that have claimed many human lives. And yet, because of the unconstitutional actions of the state, it is unlikely that these men are going to come to trial. As Danner rightly pointed out, "The use of torture deprives the society whose laws have been so egregiously violated of the possibility of rendering justice. Torture destroys justice." And this reality is perhaps, as Danner puts it, "the most important and consequential sense in which 'torture doesn't work.'"

When Barack Obama was campaigning to get elected to the White House, he wrote in *Foreign Affairs* that the task of building a better, freer world meant that the U.S. must commit itself to "ending the practices of shipping away prisoners in the dead of night to be tortured in far-off countries, of detaining thousands without charge or trial, of maintaining a network of secret prisons to jail people beyond the reach of the law." Soon after taking the oath of office, President Obama signed executive orders directing the CIA to shut down its remaining secret prisons and ordering the closing of the detention camp in Guantánamo. A few months later, in April, his administration also made public detailed memos that described the torture techniques used by the CIA in its secret prisons and elsewhere from 2002 to as late as 2005. The memos revealed that illegal interrogation techniques, like waterboarding, had indeed been regularly used against terror suspects, especially against what the Bush administration called "high-value detainees." Obama described the use of torture as "a dark and painful chapter" in the history of the United States and declared that those methods would never be used again.

But how real is the promise of change? The Obama administration has announced that it will not end renditions, and will continue to send terrorism suspects to third countries for detention and interrogation; the new president has gone so far as to also propose a new system of preventive detention of suspected terrorists; before becoming president, Obama had voted for a 2008 bill authorizing the surveillance program and he hasn't suggested new reforms; he outlawed torture but also ruled out the prosecution of the agents who had practiced torture; he has said he is not opposed to military commissions if they follow the law; he has gone back on his own promise of transparency by retracting the release of photos showing detainees at Abu Ghraib; and even if he has directed the prison in Guantánamo to be shut down, it seems it is only to be shifted somewhere closer to home, maybe in Michigan. Little wonder that after the President's May 2009 speech at the National Archives, Michael Ratner of the Center for Constitutional Rights had this to say about Obama: "He wraps himself in the Constitution, talks about American values and then proceeds to violate them."

In August 2009, a secret CIA report, written by the agency's director general in 2004, was declassified and released following legal pressure from the American Civil Liberties Union. Although the report was made public in a heavily censored form with whole pages blacked out, there was enough evidence to support the report's conclusion that the CIA investigators had used "unauthorized, improvised, inhumane" techniques of interrogation. (On one page, with the names and other details redacted, I read that the interrogator put both his hands on the detainee's neck and choked the carotid artery until the detainee passed out. This was new to me. But not the talk about mock executions. Or the threats about sexually assaulting female relatives. I had heard about those practices in India from a professor who was tortured after being mistakenly suspected of terrorism. But still it was shocking to find proof, once again, of just how flawed the idea of American exceptionalism has always been.) In response to the report, Attorney General Eric Holder announced the appointment of a prosecutor to investigate the abuses of prisoners being interrogated by CIA agents and contractors. But even in this instance, quick on the heels of the news about the criminal probe, the White House repeated the Obama mantra that on the subject of detainee interrogation the president "wants to look forward, and not back" at Bush tactics.

Perhaps Obama defenders need not have been so anxious. Joseph Margulies, a lawyer who has represented several of the Guantánamo detainees in court, explained to me in an email response to an inquiry I had sent him that the recent changes announced by the Obama administration "were more symbolic than genuine." Margulies objects to the Obama plan to set up an elite interrogation unit because, once again, as during the Bush administration, the aim is to "interrogate without regard to whether the confession will be used in court because these people will never be prosecuted." He is similarly opposed to the appointment of a prosecutor who will conduct a probe because his brief is to blame those who broke the law but not the law itself. According to Margulies, this would be no different from Abu Ghraib, where the Bush administration prosecuted "people who went beyond that which was authorized, but accepted as a given that the authorizations themselves were legitimate."

Among those that Margulies has represented is Abu Zubaydah, the high-value detainee who has the dubious honor of being the first U.S. prisoner to be waterboarded in the global war on terror. Zubaydah was the man for whom the so-called "torture memos" were written, although, as Jane Mayer suggests in her book *The Dark Side*, in the months immediately prior to the writing of the memos which were supposed to provide legal cover, a CIA team with a psychologist named James Mitchell on contract, had already subjected Zubaydah to brutal treatment. Shouldn't the Attorney General's office be pursuing legal action against Zubaydah's torturers as well as those who wrote the memos to make his torture possible?

Margulies says no. He explained his thinking to me thus: "I believe that transparency and retribution operate on two ends of a spectrum, and that democracy is better served with a system that maximizes transparency and minimizes retribution. For that reason, I'm all in favor of a full, public inquiry into what was done to whom, and on whose authority, but opposed to a process that takes as its philosophical starting position that a crime was committed for which punishment is appropriate. No one who is remotely familiar with the criminal justice system in this country can have any faith that a criminal prosecution would be an open and transparent process designed to answer questions and encourage public debate about either the individual actors, or the systemic realities of a post-9/11 world. It simply is not structured to achieve that outcome." His answer struck me as counterintuitive but correct. It made me think that the criminal prosecution of a figure like John Yoo might even rather easily provide a cathartic release for a conscience-stricken American public. Having banished torture from our midst as an evil practiced by rogue individuals in distant places, we would become comfortable once again with the more banal, but no less shocking, ways in which the war on terror has meant the derailment of ordinary rights for so many, including inside the United States.

I say this because my interest is in the Abul Jalals of this world. The codes that had sanctioned the vilification of those with a beard like him, or a name like his, are those codes going to change? In this book, I present portraits of a few individuals that are criminals but who also appear to be victims; if this is true, then they are victims of men who, acting in the role of confidential informants, are in every other respect just like them. Any one of them could be my friend Abul Jalal. I wonder when those conditions are going to change that make both types of men—the informer and the one he informs on—such easy prey to narratives devised by the state.

In early 2006, a clerk at a Circuit City store in New Jersey called the police after he noticed that a video that had been dropped off by a customer to be converted into a DVD showed footage of young men brandishing guns and shouting "Allahu Akbar!" The footage was from a vacation in the Poconos hills, showing the young men skiing, hiking, and playing paintball. Most of the men were Muslim Albanians from the former Yugoslavia, three of them were siblings, the Duka brothers. A fourth, Mohamed Shnewer, who was a Palestinian taxi-driver, was married to their sister. The FBI was contacted by the police and they recruited an informant to infiltrate the group. Omar, the informant, was an Egyptian immigrant with a long history of bank fraud; he told the young men that he had a past in the Egyptian military. Omar turned over more than a hundred hours of recordings of conversations with the young men. On one of the tapes, Shnewer talks about how easy it would be to kill soldiers on the nearby Fort Dix military base. A lot of the taped conversation, a journalist reports, is "the sometimes tedious chatter of young men." "They drink coffee at Dunkin' Donuts and debate the merits of Ford vs. Chevy; they drink coffee and talk about fishing. They play paintball and fire guns at snowballs lofted into the air." Shnewer, the one who had spoken about attacking Fort Dix, was driven by Omar to the military base for what they considered a reconnaissance mission. At one point, Shnewer is heard saying on tape, "I am at your services as you have more experiences than me in military bases and in life." The attacks that were discussed were never executed, of course, but the more serious question is whether the informant, who was paid $180,000 for his services, was also an instigator. The answer is not clear.

On December 22, 2008, the jury in the Fort Dix Six trial found five of the six accused guilty. Amanda Ripley, writing about the Fort Dix case in *Time*, noted that the big long-term disadvantage to the use of informants is that "if the rumors of entrapment become so corrosive that no one in the Muslim American community feels safe talking to the FBI, then the government has lost its best potential ally." Ripley went on to describe her meeting with a couple from India while she had been reporting her story:

the two were Muslim, they had immigrated from India some decades ago, and they helped found the Sunni mosque attended by the Duka brothers:

> We sat in their upscale suburban home and talked about the Dukas, whom they didn't know very well, and their fears. They were convinced that their phones were being tapped. They had stopped watching mainstream TV news and were even thinking of leaving the country. "This is a country which was great," the woman said. "That's why we all came—freedom of speech, justice, things that were not even to be found in Muslim countries. But it is vanishing every day."

✳ Have You Seen This Man?

They call out to us from the walls of our cities. If you have seen this man, please contact the police. He might be armed and is dangerous.

In today's culture, in which images of desirable bodies are on open display, drawing to their surface the public gaze, the terrorist's unglamorous image carries a whiff of the street. Despite the information provided about his name and place of birth, he is somehow more anonymous. We see him in smudgy, often out-of-date photographs and charcoal drawings; he arouses not desire but suspicion; he is wanted only by the police. The terrorist is the "missing person" of an earlier and more innocent age. The face we see on the wall is more of an absence, an absence that emerges from a fear in our hearts. Unless he is caught, we believe we won't have security.

When we see his picture on the peeling poster, the man looks like no one else around us. Or like everyone around us.

And yet we're often quite certain in our judgments about these faces when they are assumed to belong to foreigners. On December 13, 2001, a group of men armed with guns and explosives attacked the Indian Parliament. All of the attackers were killed; their identities have still not been established. But after seeing pictures of the slain assailants, Lal Krishna Advani, the home minister of India, is said to have remarked that the men "looked like Pakistani terrorists." But what do Pakistani terrorists look like? On the night of November 26, 2008, when the ten young men from Pakistan came ashore in Mumbai no one pointed at them on the streets and said "Look there, terrorists!" Each of the ten gunman was carrying a heavy bag which contained, among other items, a Kalashnikov, a 9-millimeter pistol, ammunition, hand grenades, dried fruits, and steel ball bearings. In a documentary about the attacks made by Channel Four, a young woman who was sitting in Leopold Cafe when it came under fire tells the camera that she had noticed one terrorist when he arrived at the restaurant. She remembered seeing a man wearing "a beige shirt and blue cargo pants" who was "very good-looking, very handsome." Unlike what Advani would have us believe, the woman didn't see him as a terrorist until he took out his rifle and shot her in the stomach.

Most of us have never met a terrorist. Nevertheless, we feel a closeness or familiarity with him—we believe that we understand his motives and his innermost thoughts. Shuddhabrata Sengupta has written that our bogus familiarity with terrorists is because of the circulation of identikit photographs as well as the images we see in newspapers and more so on our screens. To quote Sengupta, "We have seen the face of the terrorist so often, and so intimately, as a moving image that, in a sense, the terrorist actually lives in our own heads, and were we to ever come across his body, living or dead, or his image, we would be immediately in a position to crosscheck his features against the indelible impress of those features in our nervous systems."

Is that why the police document doesn't strive too hard for specificity? The text accompanying the image informs us, "Wears pant and shirt" (figure 1). As a writer, I wonder whether in a novel the poster would have said something like, "Likes Hindi films and perfume."

Given that our familiarity with terrorists is really only based on his (and, on rare occasion, her) appearance on the screen, it makes sense to ask what we can learn from the way in which that representation works. For the past decade and a half, Hindi films like *Roja, Mission Kashmir, Sarfarosh, Jaal, Maachis, Dil Se, Maa Tujhe Salaam, The Hero* . . . have been trying to save the Indian nation-state from terrorists. Over and over again. Hidden in the stories proffered by the films is the claim that they are giving the terrorist a human face. So that we understand. In the more tolerable of these productions, empathy is doled out in equal, democratic measure by filmmakers in a situation that is essentially undemocratic and brutal.

Among the more recent exercises in such representation was Anurag Kashyap's *Black Friday*, a film about the explosions in March 1993 that

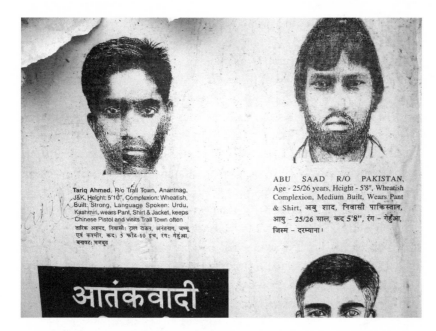

1. Amitava Kumar, "Delhi: Wears Pant and Shirt I" (2007).

shattered the city that was then still called Bombay. The specially designated anti-terrorism court delivered its verdict in September 2006. Of the
122 persons accused, 100 were convicted, even while the main accused
remained at large—a part of the exiled crime syndicate living either in
Pakistan or the Middle East.

Black Friday was suppressed by the government for two years until the
court case ended because of fear that it would prejudice the trial's outcome. The most dramatic confrontation in *Black Friday* takes place in the
interrogation room, in a conversation between a police officer and a captured terrorist. The terrorist offers his interrogator an angry testimony
about the beleaguered position of a persecuted minority. He claims that
Allah was on his side in his jihad against the Hindus who had raped and
killed with gross impunity during the riots in the city. The cop isn't a Muslim but his response is in the idiom of faith. He argues that Allah is actually on his side. The police had made two hundred arrests in two months.
The case had been easily cracked. The police officer says, "This time Allah
was with us. Allah is on the side of every honest man." God is not on the

side of killers, Hindu or Muslim, who are fooled by their leaders in the name of religion.

But this is a civics lesson. It is delivered by the secular authority who has summoned his handcuffed opponent to the police station to disarm him ideologically. A far more powerful introduction to the condition of the terrorist takes place in the film when he is shown as a man on the run.

His name is Badshah Khan. He is a foot soldier in India's urban jihad. In what must be one of the most melancholy passages in Indian cinema, we watch the actor Aditya Shrivastava project an uncanny sense of displacement as Badshah moves from one city to another, running out of money, running out of time. It isn't that the terrorist has run out of arguments; rather, he has run out of options. His face looks haunted. His speech becomes uncertain. For a moment, when he is speaking on the phone with his ringleader in Dubai, he breaks down and his eyes brim with tears. As the days pass, he feels a growing sense of abandonment. He becomes a man who inhabits a season of waiting while around him blow the dry leaves of despair.

The song that plays in the background—"Jung ka rang sunehra samjha / Lekin baad mein gehra samjha / Jung ka rang to kaala re" (I thought that the color of war was golden / But later I understood it better / The color of war is black)—is sadder than any hymn to a polity. It is certainly more honest than any national anthem. There is no glory for this warrior. We listen to the words of the song and we see in Badshah Khan's face the perfect embodiment of defeat.

This terrorist is an unsuitable citizen of the nation-state. Unlike his leader, who escaped to Dubai, and unlike the police, Badshah is out of place everywhere. In Calcutta, he joins some sightseers on a boat. It is immediately clear that he does not belong. Unlike the well-heeled tourist, his gaze is not curious, only furtive. His eyes meet those of a young, well-dressed woman; her look is indifferent; his marginality is tinged with a feeling of sexual impotence. Back in his dingy hotel room, he counts his remaining rupees, the sum of his dwindling fortunes.

He can't reach the leader in Dubai, the *bhai*, and using the coins in his fist, he makes desperate calls from a payphone. During one of these calls, his mother tells him that the police had come to see her. They were rude. He is able to reveal nothing to her. Each day, he walks the unfamiliar streets. At night, he sleeps among strangers on the floor.

"What do you want?" the hotel clerk had asked.

"A cheap room."

"Single or double?"

"Cheap. It is okay if it doesn't have a bed. Do you have something cheap?"

He answers to an assumed name. He doesn't know what fate awaits him. After the disorientation of these endless, unknown nights, after this confusion, the helplessness, and the excruciating balance of certainty and doubt at each moment of the hunt, prison must come as a relief.

The posters on our walls tell us nothing about the trials of Badshah Khan. As far as the posters are concerned, he probably doesn't even exist. All that the posters will tell us is "If you see something, say something." I see a man who cannot go home, a bus on a dusty road to Gorakhpur and behind one of the windows of the bus a pair of eyes that need sleep. I see the terrorist wearing a cheap polyester shirt that smells of stale sweat.

The film *Black Friday*, in which Badshah Khan steps out from the wings onto the stage of history for several minutes, is based on a bestselling book by the same name by the journalist S. Hussain Zaidi. The officers from the Central Bureau of Investigation had first given Zaidi information about Badshah, pointing out that his testimony was going to provide clinching evidence in the case, and it was only then that the journalist tracked him down in the Vile Parle area where Badshah lived with his family. Zaidi felt that Badshah, despite not being very educated, was very intelligent and had a sharp memory; this is what had caught the eye of the *bhai* too, who then incited his passions and ensured that he would remain loyal to his cause.

For Zaidi, the real Badshah Khan had a quality of daring, which is not entirely evident in the film's character: the Badshah that Zaidi met was not naïve or hesitant, which is why he had become, by the time Zaidi had finished writing the book, its protagonist and an example of the fate that follows "today's frustrated Muslim youth," driven into wrongdoing by the state's brutality and by the demagoguery of their own self-serving community leaders. When Zaidi described Badshah's physical appearance, I realized that he looked nothing like the actor in the film: Badshah was a short man, stocky, bearded, and less than thirty years old. He wore a kurta pajama and not the polyester shirt in which I had dressed him in my imagination. The Badshah that I had constructed, and possibly also the filmmaker, isn't someone that Badshah himself would have recognized.

The more recent terrorist attacks in Mumbai were unprecedented in their ferocity and lasted three days; but they shared some key elements with the events of 1993 in which Badshah had played a role. The police commissioner who had interrogated Badshah in *Black Friday*, Rakesh Maria, was again leading the investigation into the attacks. Of the ten men who had entered Mumbai on November 26, 2008, only one survived. He was Ajmal Kasab, 21, who had been captured alive by the police. Commissioner Maria later interrogated him and, as in 1993, in the scene celebrated in *Black Friday*, Maria was able to use reason to defeat dogma. At least this was the narrative that the media seized and repeated. I had several e-mail exchanges with Mumbai-based journalist Ashish Khetan, who had reported extensively on the November events, and his account of Maria's interaction with Kasab went as follows: After his arrest Kasab had shown no remorse. He was mouthing the doctrines of the Lashkar-e-Taiba leaders. Kasab believed, Khetan told me, that after his martyrdom "he would go to heaven and his face would glow like the moon and his body smell like an English garden." Maria had Kasab taken to the mortuary where the bodies of his nine companions were kept—several of them burned black in the fires that they themselves had started. Kasab spent a quiet fifteen or twenty minutes looking at the corpses. When he came back to Maria, Kasab "cried like a baby." There was no further exchange between the two that day but "after this episode Kasab was a changed man." He saw the error of his ways, and later in court, he confessed to his crimes.

Once again, I'm not much moved by the story offered by the state: it reads much like a parable for schoolkids. The flavor is wholesome and didactic—and just a little bit cloying. Against this self-mythology offered by the authorities, we have only the evidence of the tape made by the police only half an hour after Kasab was brought to the hospital on the night of his arrest. He was lying on a green hospital bed, his bare body covered by a woolen blanket. A fresh bandage is on his neck, just under his right jaw. A senior police officer named Tanaji Ghatge sits with a notepad calmly asking questions which Kasab answers candidly in a slightly high-pitched voice. He explains that his father encouraged him to join the jihad because his family would be paid money: "My father said: 'You will live the way they live. You will eat well, and wear good clothes. Live a life of comfort. Your brothers and sisters will get married.'"

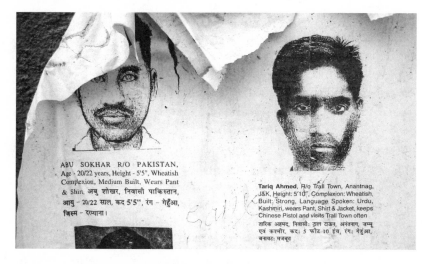

ABU SOKHAR R/O PAKISTAN,
Age - 20/22 years, Height - 5'5", Wheatish
Complexion, Medium Built, Wears Pant
& Shin, अबु शोखर, निवासी पाकिस्तान,
आयु – 20/22 साल, कद 5'5", रंग – गेहुँआ,
जिस्म – दरप्याना ।

Tariq Ahmed, R/o Trall Town, Anantnag,
J&K, Height: 5'10", Complexion: Wheatish,
Built: Strong, Language Spoken: Urdu,
Kashmiri, wears Pant, Shirt & Jacket, keeps
Chinese Pistol and visits Trall Town often
तारिक अहमद, निवासी: ट्रल टाउन, अनंतनाग, जम्मू
एवं कश्मीर, कद: 5 फीट 10 इंच, रंग: गेहुँआ,
बनावट: मजबूत

2. Amitava Kumar, "Delhi: Wears Pant and Shirt II" (2007).

The encounter stirs no pathos. The tape of Kasab offering his confession is an important part of what, according to the *New York Times*, was possibly "the most well-documented terrorist attack anywhere." The tape might incite rage, or leave one cold, but not evoke any empathy. Why? Is it only because I have watched the CCTV footage of Kasab, a Pakistani terrorist, walking around in the train terminus, calmly carrying out what was a massacre? I think it is partly that. But part of the reason I'm left untouched is that in the confession that was being broadcast on my screen Kasab was played by Kasab. Unlike the scenes from *Black Friday* that had so fascinated me, here the terrorist wasn't the actor Aditya Shrivastava. I am not moved by the confession because there is no art here. It could just as easily have been a mugshot. And besides, the camera angle is all wrong (figure 2).

On the same day that I took the pictures of the posters in Delhi, I met a man named S. A. R. Geelani. His was a name that I had first heard when, a day or two after the attack on the Parliament in Delhi, there was an announcement of an arrest of a lecturer of Arabic at a local college. That man was Geelani. He was said to have been in contact with the slain terrorists on his mobile phone. He had also made calls to Pakistan. The newspapers said that he was linked to the terrorist groups Jaish-e-Mohammed and Lashkar-e-Taiba. One newspaper even claimed that Geelani had met

Ahmad Omar Saeed Sheikh, the man who would later be charged with the murder of the American journalist Daniel Pearl.

Not one of these claims was true.

The press had been utterly subservient to the interests of the Delhi police, who had badly needed to crack the case. Any Kashmiri Muslim would do. Geelani was arrested and tortured; he was summarily condemned to death; it would be almost two years before the charges were thrown out by the Delhi High Court and Geelani was allowed to step out of prison. Why did this strange fate befall this man?

When he was arrested, two days after the attack on the Parliament, Geelani was carrying a hearing aid for a relative in Kashmir. He was in a bus going to the Tis Hazari bus depot to hand the small package to a brother who was leaving that afternoon. Geelani also had on his person his Ph.D. thesis, four hundred manuscript pages that he was taking to a man in Old Delhi for Arabic typing. (The thesis was a comparative study of the biographies of the Prophet Muhammad written in Egypt and India in the twentieth century. The manuscript was confiscated upon his arrest and never returned to him.) That day was the last Friday of the month of Ramadan, and Geelani had thought that he would stop at a mosque near the university before going on to the bus depot. A man came and sat next to him in the bus, and then, at a later stop, asked Geelani to get down. All that the man would reveal to Geelani was that he was from the police and his superior was following them in a car.

There was a white Maruti van parked behind the bus. When Geelani went close, he saw that the three men in the car had their revolvers out. He was pushed in, and the instant he was inside they began to empty his pockets. Geelani's first thought was that he was being robbed. But he was surprised by the litany of abuse. He told the men that he had been headed to the mosque. He suggested that they could let him pray first, and he would come with them to the police station. But this idea was dismissed. One of the men said to Geelani that now even Allah couldn't save him.

They first took him to the bus depot, where Geelani was asked to identify his relatives. And then he was taken away in the same car. Once, close to the Gandhi Memorial at Rajghat, the car stopped and a traffic policeman asked the driver to move to the side. The man sitting in front chided the traffic policeman with a great show of authority and then got out of the car to make calls on his phone. At that moment Geelani abandoned the fantasy that he was only being robbed.

But he didn't know where he was being taken. They soon pushed him down on the seat and covered his head with a khaki-colored half-sleeve vest. No one was hitting him so far. All he had received was verbal abuse. He was being called a traitor and a terrorist. Then, the car was traveling on a bumpy road. When it stopped and Geelani was taken out, he saw that they were probably at a farmhouse. They were in a large compound ringed with trees. There was lush green grass on the lawn. In front of him was a house on whose verandah several men were waiting. These men were older, more senior officers from different agencies, and everyone was in plainclothes.

Geelani reminded me that it was a winter evening. He was still standing beside the car when all his clothes, including his underwear, were removed. Using a rope, they tied his hands behind his back. The abuse now fell on him in a volley and nearly everyone there began to hit him. He was being asked to confess his role in the attack on the Parliament the previous day.

By the time he reached the verandah, Geelani had fallen down. There, his feet were tied together. An iron rod was inserted between his legs and he was hung upside down. The blows that were being administered were primarily on the soles of his feet. When he felt he was about to lose consciousness, Geelani asked for water. Because it was the month of Ramadan, he had been fasting and was incredibly thirsty. He had not broken his fast even though it was now night. When he said he needed a drink, the cops threw cold water on his body.

As a result of what his torturers did next, with two persons holding his arms while a third kicked him on the back until he fell down, Geelani suffered three slipped discs. The beating continued for several hours, and then, as is perhaps inevitable, the policemen got tired and ordered tea. When the tea arrived, Geelani was given a cup, and he recognized that the sugar sachet bore the name of a subsidiary of a famous five-star hotel in Delhi.

The arrest had taken place on the basis of a small piece of questionable evidence. The Indian authorities regularly monitor calls made from the Kashmir Valley. A call that they had intercepted on the day following the attacks had been made by Geelani's youngest brother. The total duration of the talk was just a little over two minutes. Geelani was in a DTC bus at the time his brother called with a request for a prospectus and a syllabus. Geelani asked his brother to call later because the telephone rates were likely to be lower. Then, according to the transcripts, the caller asked, "What has happened?" Geelani asked, "What, in Delhi?" His brother asked again, "What has happened in Delhi?" Geelani replied with a laugh. His brother said, "You should relax now." The conversation, all of it in Kashmiri, then shifted to another matter.

When I asked Geelani about it, he told me that the reference to what had happened in Delhi was actually about a domestic squabble. Geelani's wife had been upset that they had not gone to Kashmir for the Eid holidays. The younger brother was aware of this rift and was inquiring about it. But the unexamined and uncorroborated piece of conversation was taken as ready evidence of guilt by the police and led to the torture.

On that first night, when physical torture failed to elicit a confession, a change of tactics became necessary. A senior officer said that he would rape Geelani's wife in front of him, and then, dialing a number on his cell phone, he ordered Geelani's family to be brought there. After a while, Geelani was blindfolded and taken out to a car. They arrived at another house where, after he had climbed some steps, Geelani was led inside and his blindfold removed. His wife and two children, a son aged four and a daughter younger by a year or so, were standing in the room, looking terrified; Geelani's clothes had been returned, and his spectacles, and he was deeply troubled that his children were seeing him handcuffed and bloody.

Geelani is a short, soft-spoken man with a surpassing clarity about the world. Many months after his wrongful arrest, when he was finally granted freedom, Geelani had said, "The acquittal of an innocent man is not an occasion for celebration, but a cause for reflection." I could not forget that remark. Upon meeting Geelani for the first time at the Gandhi Peace Foundation, I immediately felt his warmth and also his sense of personal dignity. I wasn't surprised when Geelani revealed to me, after I had pressed him on it, that he had tried to convince his interrogators that it would be wrong to take him to his family that night. He had told them in Hindi, "The picture that will be formed in my children's minds, especially about the police and about this country, will be a very bad one. You are not doing the right thing."

The policemen paid no heed to his appeal. They told Geelani's wife to ask her husband to confess. Geelani saw that his wife was trembling. When she spoke to him, it was in Kashmiri, and she asked her husband why he wasn't doing what these men were asking. But Geelani didn't give in. He was taken to a damp maximum security cell in Tihar Jail where he was kept in isolation. This was the same cell where Maqbool Butt, the leader whose death many credit as the beginning of the protest movement in Kashmir, had been held before his execution. The authorities were probably trying to break Geelani, but he had only felt encouraged in that dank room. There were other Kashmiris jailed in Tihar and Geelani would hear their voices greeting him. "Professor sahib," the shouts would ring down unseen corridors. He felt he enjoyed a great sense of solidarity.

When Geelani was acquitted and released in October 2003, he became the victim of a bizarre and nearly fatal attack. While he was leaving the home of his lawyer one evening, an unknown gunman stepped out of the shadows and shot five bullets into him. (Geelani still has three in his body.) The Special Cell of the Delhi Police, which had earlier tortured him, acted as if Geelani was the prime suspect in his own assassination. They confiscated his computer and took away his car. Hundreds of protesters gathered outside the hospital where Geelani was fighting for his life and called for an inquiry into the assassination. (A strong cause for distrust was that the man who had arrested Geelani in 2001 was Rajbir Singh, of the Special Cell of Delhi Police, a man notorious for his "encounter killings," or extrajudicial executions, of suspected terrorists. Another footnote: In late March 2008, Singh was shot to death by a man with whom he had been involved in an illegal land deal. The weapon used was a government-issue revolver that had been reported missing by a senior police official.) The writer Arundhati Roy wrote of the attempt on Geelani's life: "I have no idea who pumped those bullets into S. A. R. Geelani. However, in deference to the general public unease with the Special Cell, the investigation ought to be conducted by an agency other than the Delhi Police. While it may be unfair to accuse them without evidence, they certainly cannot be considered above suspicion, and must be investigated."

No such investigation was undertaken, and, as many have pointed out, no newspaper or other media outlet offered an apology for having printed lies about the case. Geelani told me that once he had bumped into one of his interrogators when he had gone to an airline office. The policeman folded his hands in greeting and asked if Geelani had recognized him. Geelani assured the man that he was likely to never forget him. The man then said that what had happened with Geelani was wrong. In response, Geelani asked the policeman if he and his colleagues felt that what they were doing was really of any benefit to the nation.

"But not everyone is innocent," the man protested.

"No, but more than 95 percent are," Geelani remembered telling him. According to Talal Asad,

> When terrorists are seen as people engaged in conspiracies, one is induced to look for signs that point to something hidden (their motives are unexpressed). How might these be found? Alternatively, how can one do a proper reading of signs to discover the threats posed by secret motives? In the United States, the Patriot Act, passed to deal with terrorists, provides the practical framework for undertaking such readings. According to many critics, the Patriot Act is an attack on constitutional rights. But this kind of complaint rarely attends to the working of power/knowledge in the modern state. The project of "Defending America" calls for techniques aimed at discovering the objects that threaten. The interrogation center is not merely a source of information and a place where abuse may happen. It is the site where a particular kind of identity is typified and dealt with and where the secrets of a danger are laid bare in a war against terror, which is a permanent state.

The attack on the Indian Parliament on December 13, 2001, after which Geelani had been arrested, was quickly used by the Indian media to claim parity with New Yorkers and America. The cover story in the news weekly *India Today* ended with the following words about the Parliament building: "It has become India's own Ground Zero." And the Indian state, quick to adopt what had suddenly begun to appear as a mandatory dress code for an aspiring superpower, proclaimed a war on terror. Not only were new laws put into effect, allowing detention for 120 days without the necessity of charges being filed in court, but the government also suspended diplomatic relations with Pakistan, recalling its high commissioner from Karachi. Half a million troops were mobilized, the weaponry massed and bristling alongside the Pakistan border. News reports the world over buzzed with talk of an anticipated breakout of nuclear war.

Arguably, the bellicosity of the Indian leaders appeared familiar and even natural because it mimicked President Bush's open aggression against Afghanistan and then Iraq. But the stance also seemed logical because India wasn't the only country doing the war dance. In his book *Guantánamo and the Abuse of Presidential Power*, Joseph Margulies notes how Charles Taylor, Liberia's president at the time, claimed shortly after September 11 that opposition to his rule was in fact part of a global terrorist threat. Taylor even designated a respected journalist who was critical of his rule an "unlawful combatant." In Zimbabwe, Robert Mugabe called foreign journalists "terrorist sympathizers." Mugabe said, "We agree with President Bush. Anyone who in any way finances, harbors, or defends terrorists is himself a terrorist." A week after the attacks of September 11, the Eritrean government arrested a group of dissident politicians and later suggested that they were agents of Osama bin Laden.

When the attack on the Indian Parliament took place, the first detention camp was yet to come into being at Guantánamo. It was not until the following month, January 2002, that the first prisoners arrived at the hastily built Camp X-Ray. But in 2007, when I met Geelani and he narrated to me what he had told his former interrogator about the percentage of the tortured Kashmiris who were innocent, I immediately thought of those kept in indefinite detention at Guantánamo. This was because by this late date those men whose pictures we had all seen, their features indistinguishable in orange jumpsuits behind walls of steel mesh topped with razor wire, had been denied even the knowledge of the charges against them. Against the arrogant assumption that a strong state can act with impunity all that those prisoners had going for them was the paltry presentation of facts. The right to a fair hearing in court was being denied to these men, whom Donald Rumsfeld had called "the worst of the worst," but according to a revealing study released by the Seton Hall Law School in 2006, the U.S. government's own declassified documents showed the following:

1. Fifty-five percent of the detainees are not determined to have committed any hostile acts against the United States or its coalition allies.
2. Only 8 percent of the detainees were characterized as al Qaeda fighters. Of the remaining detainees, 40 percent have no definitive connection with al Qaeda at all and 18 percent have no definitive affiliation with either al Qaeda or the Taliban.
3. Only 5 percent of the detainees were captured by the United States forces. Eighty-six percent of the detainees were arrested by either Pakistan or the

Northern Alliance and turned over to U.S. custody at a time when the United States was offering large bounties for capture of suspected enemies.

A principal author of the study was Mark Denbeaux, a law professor at Seton Hall, who, more than a year after the release of that report, testified in front of the Senate Armed Services Committee. On that occasion, Denbeaux said that because the Supreme Court had recognized that the Guantánamo detainees had habeas corpus rights, the U.S government had to make public documents revealing "that almost everything said by our highest officials about who was detained at Guantánamo and why they were detained was false."

In his testimony, Professor Denbeaux said that one of his students asked him, "Where are the bad guys?" The student then showed him the government evidence against one of the detainees. It was limited to the charge that the detainee had been a cook's assistant for the Taliban forces in Narim, Afghanistan. The student had said to Denbeaux, "Okay. We have the assistant cook. Where is Mr. Big? Where is the cook?" The professor told the Senate Committee, "All Americans should ask that question. I have no answer."

If you don't want to be sent in shackles to be interrogated in a shed in Guantánamo, you can photograph every meal you eat and every urinal you use and upload it immediately on your website. A GPS-based device on your phone can broadcast on the site your exact location at any given time of day or night. You can make public your phone records as well as every purchase you make on your debit card. You can adopt this form of self-surveillance as a strategy not so much because you know that the government monitors your movements, but because it gets things wrong. That is why it is the government. You can monitor yourself much more accurately.

You do this if you are Hasan Elahi.

Elahi is a thirty-seven-year-old conceptual artist who teaches art and visual theory at San Jose State University in California. He was born in Bangladesh and grew up in New York. Like many other Muslims in the days following the attacks of September 11, Elahi found his name on the government's terrorist watch list. In response, he decided to open nearly every aspect of his life on his website, TrackingTransience.net.

At that site one can find a record of the coffee he has bought or the

3. Hasan Elahi, "Altitude." Used with permission of the artist.

amount of cash he has withdrawn in the past week. Over twenty thousand images on the site are time-stamped and give information about the places he has been and meals he has consumed (figure 3). In May 2007, when I met Elahi in a restaurant for lunch, he took a picture of his salad—smoked salmon with strawberry dressing—and then of the urinal in the men's room. The pictures were uploaded on his site. Having beforehand perused the list of his recent purchases, I was able to confirm that the camera he was using, a brand-new Canon G7, was one that he had acquired the previous week at a shop in New York City.

The Orwell Project, which is the name that Elahi has given to his exercise, is in reality a work of collaboration between the artist and the FBI. It was the latter who inspired this work that is part performance, part

4. Hasan Elahi, video still from *Flow—Wet Feet (Dry Feet)*. (Infinite loop, originally shot in 1999 on the exact location of an incident on Sunrise Beach, Florida where the U.S. Coast Guard had used water cannon to force Cuban refugees back into the water. 1999/2004/2006). Used with permission of the artist.

protest. On June 19, 2002, Hasan Elahi returned to the United States from an artists' residency program in Senegal, and, on arrival at the airport in Detroit, was detained for questioning. He became the subject of an FBI investigation that went on for six months and concluded with nine polygraph tests administered within the space of one day. The owners of a locker facility where he rented a locker had wrongly informed the police, on September 12, 2001, that an "Arab" man had fled the country and had left explosives behind. In order to prove to his interrogators, over the course of dozens of interviews, what he had been doing on that particular day as well as the days that followed, Elahi showed them all the information that he had available on his PDA—the record of his appointments, his itineraries, his phone calls. And when the investigation was over, Elahi began working on documenting publicly his every move. He was motivated partly by concern that his unpleasant experience with the FBI could easily be repeated, but partly also by the subversive desire to hold a mirror to the agencies that watch us. His aim is to overwhelm those who have him under surveillance—the log for his site, incidentally, reveals addresses that belong to a variety of U.S. government agencies—with the information they need. With an expression of a happy cheerfulness on his face, Elahi said to me, "If 300 million people were to offer up the details of their private lives, you would need to hire another 300 million people just to keep up."

PART I ✳ Lakhani

1 ✳ Birth of a Salesman

So, sadly, the dreamers and the haters are not two
groups. They are often one and the same persons.
—Arjun Appadurai, *Fear of Small Numbers*

The U.S. government's exhibit 1002 in *United States of America v. Hemant
Lakhani* was a document from the commissary in the Corrections Bureau
in Passaic County, New Jersey. It indicated that on March 16, 2005, in
the "early afternoon hours the defendant went to the commissary and
notwithstanding his medical condition ordered four bags of hot buffalo chips." That same afternoon, the defendant also purchased one bag
of crunchy cheese chips. Assistant U.S. Attorney Stuart Rabner flipped
through the rest of the pages of exhibit 1002. On March 21, Rabner told
the U.S. Court of Appeals for the Third Circuit, the defendant had received five bags of hot buffalo chips, five bags of salty peanuts, and five
bags of crunchy cheese chips. On March 28, he received one cheese pizza,
and again, five bags each of hot buffalo chips, salted peanuts, and crunchy
cheese chips—and five apple pies. Turning to another page, Rabner said
that on April 8 the defendant had ordered five bags of hot buffalo chips,
five bags of salted peanuts, and two bags of crunchy cheese chips. And
then on April 11, the food items ordered were five bags of hot buffalo
chips, five bags of salted peanuts, three apple pies, two honey buns, and
a cheese pizza.

"The defendant's conduct," the prosecutor argued, "can indeed be determined to be a contributing factor to the swollen legs that he now complains about and on which basis he seeks an adjournment of this trial. He should not be allowed."

Hemant Lakhani's diet was under scrutiny because he had undergone three surgeries in three weeks. The trial had begun in early January, but only ten days later the defendant had needed to be hospitalized. On the morning of January 14, a deputy marshal informed the court that the defendant had been admitted the previous evening at the St. Barnabas Medical Center in New Jersey with a variety of problems: a hernia, a congenital heart condition, and renal failure. Speaking on record four days later, Lakhani's doctor reminded the court that his patient was nearly seventy. He was probably suffering from hypertension. And it was possible that his heart needed surgical treatment. Later that week, Lakhani underwent an angioplasty and a pacemaker was inserted into his body. He was having problems with one of his knees and a rheumatologist had been pressed into service. The court couldn't meet for three weeks because the defendant had needed time to recuperate.

Henry Klingeman, the defendant's lawyer, stated that his client had described the jail food as "inedible," and had complained that he wasn't given rice, which had "been a staple of his diet for his entire life." The commissary food was used as a "supplement" and, because he had a "sweet tooth," he used to order apple pies.

The judge in the case, Katherine Hayden, took a considered view of the medical opinion she had been provided about the defendant. She declared that Lakhani was "ready to go" and commented with some concern that the diet the defendant had chosen was "loaded with salt" and "loaded with sugar." She noted that Lakhani had more than once refused nutritious meals consisting of salad, bread, beans, apples, cookies, and hard-boiled eggs. With adequate good reason, the appeal to adjourn was denied by the judge.

Judicial trials by their very nature are about acts. They concern themselves with what has actually been done by an individual or group. But the Lakhani trial from the very beginning had seemed to be about who he was rather than what he had done. He had been indicted for providing material aid to terrorists, unlawful brokering, and money laundering, but, because much of the wrongdoing had been at the suggestion of an undercover government agent, the real argument was that he had the immoral nature of someone who might be a terrorist. Even when it came to the slightly farcical matter of his diet, there was no doubt that what was being scrutinized was the defendant's character. In effect, the prosecution was saying, "Look, this person is irresponsible. He lies. He complains about the food in prison and then tucks away several bags of buffalo chips. You can't trust him."

More than four months earlier, when the trial began, FBI agents had brought in a wooden box and put it down heavily in the center of the courtroom. The prosecutors then proceeded to take out of the box a long green steel tube and showed it to the jurors. This object was an SA18 Igla shoulder-fired missile. Assistant U.S. Attorney Rabner told the court that Hemant Lakhani had sold the missile to a man whom he believed was a terrorist. Lakhani had also expressed his willingness to broker the sale of two hundred more such missiles.

The trial was taking place in a courthouse that would have been sitting in the shadow of the World Trade Center towers if they had still been there. At one point in the trial, the prosecutors played the videotape that was recorded by a secret camera during the final meeting between the defendant Lakhani and an FBI informant named Muhammad Habib Rehman. The meeting had taken place in a suite booked by Rehman in the Wyndham Hotel in Elizabeth, New Jersey. Strategically, the room overlooked the runways of the Newark International Airport. Lakhani had entered the room and discovered that the missile, which he had last seen in Russia, had indeed made it to the United States. Here are some lines from the grainy black and white videotape played for the jury:

LAKHANI: This thing is now in front of us.

REHMAN: And also the airport is in front of us.

LAKHANI: Yes, if we strike fifty at one time simultaneously, it will fuck their mother. . . . It will shake them. Then they will run. Where will they run?

And:

REHMAN: Boss, look at this now . . . Just see how many aircraft are parked there.

LAKHANI: It will fuck their mother if one or two fall down . . . If it happens ten or fifteen places simultaneously at the same time, say Sunday morning at 10 o'clock. . . . The people will be scared to death that how this could have happened. They will realize that you people are wide awake, alive and vibrant. They will know that you people are not yet dead. . . . What will happen . . . In this case, the magnitude will be very big. It means if fifteen planes come down at the same time, they will be shaken. It will fuck their mother. They will be wondering from where it came, how it came. That will be something.

The government prosecutor paused to ask the FBI informant Rehman, who was at that time on the witness stand, to take note of the gesture Lakhani had made with his hands to indicate how badly the Americans would be shaken. After that, Rehman explained how he had left the hotel room and had given to the FBI agents outside the room the wire that he was wearing on his body. On the government's videotape, half a dozen FBI agents can be seen entering the hotel room and arresting a stunned and docile Lakhani.

The investigation that ended with Lakhani's arrest on August 12, 2003, had begun in the weeks immediately following the attacks of September 11. The informant Habib Rehman had been in touch with an Indian gangster living in Dubai. The Indian man, whose name was Abdul Qayyum, had been a part of the gang responsible for the Bombay blasts in 1993. He was now in exile. The informant Rehman first heard of Lakhani in a long-distance phone conversation with Qayyum in Dubai. And it was Qayyum who told Lakhani about Rehman, repeating to Lakhani what Rehman had said about himself, that he was a powerful man in America. When Lakhani contacted Rehman, he told him that he was a businessman dealing in groceries, textile, oil, and weapons. They were talking in Hindi and, according to Rehman, the term Lakhani had used for the last trade was "mara-mari," which means "killing." This happened during their first phone conversation and later that day Rehman got in touch with his FBI handlers.

The FBI soon provided Rehman with a tape recorder to begin recording his conversations with Lakhani. Rehman told Lakhani that he was a representative of a Somalian organization called the Ogaden National Liberation Front and—although this isn't true of the actual group that has that name—that this was a terrorist group with links to al Qaeda. This group needed weapons. "The main thing," Rehman told Lakhani, "is anti-aircraft guns and missiles." Lakhani responded by asking how many were needed, and Rehman said that probably twenty to fifty missiles, but more of the anti-aircraft guns, maybe two to three hundred. Lakhani said, "You will get whatever quantity you ask."

Rehman had told the FBI agents that Lakhani was a main weapons trafficker living in London and supplying arms to Pakistani and Indian criminals and extremists, as well as terrorists in Nepal and the United Arab Emirates. He had also told them that Lakhani sold weapons to the Ukrainian government. He informed the special agent investigating the case that Lakhani was worth $300 to $400 million dollars.

Rehman and Lakhani had over 200 conversations over the next 22 months. They also met half a dozen times during this time, and these meetings were secretly recorded too. There were 154 tapes of these conversations, and the transcripts of these tapes, duly translated, filled three three-ring binders that were given to the members of the jury. It was to these transcripts that the jurors would turn when the prosecutor asked the witness to look at the lines, for instance, when Lakhani (unconsciously taking a leaf out of Ambrose Bierce, who had commented "War is God's way of teaching Americans geography") said to Rehman, "Now they know where Afghanistan is. Bin Laden taught them where Afghanistan is." But Klingeman, Lakhani's lawyer, read those conversations differently. As far as Lakhani was concerned, it was mere talk. Pointing to a transcript of a conversation on January 7, 2002, Klingeman asked Rehman, "He spends a good deal of time telling you what he's about, what he does?" When Rehman had asked him whether he had an office in Ukraine, Lakhani had said that he did. In the courtroom, Klingeman questioned Rehman about having ever come across any evidence, "any stationery, any letterhead, any mail, any indication at all" that Lakhani actually had an office in Ukraine. If Lakhani was really a businessman, why did he not even have a business card? In fact, he didn't have an office in London either. The faxes he sent Rehman were from different numbers, often from a friend's office. Had Rehman ever heard about an employee or staff that Lakhani employed? Did he ever supply a company name? To all these questions, Rehman answered in the negative.

KLINGEMAN: And I take it you never visited him in London?
REHMAN: No, sir.

KLINGEMAN: Have you seen pictures of his home, his home in [the] North London suburb of Hendon?

REHMAN: Later on I saw in the newspaper.

KLINGEMAN: So you realize it's a modest suburban single family home?

REHMAN: Yes, sir.

KLINGEMAN: And when he met with you the very first time . . . you brought him the very expensive scotch, right?

REHMAN: Yes, sir.

KLINGEMAN: That's right. Johnny Walker Blue?

REHMAN: Yes, sir.

KLINGEMAN: Did Mr. Lakhani ever reciprocate with any gifts of his own to you?

REHMAN: Yes, sir.

KLINGEMAN: That is right. Sweets?

REHMAN: Yes, sir.

KLINGEMAN: Homemade treats?

REHMAN: Yes, sir.

Lakhani's lawyer had begun the cross-examination by asking the FBI informant whether, at any time during the nearly twenty-two months that he had known Lakhani, the latter had delivered any missiles, nuclear material, armored vehicles, bullets, or anything that related to military hardware. The answer was no. But, quite apart from this mode of legal inquiry, like the government's lawyer before him, Klingeman was interested in presenting to the members of the jury a portrait of a person. He asked Rehman whether he had observed how Lakhani used to dress. Hadn't Lakhani told him that he was in the clothing trade all his life? Did he dress well? Had Rehman noticed the torn sleeves, the stains, the frayed cuffs?

The FBI agents who had guided the investigation were sitting in the gallery. The question was in reality addressed to them. Why had they believed the informant's report that Lakhani had deep pockets? The FBI had given Lakhani an initial $30,000 through the informant; an additional $55,000 was needed to purchase the missile. When Rehman said to Lakhani that the latter could put some of his own money into the deal, Lakhani had replied, "I can't arrange that kind of money." But Rehman was insistent. And Lakhani had pleaded with him, "No, I can't. Believe me. I am telling the truth. Now you see, it is all paper transaction. You see in my shop you will find only small amount of cash and nothing else." Even if this didn't arouse the government's suspicion about Lakhani, we're still left with the question of why they had gone on believing the defendant's claims when he had said that everything was readily available and yet delivered nothing. Had they been taken in by his boasting? Did they *want* to be taken in by his boasting?

The house in London that Lakhani had owned at the time of his arrest was soon put up for sale. It is now owned by a Jewish couple who run a small gas supply company. When the police arrived at the house after Lakhani's arrest, they found a fifteen-year-old BMW parked in the driveway; now, a black van with a gas cylinder painted on it stands in front of the garage. The new owners have painted the gray walls of the house white and they have installed a modish wooden door in the front. The elegant new door looks almost out of place. The house is close to the Hendon Central tube station and the neighborhood is a fairly mixed one, with a solid presence of immigrants from Eastern Europe and South Asia. It is difficult to stand in front of the house and believe, as Lakhani had claimed in his conversations with Rehman, that he was a friend of the Libyan dictator, Moammar Ghaddafi. Ditto the royal family in Dubai, the former Pakistani prime minister Benazir Bhutto, the Nigerian president Olesegun Obasanjo, and the Angolan president José Eduardo dos Santos. Lakhani had told Rehman that he had lunched with Tony Blair. "In all of the time that you spent with him at these meetings," Klingeman asked Rehman, "did he ever take a phone call from any of those folks?" Rehman replied, "I don't recall." Klingeman, deadpanning, "You don't recall whether he'd got a call from Tony Blair in the middle of talking to you?" And Rehman, "I don't think so."

Lakhani met Rehman for the first time at the Hilton in downtown Newark on January 22, 2002. Rehman was wearing a wire and the meeting was secretly being videotaped. During this conversation, Lakhani was cheerful and optimistic. He told Rehman that arms trading allowed for a lot of profit. He said, "In this business you can make 300 percent." Lakhani was carrying a brochure of an arms-seller in Ukraine, and because there was a picture of a submarine among the weapons shown in the brochure, Rehman asked whether the company manufactured them. Lakhani said that the company had expertise in making submarines and that he could arrange a sale if Rehman needed them. At that time Rehman was working as an informant in another case where he had heard talk of anti-aircraft guns and missiles, and so, instead of submarines, he asked for a missile, adding "something sinister, just like Stinger." But unlike what he had told Lakhani earlier, it wasn't twenty to fifty missiles that Rehman needed; in court, one would do just fine as evidence and that is what the FBI paid for, giving Lakhani over $86,000, both through a bank transfer and through the informal system of brokerage called hawala.

More than a year passed, and there was no missile. Lakhani was unable to find a seller. It was not until mid-January 2003, that the Russian Federation's Federal Security Services, formerly the KGB, got wind that Lakhani was looking to buy an Igla missile. According to the Russians, Lakhani had contacted a dubious company in Cyprus named Laberia, which was owned by a Russian and an Israeli. When the FBI got in touch with the Russians about what Lakhani was trying to do on their soil, they sent two undercover officers to him posing as illegal arms dealers named Aleksey and Vladimir. The Russians were cooperating with the FBI, but Vladimir complained to his supervisor on tape, saying Lakhani "fucking drove me nuts, the bitch." (The supervisor was assisting in the removal of the wire from Vladimir's body when this conversation took place and it became a part of the government's transcript. Vladimir says that Lakhani was "such a tedious guy overall, much of this has become incomprehensible to me even more." When asked about this statement in court, the supervisor said that what Vladimir was really saying was that Lakhani was "an impulsive and aggressive individual, not more, not less. That meant that it was a very dangerous individual who was trying to obtain a missile in a way that should never be done.") On July 14, 2003, the Russians arranged for Lakhani and Rehman to inspect the missile in St. Petersburg. The trip had been paid for by Rehman. The missile that the two men saw had been filled with sand instead of explosives, but when Lakhani picked up the launcher by the wrong end and swung it around, the Russian agents stuck to their roles and ducked for cover. The missile container was shipped to the United States without the dud weapon in it. And later, it was not Lakhani but the FBI that brought the dummy missile to the United States and displayed it in the New Jersey courtroom on the first day of the trial.

In Russia, Lakhani had kept telling the undercover Russian agents that he was prepared to give them bank checks for the missile. But they wanted cash, even though a bank check is easier to trace, because the agents wanted to behave like authentic criminals. It was actually Lakhani who didn't really have a clue about how real criminals behave. So, as payment, he gave Vladimir a promissory note written on a slip of paper, which was shown to the members of the jury as government exhibit 53: "I Hemant Shantilal Lakhani hereby promise to pay Mr. Vladimir the sum of 70,000 (seventy thousand dollars) for the supply of goods and parts, and I will release this sum upon receiving the necessary shipping documents in St. Petersburg."

It is perhaps understandable then that Lakhani appeared taken aback when, on the day of his arrest, he stepped into the hotel room where Rehman was waiting for him and saw, sitting on a small sofa, the missile container that he had last seen in St. Petersburg. Lakhani pointed to the container and said, "This box . . . How it arrive here? . . . I never thought it would be sitting here as your guest." And Rehman responded, "Boss, what did I tell you? I told you you can smuggle anything into America. Didn't I tell you? The stuff is right in front of you." To which, Lakhani could only say, "I can't believe what we have done."

During the cross-examination, Klingeman drew Rehman's attention to Lakhani's plain mystification or wonderment about the missile sitting in the hotel room. Lakhani had asked Rehman, "How did you bring it here?" To which Rehman replied that his men had taken care of the situation, and then he said that Lakhani had made a mistake, sending the missile to Baltimore instead of Newark. Lakhani had said lamely, "I don't know the names of the ports here."

When Rehman began opening the missile container, Lakhani protested fearfully, "No, don't open it. No. No. No, don't." But Rehman proceeded to take the missile out. Lakhani had forgotten to include the manual; neither he nor Rehman knew anything about the weapon. It was at this point that one gets a very clear sense of the man whom the U.S. government had been presenting as a sophisticated arms dealer. Here is the detail of the conversation from the courtroom about what transpired minutes before Lakhani's arrest in the hotel room in New Jersey:

KLINGEMAN: You tell Mr. Lakhani that the missile has a serial number on it, right?

REHMAN: Yes, sir.

KLINGEMAN: And he asks you a question. "What does it mean?"

REHMAN: Yes, sir.

KLINGEMAN: And you said, "This is the serial number." And you pointed as we could observe on the video. And then you say, "We don't need it."

REHMAN: Yes, sir.

KLINGEMAN: And he asks you another question, "Why not?" And you say, "Because . . ." And then the light bulb goes off, and Mr. Lakhani said, "It can be caught." Right? And you say, "In America, when it comes here, we don't need the serial number."

REHMAN: Yes, sir.

KLINGEMAN: And he says, "It is good that you told me."

REHMAN: Yes, sir.

Like Lakhani, the informant Habib Rehman was a failed businessman. During the trial, Rabner, the government attorney, asked Rehman about the work he had been doing in the United States when he wasn't assisting the FBI or the DEA. And Rehman had replied, "In the beginning I started floral business. And after that, I did a jewelry business. After that, I did grocery import business. And which includes rice and spices." The question had been intended to preemptively bring into the open a possible weakness in the government's case. Rehman had not only failed in business, he had also had civil lawsuits filed against him because of his bad trade dealings. This was more serious than the defendant's fondness for buffalo chips; Rehman's past suggested that he was an unscrupulous business partner. Rabner must have been aware that Klingeman was going to grill the informant on his business practices and raise the suspicion that Lakhani had been lured into crime. So, he asked Rehman if, during 2002, a New York businessman had invested $30,000 in a rice-importing business with him. The answer was yes. Was the investor pleased with him? Rehman said no. Rabner asked Rehman if he was able to return the money. Again, no. In response to the question whether he had paid back any part of the money, Rehman said, "Until now, I have paid him $2,500." Then, Rabner asked Rehman if, at an earlier time, in 1999, he had gone into a rice-importing business and how long that business had lasted. A few months, Rehman replied. Rabner asked, "And on what terms had the business ended?" "On bad terms," Rehman replied.

And, like a schoolteacher gently urging a pupil to make greater, more self-incriminatory confessions, Rabner inquired if there were other businesses that had ended with lawsuits and Rehman said yes. Then, Rehman was asked if these civil lawsuits had ended with judgments going against him and the amount of money that he needed to pay. The answer he gave was "Yes, sir . . . Approximately $120,000."

Muhammad Habib Rehman was born in Faisalabad, Pakistan, and received a high school education. His father and siblings dealt in gems. Some members of his family were drug smugglers and as a young man Rehman would travel to places like Dubai to collect the money owed to his uncles for the hashish they had sent out. Later, he began to help with the smuggling but took care to inform the customs officials, who paid him $80,000 over a period of several years. He had embarked on the career of an informant. At the end of the 1980s, Rehman began to assist American DEA officials working in Pakistan. (One of them was a man in Minnesota, Charles Lee, who, sometime later, would enter into a rice-importing business with Rehman and complain of being defrauded by him. During the Lakhani trial, Lee testified for the defense against Rehman.) That work was going well but one day, suddenly, Rehman was summoned to the American embassy and informed that his business associates were about to kill him. Within twenty-four hours, the U.S. government moved Rehman and his family from Pakistan to America. He has never returned.

During cross-examination, Rehman was asked by the defense lawyer whether it would be right to say that he had earned between $450,000 and $470,000 as an informant. The answer was yes. During the Lakhani investigation, Rehman was being paid $6,000 every month. But there were financial difficulties. Rehman's son had fallen sick and he had needed to purchase health insurance, but when applying for it he had lied about the medical condition and was then sued by the insurance company. The cost of the medical treatment had come to around $500,000. Weeks before the trial began, the FBI came and asked him about his insurance fraud, and as a result Rehman quickly reached an agreement with the hospital to pay $25,000. Speaking on oath in the courtroom, Rehman said in response to the barrage of questions directed at him about his insurance application, "I accept I lied."

When the court assembled again a few days later, there were further revelations about outstanding cases against Rehman in New York, Minnesota, Wisconsin, and even Kansas. The amounts of payment that Rehman needed to make ranged from $70,080.55 to $1,440.24. He hadn't made any of those payments. Although Rehman had entered the United States in 1996 and had begun earning an income, he hadn't filed his federal income tax returns in 1997. Nor did he file them in 1998 and 1999. His returns for the years 2001, 2002, and 2003 were all submitted in October 2004 after the FBI, anticipating Rehman's participation in the Lakhani trial, instructed him to do so. Yet, at the time he was testifying in court, Rehman still owed around $7,000 to the IRS.

Trouble with money notwithstanding, Rehman said he wasn't doing the work of an informant for the money. (In this respect too, he was like the man he helped put away for life. Lakhani told me when I met him in prison that his lawyer had been wrong to "parade" him as "a pauper." In his view, it was not him but Rehman who had wanted to make money. "I'm a very honest person, you can see inside," Lakhani said, clutching at the collar of his cream-colored prison shirt. And then, he said that he had a platinum credit card from British Airways, as if this was what explained the difference between him and Rehman. He raised his voice and said twice, still talking of British Airways, "They used to keep their plane waiting for me.") When Lakhani's lawyer asked Rehman what he had meant when he had said that his work "earned respect," Rehman shot back, "What do you think, sir, this work is not good work? . . . To stop a crime or any bad thing is the biggest respect in the world."

KLINGEMAN: Well, when you say respect you're presumably talking about the way others view you, correct?

REHMAN: I—when I speak respect I mean that in the eyes of the world what they see.

KLINGEMAN: Right, how others view you?

REHMAN: Yes, sir.

KLINGEMAN: But the fact is you don't tell anybody that you're an informant, do you?

REHMAN: No, I don't tell.

KLINGEMAN: Of course not. Do you put down on applications, for example, where it says occupation, informant?

REHMAN: No, sir.

KLINGEMAN: Do you go to parties and talk to people about what you do for a living and tell them that you're an informant?

REHMAN: No, sir.

KLINGEMAN: So again, who shows you respect for what you do?

REHMAN: Whenever you see any crime behind it there's an informant and when someone is arrested. And when any time someone stops the crime behind it there's an informant. And the whole world respects him. That— when I say respect that's what I mean.

I was struck by this exchange, mostly because it showed the informant as the mirror image of the defendant: a man of small means, beset with difficulties, projecting himself onto a grand stage. Each one was a failed man in many ways, a failed man, with more than a touch of desperation, dreaming of success. Both were immigrants, afraid of their perceived worthlessness, worried at the ways in which each plan they had devised had proved ineffectual. Each one tried to impress the other about how he was at home in the West. The two had their origins in enemy countries divided by a border; not once did they talk of their own religious difference or say anything bad about the other's faith or religion. The two men were worried about their families and both were committed to the cheap art of the hustle. Each believed in making a deal. Each was lying for a cause, if dreaming of a better life can be described as a cause. I wonder whether at any time during their association as business partners, there had been a moment when one of them had seen himself in the other, and whether this recognition had made him flinch.

One night in early July 2006, I took down from a shelf in my study V. S. Naipaul's *Among the Believers*, searching for the account of an interview Naipaul had conducted in Iran with Ayatollah Khalkhalli, Khomeini's hanging judge. The ayatollah had been rude and abrupt with Naipaul, and he had demanded, with Naipaul seated in front of him, that the questions for him be written down first. This is how Naipaul reports on what followed: "I could think of nothing extraordinary; I decided to be direct. On a sheet of hotel paper, which I had brought with me, I wrote: *Where were you born? What made you decide to take up religious studies? What did your father do? Where did you study? Where did you first preach? How did you become an ayatollah? What was your happiest day?*"

The simplicity of those questions, their plain curiosity, and the surprise at the end, appealed to me. And that night in July, hours before my trip to Springfield, Missouri, where Lakhani is an inmate in a federal detention facility, I copied out Naipaul's passage in my notebook. When I met Lakhani, I followed the same order: *Where were you born? What was your first job? When did you come to the West? How did you meet the FBI informant? What was your happiest day?* Like the ayatollah in Naipaul's book, Lakhani didn't answer each of my questions directly, often speaking only in generalities that were difficult to pin down; and for long bursts he fulminated angrily against his lawyer (whom he called a "first-class idiot") and against the informant (whose name he didn't mention once, often only identifying him by his religion, calling him "Mr. Musalman"); but the presence of those questions on the page in front of me had imposed a structure on our conversation.

During the meeting, Lakhani and I sat divided by a bulletproof glass window, and we had to use the prison phone to talk. I was allowed to speak only in English. (Later, Lakhani's wife, Kusum, would tell me that this rule meant that she could no longer talk to her husband in their native tongue, Gujarati. "In a way, I have lost a language," she said. In their conversations on the phone, she felt odd saying to him what she had so far said in English only to strangers, "It is raining very heavily" or "It is very hot today.") Lakhani looked much thinner than he had in the photos taken at the time of his arrest; his hair had turned completely white and lay in silvery curls at the top of his forehead. He told me that he had been born in 1935, in Porbander, the coastal town in Gujarat that was also the birthplace of Mahatma Gandhi. He lived in a joint family and remembered that at seven each morning the priest arrived to teach the children how to read from the *Gita*. His father was an engineer for the Bombay Housing Board, and had been responsible, Lakhani said, for subsidized housing for the poor in Bombay.

I asked, "What games did you play? Were there cricketers that you liked?"

Lakhani smiled and rattled off the names of the legends of the 1940 and 1950s: "Vijay Merchant, Vijay Manjrekar, Lala Amarnath. Believe me, you ask me about . . ." He stopped and, for the first time in our conversation, began to cry.

His father died when Lakhani was fifteen and he went to study at the Government Law College in Bombay. His ambition was to be the attorney general. He said that he was a good student, adding, "I've never been number one, I've never been number three." In Bombay, he enjoyed the good life, watching Hollywood films at the Metro and New Empire theaters, films like *Guys and Dolls*, with Marlon Brando in it, and the hugely popular war film *The Bridge on the River Kwai*. No one in Lakhani's family had ever gone abroad, and he was the first one to leave for London. He enrolled in economics at the London School of Economics, but he was homesick and his studies didn't go anywhere. All around him, young Indian men were dating white women, but he waited to marry a Gujarati girl.

A family friend then set him up in a Jewish clothing company called Carnegie Models; this was his first job. He said, "I am basically an intelligent man. I am a good salesman. I am a good PR man." When he said this, Lakhani looked at the prison official standing behind me, who was there to observe our meeting. The official was silent and unresponsive, but Lakhani asked him in a coaxing, pleading way, "Isn't that true?"

Lakhani recalled that he sold seventy-five-shilling woolen dresses for women, "round neck, three-fourth sleeve, good waist," to a buyer in Sweden. He sold around seven thousand pieces of this single dress. After seven or eight years, he started his own company, Ric-Rac. He became boastful again. He said things that were untrue. He said, "I brought Indian cheesecloth to England. I was the king. I was the first Indian to own a Rolls Royce. During the 1970s, I was the richest man in London."

In the 1980s, however, things took a downturn. An order worth one million pounds was cancelled, and Lakhani's business sank under "a mountain of debts." He began selling rice and spices to Arab countries. And fate once again turned a corner and he was rich again, taking holidays with his family in the south of France. Each year, he said, "From August 15 to August end, I had a suite reserved for me in the Majestic Hotel in Cannes." There was a recession in Dubai in the late 1980s, but then the Russian market opened up and the same thing happened in Germany when the Berlin Wall fell. For four years, Lakhani made "a lot of money." Then, the Indian economy was liberalized and Lakhani invested in it. He bought a small airline company and called it Up Airways. But that business went down quickly. And that's when he made the wrong contacts. Lakhani said that Delhi was like Washington, D.C., full of lobbyists, and he had been led to the FBI informant whom he now called "a third-class bastard."

I had reached the end of my list of questions. I asked Lakhani, "What was your happiest day?"

Did he misunderstand my question? Because he smiled for a while. Then he said, "Will you be happy if you're here?"

I said, "That is was not what I meant. Were you not happy before?"

He said, "I'm happy here also. This body is not mine. This is not Lakhani. They will not put *me* in a cemetery."

He stopped and I thought he was going to cry. He wiped his eyes and smiled again. He said, "I have never been unhappy in my life."

He began to repeat that had he not met the FBI informant, this wouldn't have happened to him. He had made a mistake. My time was up and I said that I would come back the next day. Lakhani repeated to me that I was to call his wife, who was visiting their son in New York City, and remind her to call him between four and five that evening. He was allowed one weekly call and if she didn't pick up the phone and the answering machine came on he would have to wait another week to talk to her. I began to gather my papers and Lakhani began to press me to stay a little longer. I looked back at the prison official, but he simply pursed his lips to say that there was no more time left. Lakhani began to beg him, calling him "Brother" and then "Boss," urging him to let me stay a few minutes longer.

In Springfield, across the street from the prison, there was a strip club called Teasers. The use of "black light" inside made the dancers' thongs and teeth glow like the fluorescent stickers that bikers wear at night on their jackets. The young women, thin and topless, had masked their skin with powdery glitter. It was a slow night, despite it being the weekend, with only a handful of customers. The taste in music at this establishment was rather literal: the songs being played were "I'm N Luv (Wit a Stripper)" by T-Pain and "I'm a Stripper" by 7 Crystal Method. One of the women working that night came over and asked if I'd buy her a drink. When we were settled with our beverages, she said, "My stage name is Ivory. Because of my skin. I don't tan." Ivory said that she wanted to go to India, and added, by way of explanation, that she loved animals and architecture. When she saw me looking around at the walls and the furniture, she called Teasers a "shithole" and then asked me what it was that had brought me to her town. I had interviewed an inmate, I said, gesturing in the direction of the prison. She wanted to know why the man was inside, and I, unable to think of anything else, replied that he had tried to sell a missile to a terrorist. Ivory stopped sucking on the straw in her Red-Bull-and-vodka and said, "That's not cool." And then, after a brief pause, she asked cheerfully, "So, how was your Fourth of July?"

Ivory's last question began to appear more and more inspirational to me the next morning when, sitting across the glass partition from Lakhani, I had to endure an hour or more of ceaseless invective against his Jewish lawyer (whom he alleged was in cahoots with the prosecutors) and the Muslim informant (who had used duplicity and greed to mislead him). I had entered the interviewing room that day and even before I had sat down Lakhani had asked, "Did my lawyer tell you about the oil refinery?" I said, "No." And Lakhani said, "He is a bastard. He is a bastard." I didn't know what he was talking about and told him so. Lakhani began to narrate to me a complicated story about how he had made a deal with the government of the United Arab Emirates about investing in an oil refinery and had been in Abu Dhabi finalizing that deal when Rehman came into his life. He wanted me to note that it was not him that the FBI had been after but the Ukrainian state-owned company that was selling arms all over the world. The president of Ukraine had been selling arms to Iraq, and the Americans were nervous, and the FBI had failed in its attempt to catch the real culprit and had ended up with Lakhani. He said, "This is the truth, nothing else."

I tried, more than once, to seek clarifications. But each time, my questions would be brushed aside. "Listen to me," Lakhani would say, and then he'd cite another random fact or detail of case history. He rambled endlessly and appeared obsessive, but he had a wonderful memory. He recited the phone number of a man in London with whom he hadn't spoken for years. Nothing that he said about his case seemed coherent or easy to follow, but everything he said came with precise references to dates or court-transcript page numbers.

His lower jaw was missing a tooth in the front and spittle dribbled out when he spoke in a rage against what had happened in his past. But Lakhani wasn't angry with himself. Most of his anger was reserved for his lawyer. He said, "I'm moving around with top-most people. It was the worst defense. I made twenty-two trips to Ukraine. Did my lawyer pay for them? Scotland Yard had issued twenty-two passports to me." There was no admission of guilt, partial or otherwise, and I suddenly began to think how easy it would have been for a jury to dislike this man, even if he wasn't the terrorist that the government wanted to believe he was.

And yet, was it only delusion on Lakhani's part as I was tempted to believe, or something else, more of a stubborn pride, perhaps, that insisted that he wasn't the man the government said he was? I don't know. A week later, while talking to his wife, I learned that at various times Lakhani had agreed to plead guilty and then changed his mind. If he had indeed done that, he would have gotten only a few years in prison at most; the way things turned out, Lakhani is scheduled for release in 2044. (At the sentencing, Lakhani had appealed to the judge, saying, "I don't want to die here in this country. Everybody would like to die in their own country.") Kusum Lakhani told me that she had gone with the lawyer Henry Klingeman to the hospital where Lakhani was being treated during the trial; her husband had tubes attached to his body and he promised her that the moment he was out from the hospital he would plead guilty. That didn't happen. And then, the weekend before the presidential elections, with Bush facing a close race, the government made a new offer of a plea bargain. Kusum Lakhani had received a call at two-thirty in the morning. She was in London. Klingeman told her that Lakhani was going to plead guilty the next day and he was going to call the media. But, again, Lakhani decided to press instead for his innocence. (I later asked Klingeman about this, but he denied ever telling Mrs. Lakhani that her husband was pleading guilty as neither Lakhani nor the government ever seriously considered making an agreement.)

When I first saw Kusum Lakhani, a small Indian woman waiting for me by the side of a street in Manhattan, she reminded me of my mother. Over lunch, she said to me in Hindi, "Upar se aasman phat gaya, neeche se zameen hut gayee" (The sky split over our heads, the ground shifted under our feet). Then, turning to English, she asked me, "You know the meaning of loss?" The last word was pronounced to rhyme with "shows." Kusum had come wearing some mascara, but she cried often and the make-up spread, giving her a more grieving air. Then, she began to tell me about the day Lakhani was arrested. The festival of Raksha Bandhan was being celebrated that day and she had been fasting; just that morning, the couple had arrived in New York from London, and while Kusum sat with her son, her husband rushed to the Wyndham Hotel in New Jersey where Rehman was waiting. After some time, the FBI had come to the apartment, and then the television cameras.

At her husband's sentencing, Kusum Lakhani too had spoken a few words: "Please excuse me my India accent. Of this I am very proud. If I may use offending words, please forgive me in explaining if I am not able to. Only thing I want to say, we do not belong to any of the terrorists group. . . . We are normal people. We live normally. We have good life in London. . . . We are God-fearing people. . . . My husband of course got in with the wrong people, which was all set up, of course you know it so I don't have to say anything." In her conversation with me, like her husband, she shared her suspicions about both the FBI informant and the defense lawyer. During the trial, she had often seen her lawyer talking or exchanging jokes with the prosecutors, and this had made her realize that they were colluding against her husband. Both Klingeman and Rabner were Jewish, she told me, as if that explained it. The informant was a Muslim. Kusum Lakhani's family had suffered during the Partition, moving from Karachi in the newly created country of Pakistan. When her husband had spoken like this, his language was so aggressive and abusive that it had been easy for me to dismiss it, but listening to Mrs. Lakhani's simpler, wholly sincere words of prejudice, I didn't quite know how to respond. She was addressing me as a Hindu man, but I couldn't find a way of mentioning to her that my wife was a Pakistani Muslim and, oddly enough, the longer I listened to the anxious, conservative, even bigoted woman sitting in front of me, the more I felt that it was I who was being dishonest.

A few months later, I was in a wine-store one evening, in the aisle containing California Chardonnays, when my cell-phone rang. It was Kusum Lakhani, wanting to know if I had written anything about her husband. I was able to say nothing assuring to her, and to make matters worse, I mentioned that I was upset that her husband had sent several accusatory letters to me from prison. Hemant Lakhani had wanted to know why I was interviewing his lawyer: he wanted me to regard him as the sole source of information about his case. Cruelly, I told Mrs. Lakhani that I felt no inclination to talk to her husband ever again. Although I haven't indeed spoken again to Lakhani or his wife, I'm often reminded of them, and I'm reminded of their nemesis, the informant Rehman.

For instance, in May 2009, when I heard the news that four men, all black Muslims, had been arrested for participating in a plot to bomb New York City synagogues and shooting down military planes. The plot had been revealed with the help of a confidential informant. Then, the following day, a news-report revealed that all of the accused were former convicts. One of them was schizophrenic and had been recently convicted of purse-snatching; when a friend visited his apartment after the arrests, he found urine stored in bottles and raw chicken on the stovetop. Another man was a crack addict. The federal authorities had provided the accused, with the help of the informant, fake bombs and even a fake heat-seeking Stinger missile. The men were arrested after they had planted the mock explosive devices in cars parked outside a synagogue. My interest flared when I read that the informant was a Pakistani man who had first met the men in a mosque. Had Rehman returned to do duty for the FBI? The news-report mentioned that the informant had earlier been arrested on charges of identity theft and turned into a government informant. He would come to the mosque and offer to take worshippers out for meals; his talk was about violence and jihad. The imam at the mosque said that the stranger's behavior was "suspicious" and that the members of the mosque "believed he was a government agent." The informant would take the accused to Danny's Restaurant; he usually paid for the group and the restaurant owner thought that he was the boss. This would have pleased Rehman, I thought. But the following day, in another report in the *New York Times*, the informant was identified as Shahed Hussain, and I felt a little disappointed. Except that there wasn't much to distinguish between the two men: both Rehman and Hussain played at being wealthy at the government's (read taxpayers') expense. Both had committed crimes that drew the attention of the authorities; and to escape deportation or other punishment, they lured their vulnerable targets with gifts and promises. I could imagine myself sitting at another trial months later where it would be unclear how motivated the accused would have been if the informant hadn't played his crucial role, and this question would only be a part of the greater mystery of the way in which the war on terror was being conducted.

There was one further twist to the story. A writer for the *Village Voice* reported that the FBI's Special Agent Robert Fuller, the lead investigating officer in the arrest of the four men, had a controversial record. He was the subject of a lawsuit in the misidentification and arrest of a Canadian man Maher Arar, who had then been renditioned to Syria and tortured for a year. Fuller had also been a part of the team that had been warned of the presence and travels of two September 11 hijackers in the days preceding the attacks; on August 23, 2001, Fuller was assigned the task of arresting the two men but he failed to locate them on the database he used. And, in February 2004, Mohamed Alanssi, an informant working for Fuller, had tried to kill himself by setting himself on fire in front of the White House. Alanssi survived with serious burns but his suicide letter was addressed to Fuller. It said, "It is my big mistake that I have cooperated with F.B.I. The F.B.I. have already destroyed my life and my family's life and made us in a very danger position . . . I am not crazy to destroy my life and my family's life to get $100,000."

✳

"The function of law enforcement is the prevention of crime and the apprehension of criminals. Manifestly, that function does not include the manufacturing of crime."
Sherman v. United States

On May 4, 1990, an Arkansas orthodontist named William Pickard had placed an ad in *USA Today* offering to sell a banking license in Grenada. On that very day, an Indiana-based U.S. customs agent named J. Thomas Rothrock was attending a seminar on money laundering, and he saw Pickard's ad and decided that it was suspicious. It was an odd assumption for Rothrock to have made because if a banking license is useful for money laundering, it doesn't make much sense to want to sell it. Nonetheless, the agent called the number provided in the ad and pretended that he had money from an organization that needed to be deposited offshore. Rothrock spoke several times to Pickard, and, after several months, was able to induce Pickard and his partner, Arnold Hollingsworth, a farmer in Arkansas, to enter a scheme that would allow the laundering of over $200,000.

Pickard and Hollingsworth were both arrested after the two of them had made separate visits to Indianapolis to meet with Rothrock and collect large amounts of cash. An Indiana jury convicted both men and they received prison sentences. This decision was reversed, however, by the court of appeals in a landmark case. Judge Posner, writing for the majority in *Hollingsworth*, wrote:

> Predisposition is not a purely mental state, the state of being willing to swallow the government's bait. It has positional as well as dispositional force. The dictionary definitions of the word include "tendency" as well as "inclination." The defendant must be so situated by reason of previous training or experience or occupation or acquaintances that it is likely that if the government had not induced him to commit the crime some criminal would have done so; only then does a sting or other arranged crime take a dangerous person out of circulation. A public official is in a position to take bribes; a drug addict to deal drugs; a gun dealer to engage in illegal gun sales. For these and other traditional targets of stings all that must be shown to establish predisposition and thus defeat the defense of entrapment is willingness to violate the law without extraordinary inducements; ability can be presumed. It is different when the defendant is not in a position without the government's help to become involved in illegal activity. The government "may not provoke or create a crime, and then punish the criminal, its creature."

Neither Pickard nor Hollingsworth had committed any crime before and the judicial panel thought that had the government left the two to their own devices they would have only been contemplating financial ruin and not lengthy terms in prison. It was also held unlikely that in the absence of the customs agent anyone else would have appeared and guided the two men into money laundering. "No real criminal," Judge Posner wrote, "would do business with such tyros."

In his closing statement during the Lakhani trial, the defense lawyer Klingeman was echoing the *Hollingsworth* ruling when he began by reminding jurors that his client was a "willing" participant but not a "ready" one in the government sting. Facing an uphill task of convincing his audience of the defendant's complete innocence, Klingeman told the jurors that they were not being asked to like Lakhani, or respect him, or even judge him morally. They were only to ask whether Lakhani was guilty of the charges against him, and for doing that the jury must consider whether there was reasonable doubt regarding Lakhani's predisposition. There was cause for doubting whether the missile that had been brought into the courtroom on the very first day of trial could have ever entered the United States without the government bringing it in. No real terrorist would ever approach Lakhani. "There was no missile plot," Klingeman argued, "until the government created the missile plot." Pointing a finger at law enforcement's need to establish itself, after the attacks of September 11, as the protector of the people, Klingeman said that the government's role was "a lot like the fireman who lights a fire and pulls the alarm so that he could be the hero and put the fire out and rescue the people."

In the *Hollingsworth* case, one of the judges on the panel wrote a dissenting opinion in which he pointed out that the majority had created a "fictional image" of "allegedly 'innocent' would-be international financiers." The dissenting judge was of the strong opinion that "the defendants were not reluctant to engage in criminal activity and there was no inducement; the government merely presented the defendants with an opportunity to commit a crime (as they do in all 'sting operations'), an opportunity that a law-abiding citizen would have refused." Similarly, at the end of the Lakhani trial, the government attorneys presented the defendant as "the eager and enthusiastic salesman" who was "the poster child for a willing broker anxious to peddle a missile for use by terrorists." (More flamboyantly, Lakhani was called "the Energizer bunny of arms traffickers." I wonder whether the defendant found it oddly flattering.) The prosecutors emphasized Lakhani's many business contacts, his familiarity with an Indian gangster, and, above all, the statements against America on tape, remarks like "America is a village of motherfuckers."

Alert to the argument advanced by the defense about Lakhani's lack of proficiency as a criminal, assistant U.S. attorney Rabner reminded the jurors, "He's not charged with being sophisticated in his illegal arms dealings. You don't have to be sophisticated to be a criminal. You could be a dumb criminal." Here, too, the Lakhani trial seemed to be following the precedence of *Hollingsworth*. In the latter, a second dissenting opinion had the following to say: "My colleagues in the majority treat Pickard as a pathetic figure. Perhaps he is. Police are better at nabbing bumblers than accomplished criminals. Being a novice caught on an initial sally into crime is no defense, however." The only difference was that, unlike both Pickard and Hollingsworth, Hemant Lakhani wasn't acquitted. The panel of eight women and four men on the jury deliberated for seven hours over two days and declared him guilty on all counts.

Let us return to *Hollingsworth* one last time. The majority opinion in the court of appeals had asked speculatively what would have happened to Pickard and Hollingsworth had the customs agent not responded to the ad in *USA Today*. The judges conjectured that Pickard, who, despite a good medical practice, had a history of bad business investments, would have "folded his financial venture." Pickard's bid to become an international banker, the majority opinion went on to suggest unequivocally, "would have joined his other failures—his movie theaters that failed, his amusement park that failed, his apartment building that failed, his attempt to market cookbooks written by his wife that failed."

Such a sad and impressive litany.

It reminded me powerfully of Lakhani and of the reasons why, at the sentencing, the defense lawyer Klingeman likened Lakhani to Willy Loman. For hundreds of thousands of American high-school and college students reading in their literature classes Arthur Miller's *Death of a Salesman*, Willy Loman is a figure who is so uncannily familiar in his enormous futility and, equally, his flawed humanity. The lawyer in his appeal was saying to the judge that he pitied his client and wanted her to be lenient. But I've been unable to shake off the comparison for its astute link to something far greater than Lakhani and his individual record of unsuccessful striving. Happily or unhappily, failure is not unique to Lakhani. Arguably, it is the shared fate of an overwhelming part of the world's population. The tapes that the government lawyers played at the Lakhani trial, giving the jurors a taste of the defendant's rants against America, were milder, less venomous, versions of speeches pouring out of public speaker systems in various parts of the world. Doesn't that hate also spring from a species of failure, a failure in which the United States is seen as having a hand?

Writing soon after the attacks of September 11, the Turkish novelist Orhan Pamuk asked us to try and understand "why millions of people in poor countries that have been pushed to one side, and deprived of the right to decide their own histories, feel such anger at America." Often, the anger that erupts in violent protests on our television screens, with the burning of effigies of Bush and Cheney, doesn't necessarily require sympathy. This is because the display of such anger, Pamuk argues, is sometimes designed to conceal the absence of democracies in those societies and to reinforce the power of local dictators. Similarly, the presence of "superficial hostility" can be a way for the indigenous elite to mask the misuse of funds provided by international agencies, so that the bristling against a distant, foreign enemy distracts attention from the inequities at home. Nevertheless, Pamuk's main aim is to force a recognition of the conditions under which the United States is misguidedly imposing an ideology of defeat on millions of people and thereby lending support to the terrorists it is purportedly fighting against:

> There are those in the U.S. today who unconditionally support military attacks for the purpose of demonstrating America's military strength and teaching terrorists "a lesson." Some cheerfully discuss on television where American planes should bomb, as if playing a video game. Such commentators should realize that decisions to engage in war taken impulsively, and without due consideration, will intensify the hostility toward the West felt by millions of people in the Islamic countries and poverty-stricken regions of the world— people living in conditions that give rise to feelings of humiliation and inferiority. It is neither Islam nor even poverty itself that directly engenders support for terrorists whose ferocity and ingenuity are unprecedented in human history; it is, rather, the crushing humiliation that has infected the third-world countries.

Even Hemant Lekhani, with his fanciful and overreaching sense of ambition, would not have contemplated offering to politicians and policymakers, through the lesson of his trial, a salutary lesson in global geopolitics. And, if we are so inclined, we can add this to his already long list of failures. But we can perhaps readily concede that this inability to see past one's own strengths or weaknesses and engage with the wellsprings of the world's misery is a failing that Lakhani would share with those rich and powerful individuals who hold the reins of the world, and in doing this, he would have at long last found a place among those whose company he had always desired.

2 ✳ The Late Career of the Sting Operation

REHMAN: "And also get me order for night vision goggles."
LAKHANI: "What is that?"
REHMAN: "That's something for seeing at night."
LAKHANI: "Are they buying it?"
REHMAN: "Yes, they need a lot of them. It is their demand."
LAKHANI: "What, the sunglasses?"
— *United States of America v. Hemant Lakhani*

A writer was selling arms in New Delhi. He thought he needed a disguise
to go around visiting members of the defense establishment and the sleazy
middlemen, whom he called "the suitcase people," and for that purpose
he had purchased a hat and a suit, also a pair of black Gucci spectacles
from Khan Market. He had learned that the Indian army was in need of
a high-tech, hand-held thermal camera; he had gotten his team to print a
brochure with material from the Web and had invented a fictitious company called West End International with offices on Regent Street. The
company's logo was what looked like a British stone cottage: it was an
image that had originally been designed for a dummy presentation of a
book by V. S. Naipaul.

The writer was conducting interviews with politicians and army officers and recording footage of the men accepting bribes to help him win a
contract for his product. Because he was pretending to be an arms dealer

based in London, he had adopted a drawl that to his ears sounded foreign. Unlike the accent, the spycam he was using was authentic and had been bought in England.

But that didn't help with the lies he needed to tell, for he knew nothing about the device that he was hawking. In a conversation with a general who was the infantry chief of the Drass-Kargil sector in Kashmir, the writer was informed that another company had sent them a sample that had been tried in the desert terrain but had malfunctioned. The writer began to boast of the qualities that his own product possessed. He said, "What we can do in ours, which is very rare, is that we can put in movement locators. So immediately there's human movement, there will be a beep that will go off." When asked what the range of the camera was, he stammered and replied, "Unlimited." The writer's sidekick was a similarly intrepid bungler. He was asked the name of the bank he used and he replied, "Thomas Cook." Not ever having gone outside India, he was a little bit at a loss when asked by one military official where he stayed when he was in London. All he could manage was the name of a football club, Manchester United.

The writer's name was Aniruddha Bahal. In the early 1990s, he had moved to Delhi from Allahabad after the publication of his first novel, which hadn't sold well, and become an investigative journalist. He was doing print journalism, but what fascinated him were spy cameras.

In 1997 he had used a secret video device for the first time—he describes the equipment then used more like "a home theater system strapped on your body"—during an interview in London. The man he was interviewing was a Pakistani cricketer who had claimed that the Indian players were offering money to throw away matches. The recording hadn't worked due to a faulty connection. But two years later, Bahal made big news by leading an undercover operation on match fixing in Indian cricket. And then in 2001, Operation West End took place, suddenly making visible in a sensational way the corruption that everyone knew existed in Indian political life. There were arrests and courts-martial; the ruling party chief, shown accepting an envelope filled with cash and putting it in his drawer, was kicked out; the defense minister was forced to resign. Many people thought that the party that was then in power in Delhi would soon collapse. This did not happen and, in some ways, the story that dominated the years that followed was about the official harassment that was meted out to the journalists. Nevertheless, Operation West End was the first real introduction that the broad Indian public had received to the power of the media and, in particular, the phenomenon of the media sting.

Unlike the United States, where the constraints of case law limit covert sting operations largely to law-enforcement agencies, in India it is the press corps that is defining the meaning of sting. It is revealing that important sting operations are often accompanied in the media by reports on the new equipment available for use in stings. Buttonhole cameras, available in Delhi's Palika Bazaar and Nehru Place, go for anywhere between $2,000 and $14,000. But cameras hidden in cigarette packs or lighters, or even watches, are more inexpensive. Indeed, given the popularity of stings, another product that has become available on the Indian market is a video jammer for about $1,000 and a camera detector for one-fourth that price. For a much higher price, closer to $100,000, it is possible to buy a "sweeper" that is able to locate wireless tapping devices, wireless hidden cameras, laser taps, phone taps, and even real-time vehicle trackers. In late 2005, Bahal released footage of members of Parliament accepting money to raise questions in the legislature. One seller of anti-sting equipment in Delhi told a journalist that while earlier he had received two inquiries each month, after Bahal's sting he had begun getting two inquiries each day.

In the years since Operation West End, schools in India that offer diplomas in television journalism have started including courses in sting operations. Each television channel now has undercover teams. These channels have shown hidden-camera footage of a journalist who was a former convict bribing officials in Delhi's Tihar Jail; an actor leading an undercover reporter to his bed while explaining the phenomenon of the "casting couch"; Muslim clerics taking money to issue fatwas, or religious rulings, on matters ranging from how "talaq," or divorce, could be initiated through text messaging on a cell phone to how sleeping on a double bed was against the tenets of Islam; Hindu holy men sexually abusing female devotees who had wanted a cure for infertility; and politicians having sex with call girls. If there have been several stings that could be described as critical and shocking, there have also been many more that are frankly pornographic.

Often, it is hard to support the argument that an entrapment has been carried out in the public interest. Television channels have been accused of carrying out stings only to raise their ratings. Tarun Tejpal, the chief editor at Tehelka.com, the news website for which Bahal had worked on Operation West End, told me in his New Delhi office in July 2006, "There is now a sting a week. It is an epidemic on Indian television." Even while I was sitting in Tejpal's office, he turned on the television and one of the channels began to announce a sting. A reporter who earlier used to work for Tehelka had caught on camera a doctor describing the method he uses to amputate, for the right payment, the healthy limbs of beggars.

Tejpal's own company has itself carried out several undercover operations in recent years. Tehelka's hidden cameras recorded the crowing words of a Gujarat legislator who admitted having paid money to buy the silence in court of a young Muslim woman who had watched her family being murdered in a bakery in the riots of March 2002. Reporters from the same outfit were responsible for an exposé on how a government-employed doctor at Agra's mental asylum was certifying women mad because un-scrupulous husbands wanted to dump their wives. In another famous case, when the main witnesses to the shooting of a female bartender at a chic South Delhi party turned hostile, Tehelka reporters went undercover in September 2006 to present on camera evidence of the use of money and threats by the father of the accused. In the absence of credible evidence, the accused murderer, who was the son of a prominent politician, was ac-quitted. But after the Tehelka sting, the politician-father resigned, and, in a later judgment, the Delhi High Court reversed its acquittal. In another investigation in early 2007, after the arrest of a rich Punjabi businessman and his servant in a township near Delhi on suspicion of the murder of several children, the Tehelka team unearthed the phone numbers and rail-way tickets that showed how the police were accepting favors from the accused and harassing the victims.

News portals like Tehelka.com, as well as the outfit that Bahal founded on his own, Cobrapost.com, sell their footage to any one of the television channels for broadcast. A good price is often 50 lakh rupees, which is less than $100,000. It is perhaps because of the money that is paid by the tele-vision agencies, and their search for maximum viewers, that the results of the sting come to the public prepackaged as sensational news, noteworthy for its shock value. Dramatic graphics, loud music, and special effects, which on American television seem to be reserved mostly for news about war or shootings in schools, are stock fare in the presentation of stings on

Indian television. But what is more remarkable is that in nearly each of these shows, what is made visible is the apparatus of the search for news. For instance, if we return to the examples of the sting operations carried out by Tehelka, we find their investigations editor, Harinder Baweja, explaining to the television anchor, for the benefit of the audience watching the news at home, how a particular individual was trapped or how a truth was uncovered on camera. Usually this involves an explanation about the story told to cover a lie or to find access. Although the technical details about the hidden cameras are rarely divulged, there is no coyness about a reporter's impersonation or the limits to a fabrication. It is possible to think of this as yet another layer of voyeurism, but I believe what is happening instead is that a medium is finding its footing—hence the effort to argue or explain the reason for its existence at the very moment it actually claims to be triumphant. In contrast to the United States, where a whole body of legal judgments provides the foundation for entrapment by law enforcement, the new, commercialized Indian television media is finding out what the boundaries of its own practice are.

There is yet another reason too. Investigative reporters who conduct stings are interested in making transparent their modus operandi in the very process of sharing with the public the results of their sting because they need to protect themselves from legal harassment. Sitting in his new basement office in Noida, across the Yamuna from Delhi, in July 2006 Aniruddha Bahal told me that when a commission of inquiry was set up by the Indian government after Operation West End, his deposition "was longer than the Encyclopedia Britannica." He added, "Since 2001, more than five years ago now, I have spent one day a week in a legal proceeding. If I were to add up those days, it would be nearly a year." The threats could also be more immediate and physical. After one of his sting operations, there was an intelligence report that Pakistan's ISI (Inter-Services Intelligence) had organized a hit on Bahal in an effort to spread mayhem in India. A court directive was issued asking the government to provide him security cover.

When our interview was over and Bahal rose to go to the Kali Temple on Mandir Marg, two men got up from their chairs outside the office door. One was a guard in his regulation paramilitary uniform, carrying an AK-47, and another in plainclothes with a Brownie pistol under his pink shirt. But the real threat remains the law itself. In 2005, the Indian

Parliament passed the Right to Information Act, but what is still missing, Bahal argues, is a strong legal mechanism that can protect journalists from being falsely implicated in criminal cases by the police and politicians. For example, the wife of one of the army officers entrapped during Operation West End had charged that her husband had been "drugged into having sex with prostitutes and blackmailed by the Tehelka team." During the long questioning in front of the various commissions of inquiry, other, more lurid, accusations were thrown their way.

More than such accusations, however, there is danger of the ruling powers cracking down on the journalists. In July 2007, two years after Bahal had masterminded a sting in which politicians were shown on camera accepting bribes to raise questions in the Parliament, Delhi police charged his company, Cobrapost, as well as the television channel that had broadcast the footage, with the crime of abetting corruption. The undercover reporter had claimed to be a representative of a fictitious business association. I must add that the police do not appear much exercised over the fictional nature of the questions that had been submitted by the reporter and signed by the honorable members of Parliament. Here are some excerpts:

> Whether the Railway Ministry has placed any order for purchase of the Yossarian Electro Diesel engine from Germany? Is the ministry aware that the Tom Wolfe committee report in Germany has halted its induction into the Euro Rail system?
>
> Whether the Government has given sanction for the seed trial of Salinger Cotton on Monsanto? If so, has a report been prepared on Catch 22 cotton so far?
>
> Has the Ministry lifted the 1962 ban it imposed on the book *For Whom the Bell Tolls* by Ernest Hemingway and the 1975 ban on Ken Kesey's book *One Flew Over a [sic] Cuckoo's Nest* and Hunter Thompson's book *Fear and Loathing in Las Vegas*? If so, when were the bans removed?

It hasn't been all laughter and gaiety so far. Bahal and others fear a crackdown on stings also through the introduction of a proposed broadcast bill that would give the government unprecedented powers to curb media expression if any piece of broadcast, as an official statement puts it, "is likely to threaten the security and integrity of the State or threaten peace and harmony or public order in the whole or part of the country." The government's authority is going to return with a vengeance. For their part, investigative journalists have been making loud noises about "public interest" every time they speak to the public about what they do. This is because they want to affect future legislation and protect the right to conduct stings. In a magazine article published in October 2006, Bahal wrote:

> In stories where we use hidden cameras, we ascertain whether the people we are doing a particular story on have a "predisposition" to commit the particular act in question. American case law that has developed on undercover operations articulates that if law enforcement has "prior knowledge" of the intention of a person to commit a crime and the person is subsequently exposed in an undercover operation, it is not bracketed as entrapment. British law, in any case, doesn't even count entrapment as a defense for the alleged victim. In India, no case law has developed yet but any that does will or should lean on "public interest" being the defining theme in any faceoff between individual privacy and an act of corruption impacting on the public at large.

When I came across Bahal's piece, I thought of Hemant Lakhani. He is not present anywhere in this picture, but it is he who holds the key to an equation that stretches across the nations that Bahal mentions in his analysis. Lakhani's story is the lowest common denominator when you stack up different nations in a row; he, but any other figure linked to a terrorist threat might do as well, will determine the limits of a legal understanding of entrapment. Once we have stepped into the red zone of a terrorist threat, and therefore into the need for prevention, entrapment will always be seen as working in the public interest. "Public interest" is only going to be another name—in all the courts everywhere—for the nation-state's "security interest." To continue to cast the debate in terms of an older definition of public interest is to remain trapped in an argument that is already obsolete. The fact is that this new definition of public interest, where the argument is made in terms of national security, will trump all other claims every time. Not only stings, but even daily journalism is already being governed and regulated by that need of the nation-state. Are journalists like Bahal who are interested in conducting stings prepared to deal with this challenge?

After the attacks of September 11, 2001, all around us the world has been retooling itself to define public interest, but only in a limited, perverse way as a global ecology of anti-terrorism. This is what makes possible the transnational exchange of intelligence as well as the outsourcing of torture. Journalists in India, and for that matter elsewhere, cannot with a flourish forego an insistence on the private in the name of the public. A hypothetical state can in the name of anti-terrorism happily condemn, if it so wills, without granting any legal rights, hundreds of prisoners to incarceration on a little island. That is why individual civil rights will have to remain the touchstone by which any credible definition of civil society is advanced, and public interest will need to be defined more boldly as the rights that offer protection against the encroachments of a security state.

3 ✳ The Art of Surveillance

We also have to work sort of the dark side, if you will.
We're going to spend time in the shadows in the intelligence
world. A lot of what needs to be done here will have to be
done quietly, without any discussions, using sources and
methods that are available to our intelligence agencies if
we're going to be successful. That's the world these folks
operate in. —Vice President Dick Cheney, on *Meet the Press*,
September 16, 2001

I must have been in my late teens when I first read Graham Greene's novel, *The Power and the Glory*, about the "whisky priest" who is being hunted by a determined police lieutenant during the era of anticlerical violence in Mexico. The priest is a marvel of flawed humanity. He is an alcoholic and has fathered an illegitimate child, but even as he flees the fanatical power that pursues him he gives succor to those who come to him in the dark for a blessing or a mass. In the end, he is caught and executed. I cannot remember now whether I understood much of the novel or the curious search for human redemption that lies at its heart. But there was a line that the priest offered that has always stayed with me: "Hate was just a failure of the imagination." When I went looking for those lines again, I found that they occur in the context of the priest trying to imagine a face, and inevitably finding evidence of grace: "He couldn't see her in the darkness, but there were plenty of faces he could remember from the old days which fitted the voice. When you visualized a man or woman carefully, you could always begin to feel pity—that was a quality God's image carried with it. When you saw the lines at the corners of the eyes, the shape of the mouth, how the hair grew, it was impossible to hate. Hate was just a failure of imagination." While reading those lines now, I recognize it as a writer's vision, a vision fueled by the belief that detail and voice, and all that we think of as face, would deliver the whole human to you, and behind that, the whole of humanity. It is a belief that, from a writer's viewpoint, is oddly narcissistic. And yet filled with supreme humility—there is a complete absence of hierarchy and also the absence of judgment, there is no distinction drawn between the high and low, the good or bad.

In the years after the attacks of September 11, I have returned to Greene's dictum to ask how artists and writers, those who are conventionally regarded as the imaginative lot, would help us disturb the algebra of hate. Perhaps the same writerly narcissism that I suspected in Greene is at work here: the desire for detail and voice behind the actors participating in the war on terror. Once I had embarked on this project, one of the first things I learned was that it is not only the pursuer and the pursued who are the participants in that war, it is all of us. All of us who hear an announcement on the public address system while we are waiting for a train; any one of us reading a newspaper or watching the news on the television; it is also all of us who have seen the orange jumpsuits and been told about what it means to inhabit a world of total sensory deprivation; and, last but not least, it is each one of us who has tortured another human being or, and this is more dangerous, lived in a world where torture has been practiced. What follows is the result of my investigation.

A growing body of contemporary art in America comments on post–September 11 conditions, specifically the changed realities in the nation's political and social psyche. Okwui Enwezor, in his incisive catalog statement for the Seville Biennial 2006, had identified three themes of the exhibition he was directing, and the statement captured very well the principal concerns that underlie the art that is a response to the "war on terror": first, "the construction of a gargantuan empire of secrets" that not only permitted the emergence of unconstitutional methods, like torture and extraordinary rendition, but actually allowed such arbitrary means to

5. Paul Chan, video still from untitled video on Lynne Stewart and her conviction, the law and poetry. Used with permission of the artist.

become "the principal tool of global governance"; second, the "weakening of the liberal model of open society" by the partnership of seemingly opposed forces, on the one hand, the terroristic imagination, and on the other, the zeal of the prosecuting state waging total war; third, the mediating role played by artistic practice, seeking to negotiate "the distinctions between civil society, civic space, and social reciprocity." Given these concerns, various artists have responded *both* by calibrating the vast reduction of individual freedoms in relation to the growth in ideologies of control, and, equally important, by charting new geographies of affect and intimacy, finding new languages to express protest and also love. In many cases, the artists have chosen to work on, in Dick Cheney's phrase, "the dark side" and they have borrowed techniques used by the covert agencies in the war on terror. For this and other reasons, their work has both immediacy and appeal. But what is of great interest, too, is the way in which these political artists in some measure parry the demand of politics. Many artists whose work compels attention in this context are those who refuse to be defined by dominant notions, whether of the left or the right, of what it means to be political. This is what makes their art thoughtful, and, at other times, transgressive or disturbing.

Paul Chan was born in Hong Kong in 1973 and grew up in Omaha, Nebraska. He is well-known in the contemporary art world for his video work and he is a font maker. (One of the fonts he has designed is called Politics to Come and every letter comes out as "blah." He has used this font to translate, for instance, the U.S. Constitution's Bill of Rights.) In a recent work, an untitled, seventeen-minute video, Chan interviewed the activist lawyer Lynne Stewart, who was disbarred from legal practice and faces a prison sentence after her conviction for providing "material support" to Islamic terrorists. The documentary is a self-portrait of the lawyer as an activist, but it is an unusual portrait because the film's surprise, and its charm, is that it has Stewart, a sixty-seven-year-old radical lawyer, reading poetry (figure 5). An opposition is being exploited here, between a sentence of law and a sentence that works otherwise. Hence the appearance on the screen, at the end, of a line from the philosopher Alain Badiou: "The poem is not a rule-bound crossing, but rather an offering, a lawless proposition."

Stewart's story of her current trial, as she told me in an interview in her former offices in New York, begins with an undercover informant. Emad Salem, a former Egyptian army officer turned FBI informant, had asked Sheikh Omar Abdel-Rahman, in the latter's kitchen late one night, whether it would be halal to bomb the United Nations building. Unknown to the sheikh, Salem was taping the conversation. It wasn't halal because it would be "bad for Muslims," the sheikh had replied, and then told him to target the American military instead. With this evidence in hand, when the government was about to try Sheikh Omar for conspiring to bomb New York City landmarks, Ramsey Clark, a former U.S. attorney general, contacted Lynne Stewart and asked if she'd be interested in representing the Egyptian cleric. Stewart took on the case and fought for her client, but the decks were stacked against him and he was found guilty.

Stewart believes that the sheikh was "wrongfully accused and wrongfully convicted." She told me that she "cared a lot" about her client, even though "his cause was not [her] cause." She laughed and said that the cleric, who is blind and infirm, was always trying to get her to convert to Islam. He would say, "Lynne, it is unthinkable to me that we'll be in paradise, and you will not be there." But more than the personal relationship she had developed, Stewart felt very strongly that her client hadn't received justice. The FBI, after the bombing of the World Trade Center in

1993, was desperate to nab anyone who could be described as a terrorist. The informant had been paid $1 million to deliver one lie after another. Stewart told me that in court, while cross-examining the informant, she had told the man, "You lied on your immigration status. You lied to the woman who married you." Despite what the government witness claimed, there was no concrete evidence of Sheikh Omar being involved in any actual plan to place a bomb. Stewart also believes that the use of anonymous jurors, as well as the practice of isolating jurors by having them picked up at the train station by U.S. marshals and being escorted into the court, only reinforced fear and prejudice against the Muslim defendants. The sheikh was found guilty on twenty-five counts and sentenced to multiple prison terms. In addition, the government had put other legal restrictions on Sheikh Omar; he was not allowed to communicate with the outside world, including the media. But Stewart ran afoul of that ruling when she read out to Reuters a statement that the sheikh had dictated about his opposition to a cease-fire in Egypt. The government charged and found her guilty under the Anti-Terrorism Act of 1996 with four counts of aiding and abetting a terrorist organization. Instead of the thirty years that the government wanted, the New York federal judge handed down a sentence of twenty-eight months. The former lawyer is currently free on bail pending her appeal.

In Chan's video, we watch Stewart recite John Ashbery, William Blake, and Eavan Boland. The video ends with Stewart reading a poem by Bertolt Brecht, the last poem that he wrote before his death: "And I always thought: the very simplest words / Must be enough. When I say what things are like / Everyone's heart must be torn to shreds." Both the poet Brecht and the artist Chan are aware that the simplest words are never enough. Nothing is ever enough. And yet we need to speak out. That is why we hear Stewart reading more of Brecht's words. "That you will go down if you don't stand up for yourself. / Surely you see that."

The surprise in the film is not simply that the lawyer is reading poetry, thereby coming to Stewart's life, as she put it to me, "from an oblique angle." It is also that when the poems are being read, the screen eliminates all image and begins to shimmer with color. Elsewhere in the film, when we hear Stewart speaking and then also see her on the screen, the sight and the sound do not always match. We are hearing her laugh, but in the image on the screen, she is somber, sitting in the dappled light on the steps behind her home in Brooklyn. This is as effective as having Stewart reading poetry. When I asked Chan about it, during an interview in his studio in Chelsea in February 2007, he said that with the "'misalignment' between sound and pictures what we realize is that the nature of things isn't the nature of things." Chan further explained, "As someone who does not do documentaries, or who is not a journalist, I cannot rely on a narrative or an argumentative logic that would hope to persuade and influence the material aspects of the case. My material is immaterial. It is ghostly. It is the ghostliness that tells us something not directly but indirectly, and it's the process of following this sign that gives us a chance at the tail end to see things and say things otherwise."

There is another kind of spectrality that Chan has been attending to. In the attention that has been paid to the Stewart case, what has often been overshadowed is the extraordinary injustice done to one of her co-defendants, Mohamed Yousry, a graduate student who had assisted Stewart in the Sheikh Omar defense only as a translator. For performing his work for Stewart, translating Sheikh Omar's Arabic words into English, Yousry was held guilty on all counts of having provided "material support" to terrorists. The government asked that Yousry be given twenty years. At the end, he was sentenced to a year and eight months in prison. While currently out on bail because of his pending appeal, Yousry has lost his job as a language instructor because his supervisors at CUNY's York College were advised not to honor his reappointment. The FBI seized all his dissertation work, forty-seven boxes of materials and two hard drives, and he has had to move with his family to Connecticut. Yousry had never been involved in any act of violence; he is not a member of any Islamic organization. In fact, he is not even a practicing Muslim; he is married to a Baptist and has raised his daughter as a Christian. He has publicly accused Sheikh Omar of "seeking to replace one form of authoritarianism in Egypt with another." A quiet and human portrait of Mohamed Yousry—and a sense of the enormous tragedy of his prosecution—emerges in a short documentary entitled *A Life Stands Still*. The film was made by Mary Billyou and Annelisse Fifi and is a part of a series that Chan has curated under the title *Charged in the Name of Terror: Portraits by Contemporary Artists*.

Trevor Paglen is a researcher in experimental geography at the University of California, Berkeley, and he uses equipment and techniques employed in astrophotography to take pictures of secret military bases, "black sites," and aircraft used in programs of "extraordinary rendition."

Paglen is interested in exploring what he calls, citing the famous passage from Conrad's *Heart of Darkness*, "blank spaces on the earth." In a telephone interview with me in July 2007, Paglen said that these are places that, under a new imperialism, "have been disappeared." Since the mid-1990s, the CIA has had in place a covert policy of kidnapping suspected terrorists from any part of the world and then detaining them in secret prisons called "black sites." One of the sites that Paglen has photographed is the secret prison in Afghanistan known as the Salt Pit. This was the facility that provided housing for the CIA's "high-value" detainees. On his website, Paglen writes, "To find the Salt Pit, I used a collection of commercial satellite imagery, a compass, testimonies from former prisoners, and a map drawn by a former prisoner." The map Paglen mentions had been drawn by Khaled El-Masri, a German citizen of Lebanese descent, who was kidnapped by the CIA in January 2004 and held incommunicado for four months. El-Masri was kidnapped in Macedonia, detained in Afghanistan, and eventually released in Albania. The conditions under which the Americans held El-Masri were inhuman and degrading. The prisoners held at this prison describe "a darkness so thick that they could not see their own hands; Eminem's *Slim Shady* album and other abrasive music and sounds were blasted twenty-four hours a day; interrogations were held under strobe lights; and prisoners were strapped to the ceiling."

To make it worse, no public records exist of such kidnapped persons. In CIA lingo, they are "ghost detainees." A part of Paglen's project has involved the compiling of information and photographs of the civilian airplanes used in the transportation of the secret prisoners. The CIA uses a fleet of unmarked aircraft owned by networks of front companies whose boards of directors are wholly fictitious individuals. In a gallery exhibition entitled "Missing Persons," Paglen has presented a collection of the signatures of these nonexistent people culled from business records, aircraft registrations, and corporate filings (figure 6). When he began investigating the individuals whose names appeared in such documents, Paglen found that "there was no home address, no phone number, nor any other proof that she'd existed at all." Each signature supposedly made by any one individual looks different because each one was made by a different person.

6. Trevor Paglen, "Missing Persons (2006)."
Used with permission of the artist.

If the torturers do not yet exist in the public consciousness, it is perhaps necessary to create them.

With the aid of sixty-dollar combat fatigues and stripes and military insignia that she bought online, the performance artist Coco Fusco has recreated her own identity as a militant sergeant. Sgt. Coco Fusco delivers lectures on the creative ways in which women can use sex as a torture tactic on terrorist suspects, especially on Islamic prisoners. Her performance has been inspired by what had been for Fusco the most disturbing aspect of the photographs from Abu Ghraib: the presence of women among them, not as victims but as victimizers.

7. Coco Fusco, video still from *Operation Atropos*.
Used with permission of the artist.

In a related project, Fusco has made a video entitled *Operation Atropos*, which explores the practice of interrogation (figure 7). In the summer of 2005, Fusco and six women, whom she had selected after circulating a call for volunteers on listservs, were filmed as they were interrogated at a camp run by retired military interrogators. The group running the camp calls itself "Team Delta" and its purpose is to train people in the arts of performing interrogation. Fusco paid $8,000 for the interrogation experience. Her mock-interrogators as well as her fellow participants had agreed beforehand to be filmed during their training.

In the resulting documentary, we first watch Fusco and her colleagues traveling in a van, driving into a wooded area, where they are to meet their interrogators. Suddenly, the van is held up by masked men who, amid loud shouting and violent pushing, take the women captive. The visitors are asked to strip to their underwear and they are given the orange coveralls that we have seen prisoners wearing in photos from Guantánamo. The men put hoods on the women and then handcuff them for the walk to the interrogation site. The women are playing the role of visiting members of a human rights group; the interrogators, gleefully hamming, pretend to be East European paramilitary thugs bent on extracting the names of the visiting group's local contact. The pretense is difficult to maintain under continuing duress. One woman, hooded and bound, breaks down and protests, "It's a fucking game, dude. I'm really fucking tired of doing this." But her interrogator is having none of it. He berates her in his fake accent, "Maybe you must understand that this is no game. But obviously you are too distraught to understand this. Pull yourself together. You'll find no compassion in me. You come across the border into my country. I'm a patriot."

Despite the farcical element in the exchange, the extreme experience, however voluntary, of being hooded and bound, must have revealed something new to the participants. When I mentioned this to Fusco, when I interviewed her one evening in June 2007 in her Brooklyn home, she said, "I learned how soldiers are trained, not how prisoners are treated. It is much easier to inflict pain on a prisoner if you believe that you've experienced it yourself." The Team Delta members were submitting their trainees to a form of torture because they believed that they'd thereby become better interrogators. That is what their leader meant when he told Fusco and her colleagues, "You won't be a good interrogator until you step into the shoes of the prisoner."

On the day I was meeting Fusco, the *New York Times* had printed a front-page story about the release of secret CIA documents called the "Family Jewels." Fusco talked for a while about the agency's role in wiretapping journalists and dissidents, and the acts that the U.S. government had undertaken in the past against legitimate, democratically elected governments, before returning to the origins of her film. When Fusco first read the reports coming from places like Abu Ghraib and Bagram Air Base, she felt that the moral issue aside, these reports were also disturbing and dramatic. It was "performance material." She had decided very early on that, unlike much of the Left's response to the war, her own take on the scandal would be to focus on what it meant to be an American. She said, "It is a mistake to overidentify with the victims of torture. We are not the victims of torture. We are the perpetrators of torture."

In 2008, Fusco published *A Field Guide for Female Interrogators*, which presents an illustrated manual of coercive techniques. The manual contains sixteen statements of instructions. Here is an example. "13. Stress Position. Direct sexual advances from a white Christian female generates anxiety in devout Muslim males by forcing them to confront their desire to break cultural taboos." The accompanying stock illustration shows an orange-suited, swarthy man sitting on a chair, looking uncomfortable. Leaning backward into his lap is a smiling female interrogator wearing military boots, regulation trousers, and a tank top. She has put one of her hands behind her arched, blond head, and laid the other on the crotch of her unbuttoned trousers.

> Will you search me?
> *What?*
> I want you to search me.
> *What?*
> We were rushing across the platform towards the express, and got on just as the door was closing. It was nearly empty but he remained standing, holding the overhead bar.
> *Why do you want me to search you?*
> Because you said you would.
> *I can't search you; you're a woman.*
> Oh, I didn't know that. I paused and looked down at my book, then back up at him. Will you train me?
> *What?*
> I want you to train me.
> *Look, I have to get off here.*
> I repeated my request. He mumbled something, scribbled a number on the last page of my book, and slipped out between the closing doors.

These are the opening words of a small book that, in addition to a video and a series of photographs, resulted from an unusual artistic experiment code-named "Lincoln Ocean Victor Eddy" (figure 8). The artist is Jill Magid, who was born in 1973 and lives in Brooklyn. When Magid returned home to New York City after living abroad in Amsterdam for five years she heard an announcement on the subway intercom that she hadn't heard before. The announcement informed subway users that the transit police could subject them to random searches. When Magid asked an officer to search her, he refused. But she befriended him and they often met in the underground station where the officer worked and, at other times, in his car or in a cheap cafe. In imitation of the slim, black notebook in which the officers log their entries, the artist maintained a log as a record of the 117 hours and 23 minutes that she interacted with the unnamed officer.

Adam Boy Charley David Eddy Frank George Henry Ida John King Lincoln Mary Nora Ocean Peter Queen Robert Sam Thomas Union Victor William X-ray Yellow Zebra

F **J**

8. Jill Magid, poster from "Lincoln Ocean Victor Eddy." Used with permission of the artist.

When I wake up and make coffee I think of him below me. I know that for me it is a new day and for him it is the same. Three hours later he calls. I go down the stairs, through the door, and turn the corner to his car. I open the passenger seat and get in.

For him I am time to be logged, a moment that comes or does not come, with a beginning and an ending, that is gone when I leave this apartment. For me he is a constant. He will follow this schedule for at least ten more years. He is my stability and I am his vacillation.

The letters of the word "love" when translated into the code followed by the police read "Lincoln Ocean Victor Eddy." Although Magid appears to be performing an idiosyncratic anthropology of the subway—her photographs are seldom studied compositions and look more like hurried pictures snatched as evidence—her project is wholly attuned to language and its startling possibilities. The artist deliberately interprets official or legal statements almost literally and uses that ploy to mine an utterance for all its emotional, human, specific meaning. After Magid's debut exhibition in New York City, one reviewer wrote that she seemed to be "motivated by an urge to infiltrate and personalize, if not sexualize, the anonymous social and technological systems that surround us." This reading is especially relevant to "Lincoln Ocean Victor Eddy." During an interview with me in downtown Manhattan one summer day in 2008, Magid explained that the question she had asked herself was the following one: "If you put intimacy into a system, what kind of intimacy do you get back?" The result is less a study of a system of surveillance, and more of an obsessive tracking or observation of human vulnerability. Magid told me that she had felt "totally lost" when she first heard the announcement about random searches on the subway intercom. It is difficult to imagine that she could have felt any more secure when she entered into what she calls "a real relationship" with the unnamed police officer. But her response to the threatening announcement she had heard on the intercom strikes me as being at once transgressive and touching. The seduction, the role playing, the class differences between the cosmopolitan artist and the working-class cop, as well as the tension between the two protagonists dancing to a gendered tune—all seem familiar enough, but in the context of the "war on terror," when our identities and behaviors are still being defined, the story that Magid tells us is appealing not only because it is familiar but because it is new.

"If you put intimacy into a system, what kind of intimacy do you get back?" Magid's question about feeling and vulnerability is turned on its head in the story that former Army reservist Lynndie England tells Philip Gourevitch and Errol Morris in their brilliant documentary-work, *Standard Operating Procedure*. In the prison at Abu Ghraib, England had fallen in love with Specialist Charles Graner, the man who would later be named in an Army report as "the ringleader" of the abuse of Iraqi detainees. England told Gourevitch and Morris that "the moment that changed me was meeting Graner. If I wasn't involved with Graner, I wouldn't have been in that situation. Therefore I wouldn't have been in the pictures." If England hadn't introduced intimacy into the system, she wouldn't have become involved in that other, unwanted intimacy called torture. She wouldn't have gone to prison or become the poster-girl for the Iraq War.

The photos from Abu Ghraib could be considered a part of the art of surveillance. The broader aim that *Standard Operating Procedure* fulfills is of telling us that despite denials by the likes of President Bush, the Americans practiced torture. Or, as Gourevitch wrote in an op-ed on the debate to make public the Abu Ghraib photos: soldiers like Graner performed "a great public service" by offering proof that "the Bush administration had decided to fight terror with terror, and torture with torture." But Gourevitch and Morris are also telling us more than that. They are pointing toward the large, impersonal system that has made the soldiers on the bottom rung its scapegoats. That, to my mind, is the real thrust of their attention to ordinary soldiers and their stories. As Gourevitch writes, "Photographs cannot tell stories. They can only provide evidence of stories, and evidence is mute; it demands investigation and interpretation." When I read that, and think of Lynndie England's love, her claims about what happened to her achieve a terrible sadness, prompting the thought that it is not only the Army but all of us who have rather easily made her the society's scapegoat: "I mean, yeah, I was in pictures that showed me holding a leash around the guy's neck. But that's all I did. I was convicted of being in a picture."

In the late 1960s, in New York City and later at the University of California, San Diego, where she was a student, the well-known artist Martha Rosler produced a series of images that she had entitled *Bringing the War Home*. Designed as agit prop, their goal was to mobilize support against the war in Vietnam. Now, Rosler has done a nearly identical series of collages that takes as its subject the war in Iraq. "This war is a replay of the earlier one," Rosler told me, "so I decided to swallow my pride and go back to a form I had abandoned thirty years ago" (figure 9). In her original series from the 1960s, outside the window of a suburban American home was a tropical landscape with charred corpses and tanks on the street; a Vietnamese housewife appeared to occupy an advertisement for a vacuum cleaner, except that visible on the other side of her clean drapes were armed American GIs standing in a bunker; two white boys were playing in a brightly furnished room with thick shag carpeting, but the window drape was lifted to show an anti-war protester being arrested by two policemen.

In the new series, the protester is missing, but the contrasts remain stark. Pfc. Lynndie England, leash held in left hand, stands inside a sophisticated kitchen with pictures of Abu Ghraib strewn about; an androgynous-looking model walks across a living room as if strutting on a ramp at a fashion show while in the foreground are two bent-over figures, hands bound behind them, hoods on their heads; a smiling young woman, her repeated figure forming a busy arc of happiness, sprays a room freshener in Saddam's ruined palace.

Rosler is not the only one who has found contemporary use and relevance for her early art. In a class at the California Institute of the Arts,

9. Martha Rosler, "Lounging Woman" from *Bringing the War Home: House Beautiful*, New Series (2004). Used with permission of the artist.

during the spring semester of 2007, Nancy Buchanan and Sam Durant asked their students to produce art modeled on Rosler's video from 1983, *A Simple Case for Torture, or How to Sleep at Night*. Rosler's film was a fiercely lucid response to an opinion piece in *Newsweek* written by the philosophy professor Michael Levin arguing for acceptance of torture if it could save lives. In his article, Levin had asked, "If you caught the terrorist, could you sleep nights knowing that millions died because you couldn't bring yourself to apply the electrodes?" The video by Rosler is inspired by the Nietzschean injunction to "distrust all in whom the impulse to punish is powerful." Rosler cites Levin's hypothetical story about a terrorist group kidnapping a newborn baby from a hospital. Levin had written that he had asked four mothers if they approved of torturing those kidnappers and all had said yes. But such "what-if" scenarios are suspect because they so rarely conform to actual reality, and the deeper error in Levin's thinking is repeatedly exposed by Rosler through a series of brilliantly clarifying arguments delivered as a calm voice-over while the camera pans over a scene of children playing with their parents in a public place:

> But the state and individuals must never be confused with one another. The state is not a person. It does not have an unconscious, a spouse, feelings, children, a house, pride, a body, sex organs. The state feels no pleasure, no pain. It does not experience ecstasy, love, depression, or hatred. It has neither rage nor passions. The state is not biological but social and historical. The state is not a worried, sleepless man. It is not a frantic mother. It is not a person or even a group of persons. The state does not have a right to do this or that. It has no right to seek revenge or retribution. The state has no personal rights. It has no personal opinions.

Although they possess a deceptive simplicity, these are powerful intellectual arguments. No less powerful is the way in which Rosler reframes the debate by pointing out in her film the dismal record that the United States has of supporting global human rights. Her criticism of vigilantism, death squads, and kangaroo courts in other parts of the world is linked—through rational argument, and through visual collage—to well-known history of U.S. aid to violent regimes in Latin America and elsewhere. The directness of Rosler's sentences, and their explanatory reach, give to the film a quality of easy didacticism. This allows the film to present a strong voice in the public sphere and explains why it reverberates in today's political context.

The students at the California Institute of the Arts produced short videos that shared some of the features one sees in the best of Rosler's work, a provocative combination of verbal and visual wit giving a sharp edge to powerful political expression. Here are a few examples:

Donna Golden's *A Good Night's Rest* mixes visual images with voice fragments from radio and television shows. The filmmaker provides no editorial commentary and lets her subjects voice their opinions while the images and descriptions of torture appear on screen; the voices we hear belong to anyone from President Bush talking about the necessity of torture to ordinary citizens cheerfully declaring on talk-show radio that what was happening in Abu Ghraib was comparable to a weekend in Las Vegas, something they'd pay good money to have done to them.

Drawing Lines by Carlin Wing straightforwardly provides the different meanings and usages of the word "line" present in the *New Shorter Oxford English Dictionary*. A neutral voice-over reads through the variety of meanings while, on the screen, words and images written on index cards are pinned to a notice board. The structure is very simple, but a slow tension is built through the exploration of what those ordinary words mean in the context of the current war in Iraq. The first few examples are innocent enough, suggesting simple household uses of rope or wire. But then, we are given one meaning of line as "a telegraph, or telephone, wire or cable . . ." and then "also, any wire or cable serving as a conductor of electric current," and what we see on the screen is a red line-drawing of a man strapped to an electric chair with a dark bag over his head. "A row of people or things" is accompanied by a sketch of a U.S. soldier leading a row of handcuffed and hooded Arab men. Another meaning of "line" is "a connected series of fieldworks, defenses, etc." and the visual on the screen is a long list of U.S. bases all over the world.

In yet another video, an untitled work by Jim McCardell, we are again confronted by a gap between the visual and the verbal, forcing viewers to question not only what they see but also what they believe. McCardell processes and distorts the widely circulated footage of U.S. soldiers using thermal imaging to shoot armed Iraqi insurgents hiding behind a truck filled with bombs; while the footage plays and is interrupted by iridescent grid-like frames, a female voice provides structural criticism of "geopolitical stabilization," quoting Immanuel Wallerstein, linking privatization and the spread of a global economy through the creation of a core-periphery divide. At the film's end, when the same footage is played with the original audio, we hear the exchange of commands between the U.S. soldiers and the sound of gunfire blasting away insurgents visible on the radar only as moving figures who have thrown their weapons down. By now, even words like "go forward hit him" or "smoke him" and the answering "ready to engage" and "roger" do not sound like ordinary words at all. We are inclined to think of invisible determining forces. The visual on the screen is like a moving dark spiral or tunnel. We are inside the historical processes that place a man running in the night in a field while an overwhelming power places him in the sights of a gun that he cannot even see.

And below are stills from a brief video, *A Love Story*, by Chie Yamayoshi (figure 10). The filmmaker stands among those waiting at the busy Los Angeles airport, holding a sign, welcoming an uncertain, if not impossible, future.

Paul Shambroom is a Minneapolis-based photographer who was born in New Jersey in 1956. Shambroom caught the public eye for two projects, both filmed over long stretches of time, documenting nuclear facilities and town council meetings all across America. His recent photographs, in what he calls *Security Series*, have been taken at training facilities financed by the Department of Homeland Security. These images, described by one commentator as "John Singer Sargent-meets-John Ashcroft portraits," show Hazmat-suited figures in eerie landscapes emptied of everything except a difficult-to-name dread.

When I came upon Shambroom's latest photographs, starting with an image titled "SWAT Team Approaching House, 'Terror Town,' Playas, New Mexico," I noticed how the viewer wasn't able to see a single face. That only enhanced the emptiness of the picture, despite the brightness and the brilliant blue sky. And then, when I had seen the other images in the series, a rare face or two visible only through gas masks, there was another recognition. All individuality had been removed from the frame: what we were witnessing was a condition. We were looking at a system in operation. Call it what you will, defense machine, surveillance system, counterterrorism paradigm.

Jonathan Raban's novel, *Surveillance*, published in 2006, opens with the

10. Chie Yamayoshi, video still from *A Love Story*. Used with permission of the artist.

following words: "After the explosion, the driver of the overturned school bus stood beside the wreckage, his clothes in shreds." When the driver takes his hands away from his ears, he notices that they are dripping blood. Beyond the bus, there is fire and smoke. When a child emerges from the blown-out window of the bus, the driver watches the rescue workers who come running over the moonscape of smashed glass, "sexless toddlers in silver spacesuits." The kid is grinning, as if he doesn't yet understand what has happened. The driver, we are told, is "trying to assign the name of a painter to the scene, Goya, maybe." Then, he tips his head and jiggles his pinkie in his right ear "to clear the canal of stage blood."

To the grinning kid, he says, "How're you doing, kid? . . . Better than school, huh?"

The driver's name is Tad Zachary and, Raban writes, he is "one of the six professional stars of the show titled TOPOFF 27 by the Department of Homeland Security." Although most victims are played by volunteers and homeless people, Tad and his fellow pros are paid well so that their faces may be filmed in close-up and beamed by satellite to a bunker in Washington, D.C. where the exercise is being monitored.

Tad doesn't mind the work but hates working with amateurs. They always overdo it. He is particularly irritated by the grinning kid, who is actually not an extra. Tad gives him a bit of advice about method acting, "If you're getting paid, kiddo, if you think you're an actor, you better learn to wipe that stupid grin off your face. This is a pro speaking. You're a casualty. You're probably going to be dead of radiation sickness in a week. Think of your parents. Think of the funeral. You're one unlucky kid . . ."

If we look carefully at Shambroom's pictures, it is difficult to be certain what Tad would make of them. Each image is balanced in its composition and nearly neutral in tone; the photographer gives no direct clue as to what he wants us to think (figure 11). It's almost as if we have to bring our own knowledge to bear on the subject. Do we know what these exercises funded by the Department of Homeland Security are or are not able to accomplish? In Raban's book, Tad reports that during the previous exercise, TOPOFF 26, "nearly every rescue worker had been contaminated, fatalities had vastly exceeded predictions, chains of command had broken down, hospitals overwhelmed." During my first phone conversation with Shambroom in June 2007, I learned that he too had recently read *Surveillance*. And his reading was the same as Tad's. Shambroom noted

11. Paul Shambroom, "Radiation Check, Nevada Test Site" (2005, 24 x 30 inches, inkjet on paper, original in color). Used with permission of the artist.

that the government had put all this money into combating terrorism, and the disaster that we got was Hurricane Katrina. He said, "It showed that they don't have a clue." At the same time, however, he emphasized that his photographs do not convey a clear or fixed political opinion. Even the pictures that he had taken of nuclear weapons and stockpile had been read in radically different ways by folk in the military or by the pacifists outside. Despite what he calls the "theme park" atmosphere at some of the "disaster towns" he photographed in the latest series, Shambroom told me that he very consciously avoided exploiting easy irony in the photographs. There is in those images something at once more elaborate and elusive at play. Layers of artifice are present in the portraits of the rescue workers, for instance, because Shambroom has followed some of the conventions of grand portraiture of the eighteenth and nineteenth centuries. We see the first responders in their biohazard suits, adopting the heroic poses of the figures in the paintings by Gainsborough and Reynolds — but with the historical context of those poses having already been hollowed out, what is communicated to us retains an unsettling theatrical edge (figure 12). This is not necessarily a mocking stance. It is possible to see the rescue workers as wanting to be heroic in these photographs, and also maybe in life, and perhaps that is what, despite the masked faces, the impenetrable uniforms, and the high-tech paraphernalia of counterterrorism, finally makes them human.

Having discussed scenes from Raban's novel with Shambroom, I thought it made sense to invite Raban to respond to the images in *Security Series*. This is what Raban wrote back to me:

I hadn't seen Shambroom's photographs before, and found his site enthralling—especially for the high ambiguity of interpretation that his pictures allow. On the surface, they reflect the Department of Homeland Security view of things—a world where bombs go off to devastating effect, and first responders are orderly, in control, heroic.

I read the images from a counter point-of-view—from the assumption that most terrorist attempts fizzle, first responders screw up, governments panic. Odd that I should be looking at Shambroom now, just a couple of days after the publication of pictures from the failed bombings in London and Glasgow—the dud car-bombs being loaded onto a transporter, the burning jeep, destined for inside the passenger terminal, stopped by concrete bollards outside, the chief victim a would-be martyr, now hanging on to life by a thread in the Glasgow hospital where he worked as a doctor . . .

Of course Shambroom's Terror Town exists in the shadow of 9/11—a rare attack in which, with the exception of the crashed plane in PA, pretty much everything went right for the terrorists. . . . Had they predicted the total collapse of the twin towers? I doubt it. My suspicion is that they were as stunned by the scale of the event as the rest of us, their grotesque success lay beyond their wildest dreams.

In Terror Town, the Honda and the Toyota are reduced to a few unrecognizable fragments of scorched metal, while the superhero bomb disposal guy with his robot stands at the ready—a lovely paradoxical image that neatly deconstructs both images.

Living in London in the 1970s and '80s, I grew used to, and bored by, the inconvenience of constant bomb-scares and (rarely) IRA bombs that actually went off and killed a relatively small number of people. Terrorism was a

12. Paul Shambroom, "Police SWAT, Camouflage, Terror Town, NM" (2005, 63 x 38 inches, pigmented inkjet on canvas with varnish, original in color). Used with permission of the artist.

nuisance, but it was a part of the weather. The three thousand killed on 9/11 changed that, of course, and invited us to imagine whole cities taken out by anthrax or a rogue nuclear "device"—the Terror Town world documented by Shambroom. But I'm stuck with my English skepticism: last week's failed attack strikes me as more representative of what we're up against, and the attempt to paint radical Islamism as the dangerous, world-altering-successor to Nazism and Stalinism seems wildly overblown.

I admire the cool responses of Gordon Brown and his new home secretary, Jacqui Smith: they were proportionate in a way that neither the Bush administration nor Tony Blair/John Reid have ever been. Even had the bombs gone off, I think Brown and Smith would have kept their heads.

In my book, which I see as a comedy of manners set in the shadow of the War on Terror, nothing goes right: the DHS exercise gets out of hand, surveillance catches the wrong people, "security" is a charade. The people at the center of the story are infected with the virus of the times, but muddle along with their lives, as people do.

The attacks of September 11 resulted in wars in Afghanistan and Iraq, illegal detentions and torture, extraordinary rendition, heightened security as well as new forms of surveillance, black sites, and the scandal of a small iguana-infested Cuban wasteland being turned into a prison where the United States could hold detainees, seemingly forever, without trial. The surveillance state and its agencies have given rise to new subjectivities, and images and texts that testify to this emergence have been adopted by artists and curators as the most powerful new documents of our times.

On December 4, 2006 the *New York Times* had a front-page report about a videotape that showed Jose Padilla, jailed in solitary confinement for three and a half years, being taken out of his cell in the army brig in Charleston, South Carolina. The report said, "That day, Mr. Padilla, a Brooklyn-born Muslim convert whom the Bush administration had accused of plotting a dirty bomb attack and had detained without charges, got to go to the dentist." The videotape, according to the *Times*, offered "the first concrete glimpse inside the secretive military incarceration of an American citizen whose detention without charges became a test case of President Bush's powers in the fight against terror." Padilla's lawyers had argued that as a result of torture at the hands of the military, including the extended solitary confinement, their client was so psychologically damaged that he could not stand trial. The report said, "Mr. Padilla's lawyers say they have a difficult time persuading him that they are on his side."

Within weeks of that report in the *Times*, in an article in *Artforum* in January 2007, Graham Bader mentioned the same video, writing about Padilla: "In the videotape documenting one short episode of his military detention, he is shown on his way to a root canal down the hall from his cell, wearing blackout goggles and noise-blocking headphones, thereby prevented from experiencing even briefly anything outside himself, outside his merest existence as bare life, wholly at the whim of the state." Bader's argument is that the most intensely politicized contemporary images are those that concern "the state's role in authoring the most basic experiences of life and death." As the Bush administration blatantly gained control of extravagant, far-reaching powers, including the right to illegal detention, it would follow that images, like those of "the broken figure of Jose Padilla, shuffling to the dentist down the hall from his cell," should enter critical-art discourse as new *evidence* to be examined and understood.

Thus, a photo exhibit attempts to represent the reality of Guantánamo not by showing the conditions of the detainees in the prison (the camp rules prohibit photographs that would in any way identify the individuals) but by assembling for public viewing the photographs collected by the pro bono lawyers working on behalf of the men imprisoned on the island.

Lawyers based in cities like Washington, D.C. and New York, when engaged by the families of the Guantánamo detainees, often sought photographs of their clients so that they could be sure that the men they met on the island were the same ones that they had been hired to help. There was another reason. Their clients were likely to be suspicious of them; after all, the men had been lied to and abused in different ways during their interrogation. Therefore, during the visits to the families in places like Yemen or Saudi Arabia, the lawyers took photographs of the people who had hired them. They collected pictures showing their clients during their former lives, as sons, brothers, fathers.

Margot Herster, a photographer whose husband is on one of the teams of lawyers working on behalf of prisoners in Guantánamo, has collected more than two thousand such photographs (figure 13). She has put together an archive of reports based on the lawyers' narratives about their

13. A gift Abdulaziz al-Swidi's attorneys purchased for his mother at his request; translation: "Don't despair, someone in the sky is taking care." Courtesy of Collection of Through the Walls/ Margot Herster (2007).

experiences while visiting the detainees' families as well as their work in Guantánamo. Herster and Carolyn Mara Borlenghi have compiled audio recordings of the status review sessions of several detainees' cases; they obtained declassified audio recordings of Combatant Status Review Tribunals (CSRTs) from Wilmer Hale, a law firm that had acquired them through a Freedom of Information Act request. A selection of about one hundred photographs, along with the audio and video materials, constitutes the exhibit titled Guantánamo: Pictures from Home; Questions of Justice. It debuted at the Fotofest Gallery in Houston, was on a year-long display at the Open Society in New York City, and then traveled to the Sesnon Gallery at the University of California, Santa Cruz. The video installation plays on a wall-mounted 32" x 37" flat panel television on a continuous loop. The lawyers speak to the camera about their visits to the prison-camp, their clients (one describes the suicide attempt by his client during the visit), and what the experience has meant to them as lawyers and as human beings. The audio installation, on a continuous loop, plays in an enclosed space with dim lighting. In one section of the tape, a man who is identified as Muhammad speaks in Arabic and his words are translated into English. He relates what he had earlier said to his American interrogator: "Did you say you've captured seventy percent of the members of al Qaeda? Good. That's excellent. Take my picture and my information to them and ask them if I am al Qaeda or not al Qaeda. You will feel better and I will feel better."

4 ✳ The Terror and the Pity

In a repressive society, a writer can be deeply influential,
but in a society that's filled with glut and repetition and
endless consumption, the act of terror may be the only
meaningful act. People who are in power make their
arrangements in secret, largely as a way of maintaining
and furthering that power. People who are powerless
make an open theater of violence. True terror is a language and a vision. There is a deep narrative structure to
terrorist acts, and they infiltrate and alter consciousness
in ways that writers used to aspire to. — Don DeLillo,
interview in the *New York Times*, May 19, 1991

In David Hare's *Stuff Happens*, an unnamed British character declares on
stage, "On September 11th, America changed. Yes. It got much stupider."
Of course, as the colloquial expression goes, it is more complicated than
that. When people ask whether September 11 changed everything, they
realize that there is something wrong with the question itself, but they
can't put their finger on what that might be. The shock endures despite
the attempt to explain the causes of what happened that morning. Nothing that is said about what followed, in the months and years since, finds
tidy coherence. Especially when one considers Afghanistan or Iraq, where

even to describe the disaster of present events is to misrepresent the fast unraveling of any predictable course of contemporary history.

Martin Amis once declared that "after a couple of hours at their desks, on September 12, 2001, all the writers on earth were reluctantly considering a change of occupation." Similarly, Jay McInerney wrote that most novelists he knew "went through a period of intense self-examination and self-loathing after the terrorist attacks on the World Trade Center." Ian McEwan, a winner of the Booker Prize, told an interviewer that he suddenly found it "wearisome to confront invented characters." Of course, none of these thoughts stopped any of these writers from writing. In fact, they each wrote books that were, quite explicitly, literary responses to the attacks and their aftermath.

Such curiosity, coupled with the need to act, was also present in what might be called the state's literary response. The book that resulted from the U.S. government's attempts to understand and explain the attacks was *The 9/11 Commission Report*. It begins with the following words:

> Tuesday, September 11, 2001, dawned temperate and nearly cloudless in the eastern United States. Millions of men and women readied themselves for work. Some made their way to the Twin Towers, the signature structures of the World Trade Center complex in New York City. Others went to Arlington, Virginia, to the Pentagon. Across the Potomac River, the United States Congress was back in session. At the other end of Pennsylvania Avenue, people began to line up for a White House tour. In Sarasota, Florida, President George W. Bush went for an early morning run.
>
> For those heading to the airport, weather conditions could not have been better for a safe and pleasant journey. Among the travelers were Mohamed Atta and Abdul Aziz al Omari, who arrived at the airport in Portland, Maine.

A government document, credited to a commission of ten members and an staff of eighty-two, the report was "the No. 1 *New York Times* nonfiction paperback bestseller for 11 weeks in a row" and was one of the five nominated contenders for the National Book Award for nonfiction. I learned this from a positive review of the book, in *Slate*, by Ben Yagoda who complimented the simple elegance of its sentences and the use of detail. The review also praised the cinematic structure of the story, cutting back and forth between the two parallel narratives, one about the planning and resolve of the hijackers and the second about the U.S. government's doomed attempts to stop the attacks. Yagoda called the report "a piece of literature" that had led the tradition of reconstructed nonfiction narrative "out of the wilderness."

But there is another feature of the report, one that Yagoda didn't comment upon, which made the document especially striking. In a chapter titled "Foresight—and Hindsight," the commissioners noted how the attacks had precipitated a change of perspective about how we told the story of contemporary globalization: "To us, Afghanistan seemed very far away. To members of al Qaeda, America seemed very close. In a sense, they were more globalized than we were." And, more crucially, what the report demanded on the part of Americans was a greater use of their imagination. After noting that the "imagination is not a gift usually associated with bureaucracies," the report stated that it was "crucial to find a way of routinizing, even bureaucratizing, the exercise of imagination." But to do *what* exactly?

The report was clear that the exercise of imagination "requires more than finding an expert who can imagine that aircraft could be used as weapons." One high-level official's awareness of the danger was to be attributed, the report noted, "more to Tom Clancy novels than to warnings from the intelligence community." There was strong emphasis put on the need for cooperation among the different governmental agencies, in particular the CIA and the FBI. The government had to learn to imagine the threat of terrorism by working across the foreign-domestic divide. This global strategy was best spelled out in the commission's declaration that "9/11 has taught us that terrorism against American interests 'over there' should be regarded just as we regard terrorism against America 'over here.'" More explicitly, the report stated, "the American homeland is the planet."

Yet, despite the call for greater imagination and the commitment to global analyses, the report was oddly reluctant to admit that the United States had any role to play in the rise of Islamic fundamentalism in Asia. In the chapter detailing the "history and political context" for the emergence of terrorism, the commissioners spoke of the "bankruptcy of secular, autocratic nationalism" in the Muslim world and of the uniform hostility shown by such regimes to democratic opposition. But there was nothing about the support, sometimes clandestine, sometimes open, that the United States had provided to undemocratic regimes. In discussing Iran, for example, the report stated that "Iran's 1979 revolution swept a Shia theocracy into power. Its success encouraged Sunni fundamentalists everywhere." The truth is that the Americans, during the Eisenhower administration, orchestrated the coup that overthrew the Iranian prime minister, Mohammad Mossadegh. Mossadegh was the populist leader who had nationalized Iranian oil and this was intolerable to American business. The United States extended support to the shah, who used his intelligence unit, the notorious SAVAK, to harass and kill tens of thousands of political dissidents. This systematic repression paved the way for the conservative Iranian clergy led by the Ayatollah Khomeini. *The 9/11 Commission Report* is similarly reticent about the history of American support not only for the Taliban or Osama bin Laden but also Saddam Hussein. Today, in the wake of the failures in Iraq, it is rather easy to criticize the U.S. government for its foreign policy. In the days after the September 11 attacks, such a critique was not welcome almost anywhere in America, but it is still surprising to find it entirely missing from *The 9/11 Commission Report*. The report reduces the complex political problems that lie behind the attacks to a bureaucratic one; indeed, it has succeeded too well at bureaucratizing the imagination. In a recent course I was teaching, all of my students searched in vain for any awareness on the part of the commissioners of what we had read the previous week in an essay by Arundhati Roy written in the days immediately following the attacks: "Someone recently said that if Osama bin Laden didn't exist, America would have had to invent him. But, in a way, America did invent him. He was among the jihadis who moved to Afghanistan in 1979 when the CIA commenced its operations there. Bin Laden has the distinction of being created by the CIA and wanted by the FBI."

There couldn't have been many in Washington, D.C. or, for that matter, anywhere else in the country who would have wanted to hear Arundhati Roy's charge that while bin Laden might have delivered the message to the American government, "it could well have been signed by the ghosts of the victims of America's old wars." Roy had listed several sites of American bloody interventions. Korea, Vietnam, Cambodia, Lebanon, Iraq, Palestine. And then she had added, somewhat conservatively in her own estimation, Yugoslavia, Somalia, Haiti, Chile, Nicaragua, El Salvador, the Dominican Republic, and Panama.

The *New York Times* reportedly refused to publish Roy's article. But nevertheless, even in the mainstream press, there was hunger for news from places like Kandahar or Lahore. In the absence of widely shared, credible reports, half-knowledge and prejudice were routinely on display in the media and in the broader culture. As Leon Wieseltier put it recently, "On September 10, 2001, nobody in America seemed to know anything about Islam. On September 12, 2001, everybody seemed to know everything about Islam." The books available at that time, and more would be produced in short order, tried to explain the rise of a fierce ideology. In the days after the attacks, you could be at an airport in any city in America, and you would inevitably see two things: machine guns in the hands of patrolling military, and, in the shop windows, books on Islam with covers showing bearded men or veiled women. An early favorite was Ahmed Rashid's excellent report, *Taliban*. And there were other titles by a wide variety of writers, ranging from Gilles Kepel and Olivier Roy to Bernard Lewis and Samuel Huntington. In the years that followed there would be more books that brought news from the Muslim world—works of both fiction and non-fiction by writers of widely differing talent, Khaled Hosseini, Christopher de Bellaigue, Azar Nafisi, Rory Stewart, Ayaan Hirsi Ali, Reza Aslan, Laila Lalami, and Mohsin Hamid, to name just a few—but I still vividly recall the early days, in the days and weeks after the attacks, when war was imminent and there was little to read about Afghanistan. Who were the people that we were about to bomb?

In late September 2001, an article written by John Sifton, an American aid worker in Afghanistan, appeared in the *New York Times Magazine*; the piece spoke of populations displaced by war, reduced to begging in a ruined land strewn with relics from the Cold War era. The premodern in Afghanistan coexisted with the postmodern. In the rural countryside, people lived in a way that Sifton conjectured their ancestors had lived four hundred years ago, but in Kabul, the young Talibs in black robes sped around in their "clean new Toyota pickup trucks, tricked-out, hip-hop ghetto-rigs." While reading Sifton's report, I had the sense that this was the beginning of our new "war lit." The writer had described how, upon his arrival at a hotel in a small, drought-hit Afghani town, he found himself looking at a large, somewhat ghastly landscape painting of animals standing beside a pond. The heads of the animals standing in the forest had been cut out, to comply with the Taliban's interpretation of the

Islamic law forbidding the representation of living beings. Sifton wrote, "This left a decapitated deer standing by a pond and a headless beaver sitting on a tree stump." But this encounter with bad art and medieval outrage—making for the unsettling montage of tawdry beauty and mutilation—didn't in the least prepare the visitor for the life outside and the pure shock of human suffering:

> Displaced persons without enough food to eat were drinking water taken from muddy ponds—mud really. "They're drinking mud," I said into my tape recorder. "They're drinking mud." I remember one particular experience especially. We were in a windy camp for displaced persons, and a man was showing us the graves of his three children, who had died of disease on three consecutive days: Thursday, Friday and Saturday. It was Monday, and he had buried his last child the day before. After he described all this, we stood around the graves in the strangely loud silence of the wind, hot as an oven, and the man absent-mindedly adjusted a rock atop one child's grave.
>
> It was a very emotional moment, yet I didn't really feel sad. I was just fascinated by the realness of it all. You look out an office window, and you see a displaced family living in a bombed-out school, sleeping on the balcony and cooking some birds they caught, doves. This is their life. They can't change the channel.

Sifton's report found a place on the reading list for my course on the "literature of 9/11" because it carries a terrible truth—a truth not only about bare life but also about our naïve fascination with its irrefutable, fixed reality. The image of the father standing beside the graves of his small children, each dying within days of each other, was so dire and so moving and so powerful that it would have been easy to believe that it could not be touched even by falling bombs.

But there is nothing static about tragedy. A tragic situation gets better or worse. The attacks of September 11 led to the war in Afghanistan and then the invasion of Iraq. There were other, unforeseen consequences. President Bush's war on terror unleashed hatreds elsewhere. In India, after the terrorist attack on the Indian Parliament, there were arbitrary arrests and torture of individuals who happened to be Muslims. India had discovered its own September 11. A right-wing Hindu leader attempting to clarify an earlier statement he had made said that not all Muslims were terrorists, but that all terrorists were Muslims. In Gujarat, Hindu fanatics felt emboldened to stage pogroms against their Muslim neighbors with the active support of the state. How much has changed not elsewhere but in the United States, not only in the conditions of people's lives, but in the ways that we have of talking about them?

Judith Butler has written, "In the United States we begin the story by invoking a first-person narrative point of view, and telling what happened on September 11." There are very few other narrative options available—or at least they weren't when Butler was writing, in the immediate aftermath of the attacks—for those who want to frame the story in broader terms. When we read her essay in class, Butler's argument jolted my students into a new state of awareness. I suddenly found the members of my seminar wondering about alternative ways of telling the story. Mohsin Hamid's *The Reluctant Fundamentalist* provided them a counterexample where the first-person narrative point of view is usurped by a voice from the other side. Hamid's narrator is a young Pakistani man who comes to America to get an education at Princeton; later, he finds work in an elite financial firm in New York City, and then, after the attacks of September 11, he feels increasingly estranged and returns to Lahore. The entire novel is the account of a single evening as the young man, whose name is Changez, tells his story to a silent American visitor. Part thriller, part testimonial, the book is very much a riposte to the West's vilification of Islam and Muslims; and yet, in its structure and denouement, the novel remains intentionally inconclusive, and this feature has been a part of its appeal for readers both "here" and "there."

Nevertheless, a book like *The Reluctant Fundamentalist* appears incongruous in what one might call the emerging canon of September 11 literature because the notion of a dialogue with the Other that is present at its heart is entirely missing from books like John Updike's *Terrorist*, Don DeLillo's *Falling Man*, and Martin Amis's *The Second Plane*. Islamic terrorists appear in the work of these Western writers—Muhammad Atta's fictional form finds a ghostly realization in more than one book—but they remain unreal and wholly unconvincing. One of the students in my class, after we had finished reading these novels, observed that if during the Second World War it had been imperative for the West to see the Japanese kamikaze pilots as inhuman and therefore as fanatical animals, then, by contrast, in the current ideological struggle, the Islamic suicide bomber is made real in the dominant mindset only by being made *human* in a stereo-typical manner. Amis's Atta is chronically constipated, hence the pained expression on his face. The master terrorist is, literally, laughably, "full of shit." The portrayal of the Arab terrorist ends up being more an exercise in parochialism, confirming what the writer already knows and believes in accord with the rest of the surrounding culture.

Pankaj Mishra, in the article in *The Guardian* on "9/11 fiction," which I've quoted from above, has noted that, in comparison to contemporary literature, it is in such recent films as *Syriana*, *The Constant Gardener*, and *Babel* that "the human self, inescapably plural and open-ended, increas-ingly finds itself in a bewilderingly enlarged and unforgiving arena." But we can go further. In such films, which others have seen as examples of "hyperlinked cinema," there is a deliberate and drastic use of multiple nar-ratives, characters, story lines, and globe-spanning locations. Destinies collide not so much as a way of capturing coincidence as much as to de-scribe our hyper-globalized connectedness. A more subtle point is also being made in these films about history. The various timelines being de-ployed out of sync are suggestive of a world that is somewhat conscious of being caught in the unending aftershock of catastrophe. As Michael Wood explains in his analysis of the timeline in *Babel*: "The writer's and director's continuing interest in accident has turned into something else, or perhaps was always tending towards something else: not worlds of sheer harm and disaster, but the sense that we are always about to step into an aftermath we can't imagine."

In recent years, war has provided the ever present sense of global catas-trophe, and to the extent that its effects have been hidden from the Ameri-can public it becomes a moral responsibility to find or interpret the com-plex narratives that make the world real to us. Will books and films about war serve this critical function?

Not necessarily. One of the books I have used in my class is Anthony Swofford's *Jarhead*, a memoir about the first Gulf War in which the writer punctures easy liberal assumptions about the power of art or protest. In the book's opening pages, Swofford describes how the Marines, before being shipped off to Saudi Arabia, get "fresh high-and-tight haircuts" (hence the name jarheads) and then rent all the war movies they can find downtown. The platoon drinks a lot of beer and watches films like *Apoca-lypse Now*, *Platoon*, and *Full Metal Jacket*. Swofford doesn't buy the talk that these Vietnam films are anti-war. Actually, he says, they are "all pro-war, no matter what the supposed message" because images of war are "pornography for the military man." "And as a young man raised on the films of the Vietnam War, I want ammunition and alcohol and dope, I want to screw some whores and kill some Iraqi motherfuckers."

In the face of such assertion, a certain hopelessness shadows the thought that one could achieve anything by reading or teaching, say, Michael Herr's *Dispatches*, pausing appropriately at lines like "I wasn't dumb but I sure was raw, certain connections are hard to make when you come from a place where they go around with war in their heads all the time." After all, Swofford's contention is starkly unforgiving about the illusions of a pacifist public audience: "It doesn't matter how many Mr. and Mrs. Johnsons are antiwar—the actual killers who know how to use the weapons are not."

But it is Swofford himself who offers a way out. At the book's end, recording his feelings after he returns home from war, Swofford notes, "I know that none of the rewards of victory will come my way, because there are no rewards, not on the field of battle, not for the man who fights the battle—the rewards accrue in places like Washington D.C., and Riyadh and Houston and Manhattan, south of 125th Street, and Kuwait City. The fighting man receives tokens—medals, ribbons, badges, promotions, combat pay, abrogation of taxes, a billet to Airborne School—worthless bits of nothing, as valuable as smoke." This expression of bitterness and, perhaps more surprising, the later despair about the violence and his empathy for the Iraqi dead, is more convincing precisely because it follows the gung-ho saber rattling of the earlier pages. The reader has made the journey with Swofford—because he has changed, we have changed too, more plausibly. In fact, when I read it first, I felt very strongly that Swofford's account was more needed in my class than anything written by the likes of Noam Chomsky and the rest of the admirable anti-war brigade. Chomsky and his valiant cohort do not tell my students anything that is new, nor do they force them to accept real contradictions. My students and I are all part of a group that can only deal with contradictions by triumphing over them, by erasing them, by being comfortably correct. Our chorus is an uncomplicated, righteous call: "Support Our Troops—Bring Them Home."

To attend to the narratives of the soldiers, who often join the military-industrial complex as migrants from an economy where they have a precarious toehold, is to participate in the decentering that Butler calls for. (But why focus only on class and on those battling the gravitational pull of downward mobility? In a warm, wonderfully evocative piece by Andrew O' Hagan entitled "Iraq, 2 May 2005," we are given a report on two deaths in different parts of Iraq on a single day, one of an American pilot and the other of a British infantryman. At one point, writing about his visit to the childhood home of the dead American, O'Hagan notes: "It was hard not to think of soldiers all over the world who started off in small bedrooms like the one in Cherry Hill; as I looked up at the placid walls and the tidy small space, a certain dream seemed to rise for a moment and take hold, a very domestic dream of glory. Motivations are perhaps the greatest mystery of all." *Soldiers all over the world*. They are the rich and the poor, and not only in the armies of the occupation. We take note of the Iraqi recruit from Mosul who had joined Saddam's army only three months earlier, the only breadwinner in a family of eight. Or the old Iraqi general called Detainee 10 who was resisting his removal to another part of the prison at Abu Ghraib called "the hard site" and ended with his face bludgeoned against the wall.) One of my students quoted in his paper a brief report on one of the first combat casualties in Iraq, Marine Lance Cpl. José Antonio Gutierrez: "He was an orphan and hard-knocks poet, had hopped trains at age 11 from Guatemala before crossing the border into California. His dream was to become an architect. The military had promised him an education and he had promised to bring his sister, Engracia, to the States." How do you condemn war without a shred of empathy for the soldier? It is the same story repeated from what we had earlier read in Herr's *Dispatches*: "Disgust doesn't begin to describe what they made me feel, they threw people out of helicopters, tied people up and put the dogs on them. Brutality was just a word in my mouth before that. But disgust was only one color in the whole mandala, gentleness and pity were other colors, there wasn't a color left out. I think that those people who used to say that they only wept for the Vietnamese never really wept for anyone at all if they couldn't squeeze out at least one for these men and boys when they died or had their lives cracked open for them."

Whether or not one chooses to begin a course on the "literature of September 11" with an account of a bright Tuesday morning and a plane flying low in the clear sky, it ends with a description of the prison in Guantá-namo, which Amnesty International has called "the gulag of our time." On the Mobius strip of history, terrorist violence is joined to state action. The violence practiced by the state, which was hardly ever invoked in the hours and days that followed the moment of the second plane exploding into the South Tower of the World Trade Center, comes back—the return of the repressed—in the form of the denial of basic legal rights to prisoners in Guantánamo and the numerous shocking reports of abuse by Ameri-cans at places like Bagram and Abu Ghraib.

The attacks of September 11 and the mistreatment of those imprisoned by American forces are linked events: they are present as twin events even in the stories of the arrests. Moazzam Begg, a British Muslim who was arrested in Pakistan and later ended up as a prisoner in Guantánamo, nar-rates how the U.S. agent told him at the time of his arrest: "Do you know where I've gotten these handcuffs from? . . . I was given these by the wife of a victim of the September 11th attacks." But the link can also be estab-lished through the official documents of the Bush administration, which sought legitimacy in its policies that rode roughshod over the Geneva Conventions. Consider the notorious "torture memos" drafted by John Yoo and Jay Bybee at the Justice Department's Office of Legal Counsel. The memos, which became public in June 2004, put forward a narrow definition of torture: "Physical pain amounting to torture must be equiva-lent in intensity to the pain accompanying serious physical injury, such as organ failure, impairment of bodily function, or even death. For purely mental pain or suffering to amount to torture . . . it must result in signifi-cant psychological harm of significant duration, e.g. lasting for months or even years." Equally infamously, the memo granted immunity to anyone charged with committing torture by stressing that this person would be guilty "only if he acts with the *express purpose* of inflicting severe pain or suffering." For good measure, the authors of the memo argued that even if a defendant did commit torture, he would still be immune from prose-cution if his actions were directed by the president.

The guidance provided by Yoo and Bybee began to govern all interro-gations in the war on terror. According to Philip Gourevitch and Errol Morris, who collaborated on *Standard Operating Procedure*, a work about the Abu Ghraib scandal, "The authorization of torture and decriminaliza-tion of cruel, inhuman, and degrading treatment of captives in wartime have been among the defining legacies of the current Administration; and the rules of interrogation that produced the abuses documented on the M.I. [Military Intelligence] block in the fall of 2003 were the direct expression of the hostility toward international law and military doctrine that was found in the White House, the Vice-President's office, and at the highest levels of the Justice and Defense Departments." This would also explain why it wasn't any of those who promulgated those orders were held accountable and prosecuted; those charged and punished were only the low-ranking reservist soldiers whose own photographs documented the abuse, both revealing and implicating them in the criminal acts that would otherwise have remained hidden from public view.

My students read *Inside the Wire* by Erik Saar and Viveca Novak. Saar was an army sergeant with the U.S. military in the prison at Guantánamo, supporting the intelligence and interrogations operation with his work as an Arabic translator. He had been required to submit the book's manuscript to the Pentagon for review, but nine unredacted pages were leaked to the Associated Press by a member of the Department of Defense. These pages, which appear toward the book's end, exposed for the first time the role of sexual humiliation in breaking Muslim prisoners incarcerated at Guantánamo. As the Associated Press reported in January 2005, "Female interrogators tried to break male Muslim detainees at the United States prison camp in Guantánamo Bay, Cuba, by sexually touching them, by wearing miniskirts and thong underwear, and, in one case, by smearing a Saudi man's face with red ink, which he was led to believe was menstrual blood, according to part of a draft manuscript written by a former Army sergeant."

Saar's account, very much like Swofford's *Jarhead*, is an insider's report; neither especially insightful nor particularly critical, it nevertheless succeeds, just like Swofford's book did, in presenting a patriotic soldier's journey to disillusionment. I should mention that not many of my students liked the book. I gathered that this was because even at the book's end, its self-interrogation doesn't rise above the level that even my students had outgrown. (Here's a representative sample of the introspectiveness displayed by Saar: "What the fuck did I just do? What the fuck were we doing? . . . Most of America was asleep, but I was wide awake, defending freedom, honor fucking bound.") But it is also possible that a part of the dissatisfaction we felt with Saar was that despite his linguistic skills we never got a real glimpse into the lives of the people who were held in the cages whose pictures we have all seen. In other words, as readers we found the reality censored from us. Every word that comes out of Guantánamo is heavily vetted by the Pentagon's official censors, and of course this is also true of whatever communication the prisoners receive from the outside world. What Saar doesn't tell us, for instance, is that Moazzam Begg, who was detained there for three years, received a censored letter from his seven-year-old daughter with only one legible line, which said, "I love you, Dad." When he was released and returned home to Birmingham, Begg learned from his daughter that the censored lines were a poem she had copied for him: "One, two, three, four, five, / Once I caught a fish alive. / Six, seven, eight, nine, ten, / Then I let it go again."

I told my students of having taken the train to Harlem to meet with Neha Singh Gohil, a young Sikh lawyer who was a part of a team that represented detainees in Guantánamo. Neha had described to me the ways in which the conversations with the clients on the island remained circumscribed. Many topics were strictly off limits and often, in exasperation, a prisoner would say that it was God and not lawyers who would help him. Or he would accuse them of having hidden from him during a previous visit the news that there had been an earthquake in his homeland or that a well-known political figure had been killed. Or he might ask when he would be released. But there were no answers to such questions. Gohil told me, "We can't give them hope. At one point, one of them asked for towels that didn't have holes in them. We said no. We can't get you towels. We can't get you real soap. We can't give you a pen. No wonder they told us we were useless."

Our last piece of reading in class was the interrogation log of Detainee 063 at Guantánamo. Detainee 063 was a young Saudi named Mohammed al-Qahtani, who is believed by many to be the so-called twentieth hijacker. He had attempted entry into the United States in August 2001 and been turned back at the Orlando airport — it has been confirmed that even while he was being questioned by the suspicious immigration official, Mohammed Atta was waiting for him outside in the airport's parking lot. Later, al-Qahtani was arrested in Afghanistan, while fleeing Tora Bora, although he claimed he was where he was because of his love for falconry. The log of his interrogation at Guantánamo was leaked to *Time* magazine and published in early January 2005. The log covers fifty days from

November 2002 to January 2003, a period during which the new torture techniques that Defense Secretary Donald Rumsfeld had approved were used on prisoners.

Time wrote that the log "reads like a night watchman's diary." This is because the document presents in a terse syntax, replete with acronyms and references to procedures, a record of the detainee's acts. How much did he sleep, what did he eat, the visits that he made to the bathroom or made requests for a visit to the bathroom and what exactly he did there. The document details the active as well as passive attempts to extract information from al-Qahtani. His physical condition, which was frequently examined, sometimes several times a day, is also described so that it is clear how much stress the detainee can actually take. There are lines that record the detainee's struggle with an IV drip, his refusal to drink water, his desire for water or to urinate. As if caught in a recurring dream, the prisoner is denied sleep, and this severe routine is scrupulously recorded. Once, in December, interrogation is called off for twenty-four hours when al-Qahtani is put in the hospital and a CT scan is performed. More tests are administered. But in the hospital, too, the log tells us, music is played to prevent the detainee from sleeping.

It is a remarkable text, the interrogation log, because it is also in some ways the record of an experiment. A technique of torture is tried, a result is achieved, it is explained in terms of a training manual, a different result is sought, and so forth. We read the log in search of a narrative where the subjectivity of the detainee, like that of a patient in a difficult operation, begins to emerge or express itself. When we as readers seem to find such a moment, it is impossible to know what exactly it is we are learning, and whether what we are learning is more about the detainee or his captors. The following is a part of the record from December 11, 2002:

0100: Detainee began to cry during pride and ego down. Detainee was reminded that no one loved, cared or remembered him. He was reminded that
he was less than human and that animals had more freedom and love than he
does. He was taken outside to see a family of banana rats. The banana rats were
moving around freely, playing, eating, showing concern for one another. Detainee was compared to the family of banana rats and reinforced that they had
more love, freedom, and concern than he had. Detainee began to cry during
this comparison.

This is where it ended. This was the last shot in the film. A man kneeling in his cage while the sun sets in the Caribbean Sea. We were left with this picture of a shorn sociality, of a man in isolation, contemplating banana rats. We could have been reading Beckett.

The writer named "C," whose words we are supposedly reading in J. M. Coetzee's *Diary of a Bad Year*, speculates that the general public grows tired of the lies told by those in power: when this happens, the people "long for relief from incessant prevarication." This explains their hunger ("a mild hunger," admits C parenthetically) for words and opinions from outside the political world. Those articulate creatures that he has in mind are "academics or churchmen or scientists or writers." Barely has this thought been written down on the page that he faces a question: "But how can this hunger be satisfied by the mere writer (to speak just of writers) when the grasp of facts that the writer has is usually incomplete or unsure, when his very access to the so-called facts is likely to be via media within the political field of forces, and when, half the time, he is because of his vocation as much interested in the liar and the psychology of the lie as in the truth?" There is compelling logic in the question, particularly when one ponders the last part of the query. What can a writer say about the interrogation log of Detainee 063 at Guantánamo? I try to pick up the shards of evidence offered about the detainee and find myself searching again and again for anything that can be revealed about the torturer. There is not much that I myself want to add.

I know, of course, that to read is to be in dialogue—with the writer, with other readers, and, no less important, with oneself. (In the case of Coetzee's C, the reflections on terror and freedom are curiously split on the page, sharing space with the diary of his neighbor, a young woman named Anya whom he desires. The dialogue there is between reason and lust. We are given a glimpse into the workings of the writer's mind, a mind that is in thrall to the body. Or at least to the comely neighbor's behind.) But who is one in dialogue with, and why, when one reads a record of torture?

Henri Alleg is now eighty-eight. Fifty-one years ago, he wrote *The Question*, describing his torture at the hands of French paratroopers. Alleg was an editor of a French paper at that time and wrote in favor of Algerian independence. His book has been reissued, his publishers recognizing the new relevance. (In her foreword to the new edition, Ellen Ray writes: "Well before the U.S. invasion of Iraq, the U.S. Army screened for its officers Gillo Pontecorvo's famous 1965 film, *The Battle of Algiers*, as an example of urban guerrilla warfare in an Arab Muslim nation. The film is a vivid reenactment of the French army's method of brutally crushing the insurgency in Algiers in 1957, and shows the place of torture in its strategy.") *The Question* is a profoundly moving account of Alleg's month-long ordeal and his triumph over his torturers. I met Alleg in April 2007 when he came to my college campus. He is a small man, very frail now, speaking with a soft voice, and I couldn't look at him without remembering the brutal details of his torture. At dinner he said that people often ask him what can be done to avoid torture. His reply always is "there can be no clean war in this situation." You cannot simply ban torture; you have to banish the war itself. I asked him if he had "a question" for his torturers. "I don't have much to say about that situation," he said. "I had seen these people after the sentence that gave me ten years imprisonment. They were like little schoolboys."

PART II  Siraj

5 ✳ I Have Delivered the Pizza

For those of us who work at the United States
Department of Justice, every day is September 12, 2001.
Every day is that day after. Every day requires renewed
commitment to combating and preventing terrorism.
—Alberto R. Gonzales, October 25, 2006

On the evening of January 8, 2007, a federal judge at the U.S. District
Court for the Eastern District of New York sentenced Shahawar Matin
Siraj to thirty years in prison. Siraj, a twenty-four-year-old Pakistani immigrant living in Queens, had been found guilty, after a four-week trial
in May the previous year, of participating in a conspiracy to bomb the
subway station at Thirty-Fourth Street and Herald Square in New York
City. The prosecution had presented the defendant as a young, disaffected
Muslim man who, as soon as he had received his immigration papers,
wanted to take revenge against the United States for the war in Iraq; the
defendant's lawyers didn't question that charge, or the evidence on tape
that showed their client saying things like "I want fuck this country very
badly," but they argued strenuously that the young man had been entrapped.

An informant for the New York Police Department had been paid more
than $100,000 to spy on what he heard and saw at mosques in Brooklyn

and Staten Island; and, the defense argued, this informant had shown Siraj pictures of abuse at Abu Ghraib to incite him and to involve him in a plot that Siraj, if he had been left alone, would have been unable to devise or execute by himself. The informant's name was Osama Eldawoody. He was an Egyptian-born fifty-year-old who had met and befriended Siraj at the Islamic bookstore where the latter worked. According to the testimony offered by the police "handler," Eldawoody had shared the information with the defendant that he was a nuclear engineer and could build a "dirty bomb"; later, according to another government witness, the informant had told Siraj that his imam had given him a fatwa decreeing that it was "okay to kill the killers" and, therefore, to harm the U.S. government, which was massacring Iraqis.

In the hours before the sentencing, television stations in New York played a fragment of a video that the Department of Justice had made available to the media. The black and white video had been shot from a secret camera inside the car used by the police informant and it showed the defendant discussing the plan to carry out the bombing. On the video, which had been recorded on August 23, 2004, Eldawoody was in conversation inside his Toyota Corolla with Siraj as well as a third person, James Elshafay, a friend of Siraj's who pleaded guilty and testified against the defendant. The video showed Elshafay in the seat beside the driver, and Siraj in the back: Eldawoody got out of the car and brought two backpacks from the trunk. All three were wearing Islamic prayer caps. The time was a little past nine-thirty in the evening. "These backpacks. It's this size, that's what he said," Eldawoody informed the two youths, referring to a fictitious "Brother Nazeem" whom he had presented as the leader of a terrorist outfit in upstate New York. Siraj and Elshafay were divided over the size of the backpacks for the bombs: Siraj thought they were too big while Elshafay thought they were too small. But there was no debate over the detail that one of the backpacks was to be put under a seat on the platform and the second in a garbage can. The video ended with the informant asking, his fingers unfurling dramatically in the air, "What do you think?"

The video was a part of the evidence submitted by the prosecution in court. The entire video recording of that meeting, which had been played during the trial, was about forty-five minutes long, too long to be shown as a clip on television news; but the longer conversation reveals some of the complications that inevitably color the case, even if they don't necessarily change its outcome. The full conversation brings to the fore a sense of hesitation and doubt on the defendant's part, and it demonstrates the sometimes touching, sometimes ridiculous, relationship that the defendant had with the two men who served as the government's witnesses. More than anything else, however, it raises the question whether or not acts of terror can be carried out by persons who lack sophistication and training—for if the answer is yes, the paranoia displayed by the government so far might actually appear understated, and if the answer is no, then it is clearly wrong to use informants to prosecute an individual as a bomber when there is no bomb on the scene. I'm taking the liberty of quoting at length a transcript of the conversation on video from August 23, 2004:

ELDAWOODY: Brother Nazeem upstate is very, very happy, very impressed. He says about the Verrazano, it's a little bit complicated. We are not that big, that strong, it's too heavy for us, things like that. He says, "in time." The plan is perfect, but it needs a nuclear bomb, not a regular bomb. So he says that will be later. 34th Street is on.

SIRAJ: Hmm? Tell him that we are very careful about people's lives. Have you told him this?

ELDAWOODY: We've spoken of many things.

SIRAJ: I don't want to be the one who drops it and have people die.

ELDAWOODY: No, no. He agrees, he agrees about lots of things. Because that's the principle, you know? No suiciding, no killing.

SIRAJ: No killing. Only economy problems. I'm going to work as a planner.

ELDAWOODY: Are you okay with it?

SIRAJ: I have to, you know, ask my mother's permission. Every single thing matters.

ELDAWOODY: Okay, here is the point. Are you willing to do jihad?

SIRAJ: I will work with those brothers as a planner or whatever. But dropping the bomb? I'm not sure. I have to think about it. Give me some time to feel comfortable with it.

ELDAWOODY: You don't want to put it there?

SIRAJ: No.

ELDAWOODY: Okay, I'll tell them that, because they were depending on you the most at 34th Street Station.

SIRAJ: I know about 34th Street. I can go with the brother, whatever, but I will not be the one who drops it.

ELDAWOODY: There will be two people.

SIRAJ: I will be the second person, if the other guy is dropping. No problem.

ELDAWOODY: It's not dropping. It's putting the stuff in a garbage can. Whatever makes you comfortable.

SIRAJ: I already gave the brothers the idea. They liked it, right? But the thing is, I will not be the person who puts it in the garbage can. Because if somebody dies, then the blame will come on me. Allah doesn't see those situations as accidents.

ELDAWOODY: So you are out of jihad?

SIRAJ: Planning is also jihad, brother.

ELSHAFAY: Am I going to do 34th Street?

ELDAWOODY: Yes.

ELSHAFAY: Can they maybe get someone who is more trained to do this?

SIRAJ: We're new. We don't even know what we are doing. We only know that I made the plan and we are working on the plan.

ELSHAFAY: If I'm going to do 34th Street, I want to go there a few more times. I want to check it out a little more. And if they can get someone better qualified than me to do it, then I think they should, because I'm not really experienced in this and might not know what to do. Is that okay?

ELDAWOODY: Okay. Whatever you feel. Whatever.

ELSHAFAY: I'll do it.

SIRAJ: The time to check out the station is in the morning from three o'clock to five o'clock. When the train stops, how many people get out? Find out which car is empty, so people have a chance to survive, you know. That way, it will be nice.

ELSHAFAY: I have an idea. If I go in to do it, I'll dress like a Jew. I'll have the bomb on me so it looks like a belly. I'll take it out and put it in the garbage can. I'll tuck in my shirt and walk out the 34th Street entrance.

SIRAJ: Don't put it in the belly.

ELSHAFAY: But I'm going to dress like a Jew. That way no one will check me.

SIRAJ: Jews do carry bags. See what bags they carry. What kinds of things they carry. Maybe it could be a Macy's bag.

ELSHAFAY: They'll never check a Jew, 'cause they know Jews aren't the ones doing it.

ELDAWOODY: Okay, are you going to be with him, Matin?

SIRAJ: Yeah, I can be with him.

ELSHAFAY: No. It's better if I just go in myself. Walk down there, *inshallah*, and everything will go the way Allah planned it. But I gotta get Jewish garb.

SIRAJ: The ponytails too?

ELSHAFAY: Yeah, those curls too. I gotta have 'em. Is there any way they can make the bomb look like something different?

ELDAWOODY: I don't know, but I don't think so.

ELSHAFAY: Could they make it look like a clock?

ELDAWOODY: A clock?

ELSHAFAY: 'Cause if they make it look like something different and I get checked, they just won't see that it's a bomb. They don't have X-rays there in the subway.

ELDAWOODY: I know that.

ELSHAFAY: So, yeah, definitely. If they can get the bomb to look like something different, I'll get dressed up like a Jew and go put the bomb there.

ELDAWOODY: So, Matin, what's your part? Your part is out? You don't want nothing?

SIRAJ: With the 34th thing?

ELDAWOODY: Yeah, 34th?

SIRAJ: I see you've started smoking again. You have to control yourself. It's not good for your health. Plus you have a daughter.

ELDAWOODY: No, no, no. It's under control. I'm playing with cigarettes. I was a heavy smoker, and I don't smoke now. I'm totally under control with cigarettes.

SIRAJ: It can hurt your liver, right? Cirrhosis, the nicotine.

ELDAWOODY: Smoking has nothing to do with the liver.

SIRAJ: But you cannot let that thing control you.

ELDAWOODY: Smoking is not good, but did I say that smoking is good?

ELSHAFAY: It hurts the lungs.

ELDAWOODY: But I don't inhale the smoke.

ELSHAFAY: Then you can get tongue cancer.

ELDAWOODY: Tongue?

ELSHAFAY: Tongue cancer.

ELDAWOODY: If I am dying, I am not going to die from cigarettes. I would die from other things.

ELSHAFAY: I miss Egypt.

ELDAWOODY: I do too. I really do.

The first to arrive at the sentencing were the artists for the news media, middle-aged women wearing colorful coats and sweaters, clutching to their chests drawing boards and opera glasses. Then came the journalists armed with slim notebooks and an air of competitive camaraderie. And then the government lawyers and police department officials in dark suits and polished shoes. Last, but still early, came the parents of the defendant, who sat down on the only empty bench closest to the wall at the back.

When Siraj was brought into the courtroom, he turned around to look, his eyes unfocused, at the public benches behind him. His mother, clutching prayer beads in her hands, half-rose from her seat, and Siraj acknowledged her with a hurried wave. He was wearing a blue, short-sleeve prison smock and long-sleeved gray underwear beneath it. His hair was cut short and he wore glasses that weren't very effective anymore because his eyesight had worsened in prison. Police marshals stood at every door. For a while the only sound in the courtroom came from the front bench where the artists were busily scratching crayon on paper.

The lead defense lawyer, Martin Stolar, spoke first. "The NYPD have created a crime," he said, "so that they can solve it." He reminded the court that the defendant had received low grades in school, and the plan for the bombing wasn't something that he would have himself come up with. The statements that Siraj had made were examples of "trash talking." When Stolar quoted Siraj on the video saying that he needed to ask his mother for permission, the journalists turned around in their seats to look at the Pakistani woman seated in the last row. The lawyer repeated what he had said during the trial, that his client was "not the brightest bulb in the chandelier." Then, reaching for higher ground, he ended by saying, "You should sentence a young man, not a symbol of the war on terror."

Judge Nina Gershon asked the defendant if he had anything to say. "Your honor I want to apologize. I want to apologize for all the recordings," Siraj began and then stopped. The judge directed that he be given water. After a while, having wiped away his tears, the defendant resumed, speaking in a slightly high-pitched rush, "I wish I could take those words back. At the time it happened, if the confidential informant hadn't come into my life . . . I told him clean—Mr. Eldawoody, I don't want to do it. That's on the tape. I want to ask my mother's permission. That's on tape. There are other previous conversations . . . I didn't commit the crime. I'm taking the responsibility for 34th Street, but I was manipulated by this person."

Assistant U.S. Attorney Todd Harrison was the first to speak after the defendant. Commenting on Stolar's plea that the judge must remember that she was sentencing a human being rather than a symbol, Harrison began by simply asking the judge to "sentence a person who has committed a crime." More than once, he called Siraj "calculating," saying that it was "on his own" that he had initiated and carried forward the conspiracy to bomb, and he pointed out that the defendant had hoped that "Osama bin Laden struck again." Harrison's colleague, Assistant U.S. Attorney Marshall Miller spoke next, beginning with the remark that it was "harder to imagine a more dangerous or more serious crime." "The evidence of the crime," Miller said, "comes from the defendant's mouth." He described Siraj as "the driving force" behind the conspiracy. "The attack was his brainchild," he added, "this plot was his handiwork." And then Miller addressed head-on what had been a criticism of the case, that the confidential informant had entrapped the impressionable, young defendant. Miller said that this charge was a "red herring." From the government's point of view, he said, the Siraj investigation had been a "model example of law enforcement." The government had done well; it was protecting the public. Miller told the court that the defendant had been caught on tape saying that he intended to engage in violent jihad until he achieved a martyr's death. A just sentence, Miller ended, would be one that sent Siraj to prison from thirty years to life.

Then it was time for the sentencing. The judge called the defendant's testimony "untruthful" and "willfully and intentionally false." She said Siraj was "opportunistic," "evasive," and "generally unreliable." Judge Gershon, small and dark-haired, wearing glasses, read in a low, calm voice. She paused to sip water. Her comments were openly dismissive of the defense claim that the police informant was responsible for a change in Siraj's thinking; she said that Siraj's "efforts to deny responsibility were both vigorous and untrue." While the judge was reading her statement, Siraj stood with his eyes downcast, his shoulders slumping, but everyone else in the courtroom sat motionless too, as if no one there was exempt from the purview of legal judgment.

The judge began to read her remarks about the seriousness of the intended crimes. She said, "They had the potential, if not thwarted, to wreak havoc with the New York City transportation system, indeed, the tristate-area transportation system." She added that the bombing would have led to enormous economic losses and, despite the defendant's intentions to minimize deaths, serious loss of life. Then the judge delivered the sentence. Siraj's father, his hands clenched, spoke into his wife's ear. But both of them, the husband and wife sitting by themselves, seemed unable to grasp what had happened. They showed a look of bewilderment on their faces and kept asking each other questions in Kutchi. Within their earshot, a female journalist, a young white woman, said to an older male colleague, "That was harsh." The man replied, "The kid will be fifty-three." A short, dapper man was entertaining the court artists with a story that made the ladies laugh. A little distance away, the government lawyers were shaking hands with the people who were congratulating them.

Siraj was led away by the marshals. His lawyers stepped out of the courtroom with the defendant's parents and his uncle. The couple sat down on a bench in the court's lobby and two of the lawyers on the defense team began to talk to them. Siraj's mother was crying. Her husband, Siraj Rehman, would turn one ear to whoever was speaking and then, apparently ineffectually, fiddle with his hearing aid. For a while the journalists allowed this tiny circle its privacy, but a little later, a man holding a laptop in his hand asked one of the lawyers for a statement from the parents. The mother, Shahina Parveen, stood up. Speaking in Urdu, she said, "Mera beta begunah hai" (My son is innocent). Her lawyer translated her words for the journalists. Parveen said that her son had been trapped by the NYPD through the use of a "paid informant." "It was not a fair sentence," she said, and added, "My son is not connected to any terrorist group or institution." "Mera bachcha bekasoor hai, mera ghareloo bachcha hai," she added, but the lawyer didn't think it necessary to translate those words.

Outside, in the bitterly cold night, the television cameramen and newspaper photographers were waiting for the defendant's parents. Without the lawyers present to translate, the two of them weren't talking to the journalists anymore. Parveen was wearing a slightly shabby pale brown jacket over her light blue shalwar-kameez; on her head, she had put a gray woolen cap. Her husband, holding a white polythene bag in one hand, half-supported her with the other as they walked away slowly.

Just a couple of hours earlier, I had stood there on the pavement with one of the government prosecutors and a detective. The men I was talking with had little sympathy for the argument about entrapment that was later repeated by Siraj's mother. When I had brought the subject up, the detective had smiled indulgently at my naïveté and said, "If they had stopped the 9/11 hijackers, their lawyers would no doubt have made the same case for five or six of them."

The next morning, before dawn, Siraj's parents and nineteen-year-old sister were arrested in their home. They were being detained for having overstayed their visa, but, as their lawyer later explained, the government had been aware of their status since 2002. The family had applied for asylum in the United States, long before Siraj's arrest in the bombing case, on grounds that they would face religious persecution if they returned to Pakistan. They are Ismaili Muslims, a minority in Pakistan, and had argued that this was sufficient ground for being granted asylum in the United States. As their appeal was still under consideration, the arrest was unusual and puzzling. But it was perplexing only in the abstract; there was nothing at all hidden or veiled about the timing of the action taken by the immigration authorities.

While Matin Siraj was being kept at the Metropolitan Detention Facility in Brooklyn until he was assigned to a federal facility—he is currently in the medium-security wing of the new federal prison for Arab and other inmates in Terre Haute, Indiana, where I was refused permission to interview him on the somewhat inexplicable grounds that the visit "could jeopardize security and disturb the orderly running of the institution"— his family was being kept at the Immigration and Customs Enforcement facility in Elizabeth, New Jersey.

A week after the Siraj family's arrest, they were presented in front of a judge for a bail hearing at the same facility. An activist organization of South Asians in New York City had hired a bus to bring about twenty protestors to Elizabeth. Although they were not allowed inside the yellow brick building, resembling a warehouse, where the hearing was taking place, the men and women in the group walked in a circle outside the gate, chanting slogans like "Stop Breaking Our Families Apart." A Pakistani man, who said that he was the imam of a mosque in Elmhurst, Queens, said that when he was leaving for Elizabeth that morning his wife said to him. "Don't go there. Otherwise they'll come to our house." He struggled to explain to her, and to those listening to him now, that that was exactly the reason why everyone needed to be at the protest.

While the protestors spoke to reporters, in the background large trucks entered the gates of adjoining buildings that had large signs with words like "Shipping and Receiving." The cold was of the sort that quickly numbs enthusiasm even for necessary talk, but several of the activists stuck to their task, shouting into the frigid air, stamping their feet, and clapping their gloved hands together for heat. Five Muslim men took off their shoes and, their faces turned east toward Mecca, their hands spread out in front of them, began to pray on the empty road. Behind them, commercial airlines lifted off, from the runways of Newark airport on the other side of the highways, into the cold stillness above.

It was not until the evening that the group received news that the hearing had not gone well. The judge had decided that Siraj Rehman's case would be decided not in court on appeal but administratively. The question of securing bail didn't arise for him. The bond for Shahina Parveen's release had been set at $20,000 and for their daughter, Saniya, at $15,000. The following morning, in a telephone conversation, Mona Shah, the family's lawyer, called the bond amount "ridiculously high" and "outrageous." She said about the hearing, "The government was asking so many questions that bordered on irrelevancy. This is a straightforward case." The lawyer believed that the parents were being punished even after punishment had been meted out to the son. She described her clients as being in "a state of shock, traumatized by their son's conviction," and now "absolutely terrified and absolutely broken." Twelve days later, the day after her release on payment of bond, Parveen said that the imprisonment had left her feeling humiliated and helpless, and she no longer wished to come out of her house. But it became clear that Parveen had no choice, the family had no income, and soon she began to work at the Islamic Books and Tapes, the same bookstore in Bay Ridge where her son had been employed and where the informant had befriended him.

Bay Ridge is an ethnically mixed neighborhood largely dominated by Arab immigrants; it sits on the southwestern edge of the borough of Brooklyn, almost near the end of the R line. On emerging from the Bay Ridge Avenue station, the visitor has to cross a block of apartment buildings and businesses with names like Arabesq Arab Cafe, Ramalla Coffee Shop, and Paradise Boutique, its window populated by tall, white-looking mannequins incongruously wearing the hijab, before arriving at Fifth Avenue, where, wedged between the Islamic Society of Bay Ridge Mosque and the Dog and Cat Hospital, is the bookstore owned by Matin Siraj's uncle.

The store's name is Islamic Books and Tapes, but most of the customers there seem primarily interested in buying phone cards. The plastic cards make a colorful tapestry on the wall behind the counter, and, with names like "Arabian Deluxe," "East," "Numero Uno," and "Sohni Dharti," invite customers to call countries like Morocco, Libya, Egypt, Somalia, Pakistan, and Tunisia. The Islamic prayer clock, showing the time for the *azaan*, or call to prayer, in one hundred and one cities all over the world, is sold in the store for $25.00. An old and grimy photocopying machine sits a bit further inside the store, next to a table with prayer mats and Islamic prayer caps on sale. The shelves around it are stocked with dried dates, perfume, prayer beads, shiny headdresses for women, and room fresheners.

The titles of the books and tapes appear seemingly eclectic but actually have a distinct and recognizable uniformity to them: *Don't be Sad* by Aaidh ibn Abdullah al-Qarni; *Why Darwinism Is Incompatible with the Qoran*; *Systems of Modesty and Chastity in Islam*; *Only Love Can Defeat Terrorism* by Harun Yahiya; *The Miracle of Respiration*; *Terrorism and Islam: An Islamic Perspective*; and also, evoking surprise, a feature film, *The Color of Paradise* by the famed Iranian director Majid Majidi. A rotating stand close to the cash register is stacked with children's books. The cheap books, printed on cheap paper in Daryaganj in Delhi and telling stories from the Holy Qu'ran, follow the Islamic injunction of not representing the human form. So, remarkably, *The Story of Adam and Hawwa* by one Dr. Shamim Nikhat, shows featureless mountains and calendar-art flowers and even several planets hovering above Eden, but no one whom a child reading the book can identify as Adam and Eve. The reading of the story is likely to produce, in the mind of the uninitiated, a feeling of alienation and claustrophobia.

The world outside the store is not any more inviting either. Standing at the counter and looking out of its glass windows at the street, visitors can see a row of shabby ethnic restaurants, discount stores, a place with the words "CHECKS CASHED" above the door, and a downscale furniture shop with a notice in its window that, on closer inspection, reveals the following message: "If you suspect terrorism, call NYPD 1-888-NYC-SAFE."

In 1999, Siraj's family moved to New York City from Karachi, Pakistan. They had some difficulty because Siraj's father, Siraj Rehman, didn't keep good health. He was having problems with his hearing and he had developed a hernia while working as a laundryman in Pakistan. After coming to the United States, he had found a job as a parking-lot attendant, but one day he slipped and fell, and the hernia came back and required surgery. Matin Siraj was a teenager at that time and began working as a delivery boy for Blimpie's. After that, for a year or so, he was employed at a grocery store near his aunt's house; he got work at a 99 Cent Store but was fired after a week because he didn't have a Social Security number. A brief period of unemployment followed and then Siraj started doing paperwork for a cellphone business. Then he was out of a job again. Later, when he started working at Islamic Books and Tapes in the middle of 2002, his uncle started his own cell-phone business and Siraj got involved in that, working from a space at the back of the bookstore.

While manning the sales counter at the bookstore after her release from detention in Elizabeth, Shahina Parveen spoke fondly of her earlier employment as a midwife in Pakistan. She would travel in an ambulance. She was also a beautician and performed make-up for brides ("I never took money for it"). The family had fallen on hard times, she said, and if the government broke them further, they would have to resort to begging. Then, the cold days of winter passed and it was spring, and she would assure her husband on the phone, when he called during the afternoons from jail, telling him that he should try to stay calm and read the Holy Qu'ran.

In June 2007, after more than five months in detention, her husband was also released on payment of bond. As a condition of his release, Siraj Rehman needed to wear an electronic monitoring bracelet on his leg. It looked like a very large watch strapped to his left leg; another device in his house recorded his entry and exit from his home. Rehman was to be out of the house only between eight in the morning and eleven at night. He began to use much of this time to work at Islamic Books and Tapes, resting there in the afternoon by sleeping behind the counter while his daughter dealt with customers. His health had worsened in prison. He said in Urdu, "I do not know of my tomorrow." His three hernia operations had not cured him, his blood pressure had shot up dramatically; often he felt breathless and was afraid that he was about to die. He opened his mouth and put out his tongue to show the boils that he said a doctor had decided were most likely ulcers.

Sometime in September 2003, Osama Eldawoody began to visit Islamic Books and Tapes after his routine surveillance visits to the mosque next door. According to the informant's court testimony, a few months after their first meeting, when Eldawoody told Siraj that he had a degree in nuclear engineering, the youth asked him if he knew how to design a nuclear bomb. And a few months after that, in April, Siraj excitedly gave him a CD and said that it had instructions on how to make a bomb. This CD was only a pirated copy of the popular protest manual of the 1970s, *The Anarchist Cookbook*. Nevertheless, Eldawoody called his handler and told him, "I got a really, like, crazy CD." He told the detective that Siraj was asking him if it was possible to acquire the materials needed to make a bomb described in the book.

A month later, the scandal of Abu Ghraib was everywhere in the news. The tales of abuse gave a new and different edge to the discussions between Siraj and Eldawoody. During the trial, the defendant testified that the confidential informant had shown him pictures of abuse, including one of a thirteen-year-old Iraqi girl getting raped by a dog. Eldawoody's account differed from Siraj's. He said that Siraj was enraged by the reports coming out of Abu Ghraib and had told him that after his immigration hearing was over he would go to Pakistan and join an al Qaeda training camp.

Around this time, Siraj introduced Eldawoody to his friend James Elshafay, the young man who was later charged along with Siraj but pleaded guilty and became a government witness. He was the son of an Irish American mother and an Egyptian father. His parents had separated when he was two, and for much of his life he had lived with his mother and aunt in Staten Island. When he was eleven or twelve, he gave up the Roman Catholic faith of his mother and converted to Islam. He had once received a juvenile delinquent card because he had posted notices in his neighborhood asking "Did you beat a Jew today?" Elshafay, who was in his late teens when he met Eldawoody, had earlier been in trouble because of his drinking and drug use. In addition, he had received psychiatric treatment for schizophrenia, which involved a stay in the hospital after having suffered from delusions, including imagining his mother telling him that he was Jewish. After a short visit to Egypt, he began to frequent Islamic Books and Tapes, where he would often discuss religion and politics with Siraj.

On one occasion, after talking about a bombing in Iraq, the two young men began speculating about the possibilities of carrying out a bomb attack in the United States. Elshafay borrowed a pen and paper from Siraj and drew a map of Staten Island and the bridges around it. Next he drew boxes to indicate the police stations and the jail. He told Siraj that he had a plan—although for anyone else to call it that would be delusional—to blow up the bridges and, with the help of two to three hundred people, release all the inmates from the prison and put the police inside in their place. Elshafay's map, which later became government exhibit 6 during the trial, was taken by Siraj to Eldawoody, who, in turn, replied that he would talk to his contact in upstate New York.

In his thriller titled *A Most Wanted Man*, John Le Carré writes: "Since 9/11, Hamburg's mosques had become dangerous places. Go to the wrong one, or the right one and get the wrong imam, and you could find yourself and your family on a police watch list for the rest of your life. Nobody doubted that practically every prayer row contained an informant who was earning his way with the authorities." Hamburg was the city where Mohammed Atta and two other September 11 hijackers had lived for a while, and that is the place where much of the drama and action in Le Carré's novel ensues; but even in the real world, in the United States, according to a report in *Newsweek* in early February 2003, the FBI director Robert Mueller asked all his field offices to tally the number of mosques in their localities and shift their focus from "drug and relatively minor white-collar fraud cases" to "terrorism cases, including developing undercover informants." Eldawoody's emergence followed this script, but it also introduced a complication. Eldawoody had stated in court on more than one occasion that the police instruction to him was to keep his "eyes and ears open for any radical acts." However, that isn't all that he was doing. He served as a mentor and guide to the young men he had under surveillance. This might have been because he had acquired the reputation of being a religious man. During prayers at the Bay Ridge mosque, he would weep openly. Siraj and others were affected by Eldawoody's revelation that he was suffering from cirrhosis of the liver. He was a heavy smoker, and his hands shook sometimes; it is possible that he had also told the young men that he was dying of cancer. On at least one occasion, Siraj had told Eldawoody, "I am like your son." It is arguable that for Elshafay too, who had grown up with an absent father, the informant had become a paternal figure providing guidance. In any case, what is less open to doubt is that Eldawoody regularly discoursed on religion and rules of conduct.

He had told Elshafay that "a killer gets killed in Islam." He had indicated to the two men that it was "lawful to spill a non-Muslim's blood." More than once, he told them that it was *haram* to take one's own life and consequently encouraged them to devise a plan that didn't involve suicide bombing. After Siraj told him about the Staten Island plan, Eldawoody gave Elshafay a ride in his car and began to talk about the killings of Muslims in places like Iraq. He asked the young man, "Why do they want to kill us?" It was only when this question was asked that Elshafay realized that Siraj had shared his bombing plan with Eldawoody. Again, on a separate occasion, driving on the Verrazano Bridge, Eldawoody questioned Elshafay on what would be the best place to put the bomb. The conversation nearly had a tone of benign, academic exchange. Eldawoody was like a parent helping with homework, testing the child's knowledge and intelligence, complimenting him, and stamping his authority with his own expertise.

That same month, Siraj came up with the plan to put bombs in the subway station at Thirty-Fourth Street and Herald Square. This was the station where Siraj would change trains every day. At first he had proposed that a bomb be placed in the last car of the B or D train at the Thirty-Fourth Street station, and that it be detonated as the train crossed the Manhattan Bridge. There were other targets to consider too. But Eldawoody came back to Siraj with the news that the brother in upstate New York had approved only of the Thirty-Fourth Street plan. Siraj's plan was that he would take the F train from Queens and, before he changed to the D that would take him to Bay Ridge, he would tuck a package under a bench or inside a garbage can.

While the plan was being formed, Eldawoody asked Siraj if there were surveillance cameras at the station. Siraj had seen none but a decision was taken that the two of them, along with Elshafay, would make a reconnaissance trip. On August 21, 2007, a rainy day, the three men made that trip. Siraj had asked Eldawoody to wear baseball gear and he himself tied a bandana on his head. After the visit to the station, during which detectives in plainclothes photographed the trio at the station, the men sat in Eldawoody's car and drew maps. Siraj's detailed map of the station became government exhibit 9 during the trial; it showed the entry and exit routes, and the places where the bombs would be put. James Elshafay offered to carry the bomb. Siraj said that he didn't want to do it, but he would look out for cops. Eldawoody wanted to know why he wouldn't place the bombs himself, and Siraj explained his reluctance by saying, "Brother, planning is jihad." A part of the planning that Siraj had done was that the person who would place the bomb in the station would call the person who would detonate it with the message "I have delivered the pizza." What he had not planned was his arrest, a few days before the Republican Convention in New York City, and that he would probably never walk free in this country ever again. Siraj will be fifty-three when he gets out of prison and will almost certainly be deported immediately upon his release.

Before the trial got underway, Siraj's lawyers had been worried that he would not get an impartial jury. The jurors would have heard about the case in the media and would already have made up their minds about the accused. They would have made stereotypical assumptions about a young Muslim man charged in a terrorism trial. And, undeniably, it would be difficult for them to distance themselves from their own fears if they contemplated the bombing of the subway in which they probably traveled each day. The defense lawyers submitted a questionnaire to the judge, who, after some alterations, gave it to the men and women in the jury pool. On the basis of the responses, which sometimes betrayed naked bias against their client, the number of potential jurors was whittled down from more than 160 to around 80. After further questions, this number was reduced to 12 jurors and 6 alternates. These were some of the questions that the lawyers had asked on the questionnaire:

1. Have you read, seen or heard about the case from the news, family, or friends? Have you heard anything about this case? _____ Yes _____ No If "Yes," what have you read, seen or heard about this case?

7. Based on what you have seen, read, discussed or formed an opinion about this case, would that make it difficult for you to sit as a fair and impartial juror in this case? _____ Yes _____ No Please explain:

11. Are you aware of the New York Police Department's policy of "random subway searches" to "deter terrorism?" _____ Yes _____ No

12. If "Yes," what are your thoughts on this policy?

13. Have you been subject to or observed one or more of these subway searches? _____ Yes _____ No

14. If "Yes," what was your reaction?

17. Are you aware of the bombings on the London, England and Madrid, Spain mass transportations last year? _____ Yes _____ No

18. If "Yes," will your knowledge make it difficult for you to serve as a fair and impartial juror in this case? _____ Yes _____ No
Please explain:

19. Do you personally know anyone who was killed or injured in the September 11, 2001 attacks on the World Trade Center and the Pentagon or on the flight that was downed in Pennsylvania? _____ Yes _____ No

20. If "Yes," who (without naming names): _____

21. What is your opinion about the government's "war on terrorism?"

22. Have you heard of the USA Patriot Act? _____ Yes _____ No
If "Yes," do you agree with the purposes of the Act?
_____ Yes _____ No _____ No Opinion
If "Yes" or "No," please explain:

23. Do you believe that the war in Iraq is part of the war on terrorism?
_____ Yes _____ No
Please explain:

27. Do you have any knowledge about the history and practices of the faith of Islam? _____ Yes _____ No

28. If "Yes," how knowledgeable are you and what is the source of your knowledge?

29. Do you have any Muslim friends or family members?
_____ Yes _____ No

30. When you hear that someone is Muslim does that affect your perception of that person _____ in a positive way, _____ in a negative way, _____ in no way at all?
If "positive" or "negative," please explain:

31. Do you believe that Islam endorses violence to a greater or lesser extent than other major religions?
_____ greater extent _____ lesser extent _____ same extent
_____ no opinion

32. What, if anything, do you understand the term "jihad" to mean?

33. Are you open to alternative interpretations if those are presented?
_____ Yes _____ No

34. Is there any reason why you could not be a fair and impartial juror because the defendant is Muslim? _____ Yes _____ No

If "Yes," please explain:

36. Have you or an immediate family member ever felt you were discriminated against because of your religious beliefs?

_____ Yes _____ No

If "Yes," please explain:

39. Will the fact that the defendant is an immigrant from Pakistan make it difficult for you to be a fair and impartial Juror in this case?

_____ Yes _____ No

Please explain:

41. The evidence in this case may include information provided or obtained by individual(s) working with the government in exchange for payment or other benefits.

These individuals are sometimes called "confidential informants." Do you have views against the use of evidence provided or obtained by such individuals? _____ Yes _____ No

If "Yes," please explain:

44. To your knowledge, have you, any family member or close friend, ever been the subject of surveillance (visual, electronic or photographic) by law enforcement or had your/their car or home searched by law enforcement? _____ Yes _____ No

If "Yes," please explain:

This process of questioning, which is known in legal parlance as voir dire, involves an active interrogation of the potential jurors' opinions. The questions have to be probing and are followed by demands for explanation. This is because even in conditions where a juror says that he or she is likely to be impartial, it is quite possible that the individual is either unwilling to admit biases in front of other jurors or is simply not cognizant of them. In his paper called "Trial by Jury Involving Persons Accused of Terrorism or Supporting Terrorism," Neil Vidmar of Duke University's Law School cites several examples from the surveys of jury-eligible persons in the North Virginia prosecution of John Walker Lindh, the so-called American Taliban. Here is one revealing instance of a self-professed impartial person offering a response that is in sharp contradiction to her claim:

Respondent #165 asserted she could be impartial in deciding Mr. Lindh's guilt or innocence and explained why by saying "It must be proven with facts."

Yet her just expressed responses to other questions on the survey indicated that she had a "strongly unfavorable" impression of the accused, that "he is a traitor," that he was "definitely guilty," "he killed Americans and should be shot." That a jury's not-guilty verdict would be "very unacceptable," and that he should experience "death by hanging" for the reason that "I want him to feel pain."

Vidmar also offers examples of voir dire responses from the trial of Sami Al-Arian, a Palestinian professor at the University of South Florida, who had been charged with providing support to a terrorist group. Given the amount of bias against Arabs and Muslims, and given Al-Arian's own notoriety in Florida, there was a lot of concern among the defense lawyers about whether it would be possible to select a jury that didn't show bias or even outright hostility. The trial judge sent a lengthy questionnaire, containing 83, to 500 randomly selected names using the court's normal procedures for drawing a jury panel. Of the 500 questionnaires, only 328 were returned; of this number, 34 percent declared themselves biased against the accused. Here is one example of a respondent who described herself as biased:

> Too much to state here—read and followed everything I could. I have a daughter attending USF in Tampa and the jerk was a professor there. Sami Al-Arian looks like a Moslem Radical to me; Sami is probably one of those "kill the infidels"; He's probably had a hand in fund-raising for terror organizations. . . . What do you think! I saw him all sweaty and screaming with laundry wrapped on his head on those film clips. Looked obvious to me. I think he's guilty of fund-raising for terrorists. What I've read and seen in the media you can take my vote now and save all that taxpayer money. Remember 911? I think Sami is guilty.

Vidmar's own count of biased respondents is even higher, closer to 39 percent, because he includes those potential jurors who, despite calling themselves impartial, reveal strong prejudice. Yet, despite the widespread and even endemic prejudice against Arabs, the Al-Arian trial ended with the jury unanimously finding him not guilty. Through a study of these cases, the argument that Vidmar is offering is not so much that there is obvious bias among many potential jurors in terrorism trials; rather, it is that a jury randomly selected from a population holding such biased opinion would not lead to a fair and impartial hearing. In other words, the use of voir dire and other measures appears wholly necessary.

The questionnaire designed by the Siraj defense team was presumably effective because, during its deliberations, the jury sent out notes to the judge seeking clarifications on the specific charges she had laid out for them. Midway through their discussions, the jury wanted the judge to establish clearly the time frame within which they were to evaluate the defendant's readiness or willingness to commit a terrorist crime—how far in history were they going to have to go to perform such an evaluation? Martin Stolar, Siraj's lead defense lawyer, told the *New York Times* that the notes showed that the jury system had worked. He had said this *after* the jury had returned a guilty verdict on his client. "They did not convict my client merely because he's a Muslim accused of terrorism," said Stolar. "They believed that the evidence did not make out the defense of entrapment, and they followed the law."

But a troubling issue remains. Let's go back to the questionnaire submitted to the potential jurors in the Siraj trial. The questions refer to the attacks of September 11, the Patriot Act, random searches, immigration, religious persecution, surveillance and police informants, the Iraq War. The respondents' views on such matters would determine whether they could serve on the jury. But any reasonable discussion of such issues, in particular the Iraq War and the ways in which it provided a backdrop for the defendant's actions, could not be allowed to be matters of discussion in the trial. After all, President Bush or Secretary Rumsfeld were not on trial, Siraj was. I'm not denying the practical necessities of conducting a criminal trial; I'm certainly not providing advice on how they should be run. Nevertheless, what I want to underline, if it isn't obvious, is that there were deeper questions that the Siraj trial brought to the fore, questions that the jury was constitutionally unable to recognize or address.

As an example, consider the exchange on the subject of suicide bombings between the defendant and an undercover police officer, a young man from Bangladesh recruited by the NYPD and given the street name Kamil Pasha. Pasha told the court that on one occasion Siraj had tried to justify suicide bombings by Palestinians. He had spoken of them as acts of revenge, "because the enemies have killed the family members, they raped their sisters, and that it was revenge for the bombers to get even."

Pasha added, "The defendant said that if anybody did that to his family, he would do the same thing. . . . At that point, I asked the defendant if there is going to be any suicide bombings in the United States and I recall the defendant saying, yes, there will be suicide bombings in the United States because of the U.S. support for Israel." Later, on cross-examination, Pasha was asked if he thought that Siraj was giving him his "opinion" when asked if suicide bombings were going to take place in the United States. In response, Pasha said, "That's what he said. I can't analyze that statement. I don't know." Siraj's lawyer, Stolar, persisted, "It's a political opinion, isn't it?" The government lawyer interjected with an objection, which was sustained, and Stolar decided to rephrase the question. Stolar asked Pasha, "Did you ask him for his political opinion, if he thinks that suicide bombings are going to happen in the United States?" There was another objection, and again it was sustained, yet another rephrasing, and yet another objection, which resulted in a sidebar conversation with the judge. The prosecutors were interested in letting Siraj's statement stand as evidence, while the defense lawyer was committed to shaping it as idle opinion. But surely, the wider, necessary question, once we are freed from the requirements of the trial itself, is why there have so far been no suicide bombings in the United States and whether the Siraj saga has anything to teach us in this regard.

Toward the end of Pasha's cross-examination, Stolar returned to the question from a new angle. He asked the undercover officer whether the defendant had spoken about "Muslims being victimized in this country." Pasha replied, "The defendant at times would say Muslims are being victimized in this country and other countries and that the U.S. only supported Israel." Stolar asked, "Now, that is a political statement, is it not?" Once again, Pasha said, "I can't analyze that. I am not an analyst." On further questioning, he admitted that the viewpoint that Siraj expressed was not his alone but was talked about by other people too in the Bay Ridge neighborhood. The government attorney objected and then sought permission to approach the bench. According to court records, he appealed to the judge that Stolar's questioning was "improper" because it was about "whether Matin was making a political statement . . . as to why he is saying something." The judge agreed, rightly, pointing out, "It is not up to this witness. Look, you can characterize this for argument, if you want to, that it's political. To be asking this witness who is not an expert on political opinions versus other opinions. I think it is improper. What you need to do is ask him factual questions."

Therein lies the rub. The truth is that what we recognize as fact might well be only the confirmation of what has settled in our minds as a stereotype. How has it come to be accepted as a fact that a young Muslim man is likely to be a terrorist? We recognize Matin Siraj's every word and action as irrefutable evidence of a terrorist's personality because it matches the profile we have registered on our retinas. Two days after the attacks of September 11, two Indian businessmen, both Muslims from Hyderabad, were on a train to Texas. En route, they were asked to show what was in their luggage. When the police found box cutters, hair dye, and $7,000 in cash, they declared that they had found the missing "hijacker number 20." The men had been running a newsstand, hence the box cutters; in early September, they had lost their jobs when the newsstand changed owners, and they were going to start anew in San Antonio. The men were in detention for seventeen months; there was no sign of their having engaged in terrorism and their ultimate convictions were on the minor charges of credit card fraud. One of the two men, Mohammad Azmath, told a journalist in India after his release, "I was put in a cage for three months. They would bang on the door once every thirty minutes—I never slept a wink for all that time." Azmath was one of the roughly 1,100 individuals who were taken into custody after September 11 and suffered a variety of abuse; in the time since then, the diverse body of legislation and administrative measures undertaken to target Muslims has reminded observers of the sorry history of Japanese internment during the Second World War, when the U.S. Supreme Court had offered its infamous decision that the "exclusion of those of Japanese origin was deemed necessary because of the presence of an unascertained number of disloyal members of the group."

Once we are comfortable with stereotypes, other complicating truths appear like political provocations. Consider a remark made by Aziz Huq, a legal theorist at the University of Chicago Law School, that looking for terrorists by scouring Muslim communities is "like looking for needles in a haystack." This is because the terrorists "are few and far between, and their ideological roots are difficult to mechanistically untangle from those who endorse a puritanical—but nonviolent—form of Islam. Studies of terrorist radicalization also reveal a multiplicity of individual root causes, both emotion and societal." Recent statistics support Huq's argument. He writes, "U.S. Attorneys have declined to prosecute in sixty-eight percent of terrorism referrals since 9/11." Of the 288 convictions claimed by the Justice Department, many were resolved not as terror cases but as cases involving credit card fraud and immigration illegality. Only fourteen received sentences of twenty years or more—and these include cases like Siraj, cases in which, Huq writes, "informants have played a crucial catalytic role in pushing young and impressionable men toward verbal endorsement of violent action—hence exposing them to criminal prosecution."

On June 30, 2007, a man driving a dark green Jeep Cherokee received 90 percent burns on his body outside the Glasgow airport. The man's name was Kafeel Ahmed and he had rammed his vehicle against the security bollards outside the airport. The Jeep Cherokee was filled with propane canisters, and they failed to ignite, but the driver was on fire. His mother, Dr. Zakia Ahmed, watching the news on television in India, didn't recognize him. Even four days later, after her second son, Sabeel, had been arrested, she still believed that her firstborn was in hiding, although the statement she made to a journalist contained a hint of ambiguity: "I didn't recognize the person on the ground on fire, I didn't recognize him as my son." She then said, "Mujhe pata nahin mere bachchon ko kisne gumrah kiya hai" (I don't know who led my children astray).

When I read Zakia Ahmed's words, I thought of Shahina Parveen. There were similarities between their sons, no doubt, but there were similarities also between the two mothers. Both did not recognize their sons in the figure of the foreign terrorist; both preserved in the idea of their sons having gone astray the aura of violated innocence. It is a mother's right, I suppose, and in Parveen's case, her son makes the task easier. Every time I have met with Parveen she has shown me the letters her son writes to her from prison: in nearly each one of them, in a handwriting that is still like a child's, as if he were practicing cursive writing according to the rules taught in a classroom, Siraj reminds his mother that he is good. The habit is so consistent that it seems petty to suspect that it is only a strategy devised for Siraj's appeal. In one letter, he wrote that he wanted his clothes to be given to the victims of the tsunami. He believed that the American public, which had been generous to the victims, would be blessed by Allah. In the very next line, he asked that money be sent also to Guyana, where he mentioned there had been flooding. Before ending with expressions of love for the extended family, he assured his mother: "Ma I now this is very hard for you but Allah will make this easy for us and will listen your prayer I will soon be with you again so dont take any stress because you now your son and you know that I am innecont so my trust is on Allah and he will help us. . . ."

In another letter, Siraj wrote to greet his family on Ramadan. He talked of fasting and of breaking the fast. He wrote: "Ma you know when I miss your food you use to make all my favourite food so its now more than a year I dint tast the food of your hand but when I miss your food I start thinking about the people in Kantrina and the earthquick that came in Pakistan and the other storm in Central America I heard I thank God whatever food he give me I pray for all that are suffering."

Even two years later, the letters say the same thing, and in the same language: "Ma don't take any stress just pray for me Allah know I am not what they lable me as."

Unlike Kafeel Ahmed's mother in Bangalore, Parveen says she knows who misled her son. It is the confidential informant, Osama Eldawoody. She says that Eldawoody always wanted Siraj to drink tea or coffee, but her son never drank such beverages. However, Eldawoody had also given Siraj fruits and sweets. Had he laced them with a substance that changed her son's thinking? More than once the informant had offered Siraj cookies, but Siraj hadn't eaten them; he had brought them home to show them to his mother. Parveen claimed that she had taken the cookies out of the house and put them on the street so that cats and dogs could eat them.

The Siraj family lives in a two-room apartment in a six-story brick building in Jackson Heights, Queens. On an afternoon in August, Parveen was holding an album of pictures in her hand. She said, "Eldawoody used to smoke a lot. Was there a drug in what he was smoking? Did that affect my son?"

Probably because she had worked as a nurse, Parveen wanted her children to become doctors. In a letter to his mother dated August 21, 2007, Siraj acknowledged that he wasn't able to look after his parents. But he was working toward his GED, the tests that would certify that he had high-school-level academic skills. He had added, "I just reading books many kind. I am learning science of insects and Biology book basic of becoming doctor these kind of books have a lot of knowledge. I am trying my best to stay strong against stress. Ma I miss you a lot. I miss your food a lot." This letter, touching on dreams and ambition, had cheered Parveen. (Especially because just a couple of months earlier, her son had complained that he had not been given the medication that a visiting psychologist had said he needed for "anzaity and depration.") And then, in another letter written to his lawyer just a day later, a copy of which had been mailed to Parveen, Siraj spoke happily of how he had celebrated his sister's birthday in prison. In the preceding weeks I had sent to his warden letters of introduction from the London-based editor of *Granta* magazine, and then, reading Siraj's letter, I found confirmation that he had indeed received my request: ". . . we inmates all played Bingo and I win price and realy missed my family tell my sister I said Happy Birthday I cannot talk to her on phone I will call them on friday. Martin some lady want to take my interview for Gernet magazin should I allow that even I allow by my permission the warden will not allow he already said no to WNBC the one you said I should talk with them."

I often found the chore of reading Siraj's letters wearying. Just after reading two or three sentences, I'd inevitably begin to wonder how this man could ever plan a bombing by himself. But, more usually, it was simply my impatience with a mind that seemed to have trouble distinguishing between the world and the womb. Once I had slipped into this mood, his mother's talk would quickly become tiresome. I would tell myself that I was being irrational and probably also unfair, but that didn't lessen my sense of intolerance and exasperation. Of course, there were many occasions when I'd be in conversation with Siraj's mother and she would strike me as a victim of the war on terror. I didn't presume her son's innocence; rather, even with his guilt, it was still very clear that his parents had endured the consequences of a war in which their participation had been claimed without their being asked for consent. Parveen would be showing me pictures of weddings in Karachi, or the photographs from her youth, a time when she would point out she was much thinner, and I would pay attention because what I was witnessing was a return to a former, cherished life of a survivor.

Yes, it is true that I kept waiting for an acknowledgment of some genuine self-questioning or an explanation of what would have made Siraj vulnerable to the informant's prodding. Always, there was only a feeling of bewilderment—and talk about cookies or *lassi* laced with a mystery drug that turned boys into terrorists. But why had I expected anything else from someone that even I recognized in some measure as collateral damage in this war on terror?

In his brilliant documentary film *War at a Distance*, the German filmmaker Harun Farocki says that "war in the electronic age presents itself as an event free of people though they still may be involved." What Farocki is referring to are the "synthetic images" taken from an aircraft or a smart bomb and "purged of anything that could be a direct clue to human life." Even fields, roads, and entire villages "have been reduced to a symbolic level." A similar logic operates in the execution of the war on terror. A distancing optic allows individuals and families to blur into whole communities and nations. They are all collapsible into each other. There is an even greater violence that takes place. Certain communities and nations are *not* collapsible into each other. Muslim immigrant communities are at this moment seen as a whole separate entity existing outside the boundaries of a more authentically Western culture. The intimacy of enemies, for some reason, eludes our ideologues. We see the East and the West as self-contained, distinct civilizations that do not overlap and do not share complicated histories of mutual engagement and influence.

In the months following the attacks of September 11, I had read an interview with Frank Lindh, the father of John Walker Lindh, the young American captured in Afghanistan fighting for the Taliban. When asked about his son's startling odyssey from Marin County to the mountains of Afghanistan, Frank Lindh had said, "I can't connect the dots between where John was and where John is." This didn't surprise me, the sense of bafflement that parents reveal when accosted with news of their progeny, but then I read that Frank Lindh, back in 2000, had sent his son to Yemen with his blessing. This interested me more. In our educational institutions, and even in our homes, we talk quite often of multiculturalism or tolerance. But usually this means nothing but being open to the idea of celebrating someone else's holiday—with some matching ethnic food, if you please. For a practicing Catholic to show no hostility to his son's conversion to Islam after watching Spike Lee's biopic *Malcolm X*, and then to encourage him when he decides to study at a madrassa in Sana'a requires some genuine sense of acceptance. When I contacted Frank Lindh through his lawyers, I asked him whether he understood what his son had ended up doing, and whether he now regretted his earlier openness, which some would even call naïveté.

Lindh is a lawyer and has taken up the task, after an initial period of silence lasting more than a year, of speaking on his son's behalf, especially because John is not permitted to make any public statements or meet with the media. (He is an inmate in the super-maximum security facility in Florence, Colorado, the same prison that houses others convicted of terrorism, including Sheikh Omar Abdel-Rahman, Ramzi Yousef, Zacarias Moussaoui, Richard Colvin Reid, Theodore Kaczynski, and others. Timothy McVeigh was incarcerated there.) In early 2003, Frank Lindh took six months off from work to research and write an article about his son, a version of which was published in the *Washington Lawyer*, the publication of the D.C. Bar Association. He has since spoken at a few public meetings and in law classrooms where he emphasizes the need to guard the right to due process.

In an interview with me, Lindh recalled that on the night of December 1, 2001, he had come out of a movie theater after watching *The Man Who Wasn't There* and found a message on his cell phone from his former wife, Marilyn. She had received an email about a piece of news on the MSNBC website about a young American called Abdul Hamid who had been found at a fort outside Mazar-i-Sharif among the survivors of an uprising by Taliban prisoners. The youth in the grainy photograph of Abdul Hamid, which was the name that John had given to his captors, looked unmistakably like their son. Nothing had prepared him for this news. For the past seven months, there had been no word from John. Soon after September 11 that year, the idea of a young white American by himself in an Arabic country had become a source of worry for Lindh, but all his attempts to locate John had proved fruitless. Unknown to Lindh, his son had crossed into Afghanistan in early June that year and volunteered to fight in the Taliban army battling against the Northern Alliance. He received a short training in an al Qaeda camp, which was twice visited by Osama bin Laden. Lindh says that John believed that it was his duty as a Muslim to fight in what was an Islamic liberation movement against the northern warlords. Then, the events of September 11 took place, suddenly making the Taliban, who were playing host to bin Laden, the new enemies of the United States.

When he speaks to audiences, Lindh reminds his listeners that even up until May 2001, the U.S. government had given a $43 million grant to the Taliban to aid in opium eradication. Colin Powell had stated, "We will continue to look for ways to provide more assistance to the Afghan people." Just as John Lindh had shown his concern for innocent Afghani civilians, American leaders had showered attention on the Taliban who were fighting the Soviet-backed Northern Alliance. In July 2000, the State Department had issued a "fact sheet" that reported that the United States was "the single largest donor of humanitarian aid to the Afghan people." Frank Lindh says that John had no advance knowledge of Osama bin Laden's plan to attack the United States and that in joining the Taliban he was giving support to an army that had received assistance from the Carter administration, the Reagan administration, the first Bush administration, the Clinton administration, and the second Bush administration. Lindh says of his son, "John had no criminal intent, and he never took any action of any kind against the United States."

Very quickly after the news of his capture spread, because this was happening in the near aftermath of the attacks of September 11, John was dubbed a traitor and a terrorist, not only by the press but also by President Bush, Attorney General John Ashcroft, Defense Secretary Rumsfeld, and Senators Hillary Clinton and John McCain. "That is a completely false portrait of my son," Frank Lindh said to me. He added, "John made a bad judgment in going to Afghanistan, and he did it without my permission, but it was an idealistic decision." Lindh said that he was reluctant to speak to the media because in most reports he "simply became the idiot father who defended a terrorist." He said that he has twenty-seven scrapbooks filled with articles about John, and nearly all of them are evidence of the extreme prejudice with which he had been viewed. When I asked him whether a journalist had been correct to think of him as a fundamentalist in defense of his son, Lindh replied, "I'm very committed to making the people aware of the truth about my son. It is a difficult challenge . . ." As it happened, the Justice Department dropped nine out of the ten counts against Lindh. As a part of his plea agreement, John Lindh accepted guilt on a charge not even directly related to terrorism, violation of an executive order of 1999 forbidding American citizens from contributing "services" to the Taliban. In her book *The Dark Side*, the journalist Jane Mayer writes that the weakness of the case against Lindh had been signaled by the district court judge T. S. Ellis III, who was presiding over it. According to

Mayer, "In a sentencing hearing after the settlement, Ellis noted that the case linking Lindh to Al Qaeda 'was not strong' and that there was 'no evidence' tying him" to the death in Afghanistan of the American CIA officer, Mike Spann. Mayer reports, "When Spann's heartbroken father objected to this statement, Judge Ellis responded gently. 'He clearly is a hero,' he said, speaking of Spann. But he added pointedly, 'Of all the things he fought for, one of them is that we don't convict people in the absence of proof beyond a reasonable doubt.'"

I suggested to Lindh that his son's trials, and perhaps his own, had pushed him into the world. He had become a teacher. I asked him to tell me what he thought he had learned. Lindh paused for a while and then began to tell me a story from his childhood. Lindh has a twin brother who is crippled with cerebral palsy. On one occasion, when they were kids at church, the usher during the service thought that Lindh's brother was misbehaving. He didn't think that the kid was spastic, he thought that he was only playacting. The usher began to reprimand the boy. Lindh remembers how his father rose up from his seat, took the usher to the back, and spoke angrily to him, his finger pointing into his face.

When Lindh was telling me this story, he broke down at this point. He said that his father, John's grandfather, died before his grandson's arrest in Afghanistan. He had been a great source of strength, and he was missed by the family. Lindh is often reminded of his father because he thinks he is his father now speaking to those who have judged his son unjustly.

It would be wonderful, a writer-friend said to me, if the father of one of the terrorists were to depart from stereotype and say, "Oh yes, we saw it coming years ago. It started when he was thirteen." It wasn't Frank Lindh but Jon Stewart on *The Daily Show* who, only a few days after John's capture in Afghanistan, speculated about the arrested man's past as a teenager in Northern California. The audience cheered when Stewart joked: "In fact, notes he wrote in his classmates' yearbooks foreshadow his transformation. 'Billie, Have a porkless summer. K.I.T., John' and, of course, 'Cheryl, Next time I see you be sure you're wearing a burqa, you filthy whore. B.F.F., J.W.?'"

Then Stewart played a tape that showed Frank Lindh telling a television reporter that his son "had got caught up in something that . . . he shouldn't have been caught up in." Mocking Lindh's choice of words, Stewart pointed out that participating in a prison-riot in Mazar-i-Sharif went "a little beyond" getting "caught up in something." The latter phrase was more appropriate for "getting busted doing whippets at the 7-Eleven," or "stealing the competing High School's goat mascot," and so forth.

Such bracing humor. Poor Frank Lindh. But then one remembers that on all the other nights Jon Stewart is making fun of the other fathers, the real fathers, the ones who are the deciders. The hard fathers of the hard state. They are the ones who lay down all the rules for us, but who break them as they will.

6 ✳ A Collaborator in Kashmir

Apples still come from Kashmir
pale pink in crates in winter's market.
Each grew through the year till it absorbed
the valley's sweetness and undertaste
and reached its final shape and weight.
They are not dead, but come to fruition.
When you bite them, not blood,
but the valley's clear juice floods your mouth.
—Amit Chaudhuri, *St. Cyril Road and Other Poems*

It had been snowing in the north. There was a strong chance that flights
to Srinagar would be cancelled. Even in Jammu the weather was bad. I
had arrived there earlier in the day, March 12, 2007, to meet the governor.
He was a retired general, more than eighty years old now, and the top executive authority in the state. He recalled how, in 1947, when he was only
twenty-one or twenty-two, he had organized an airlift to counter Pakistani agents who had infiltrated the border. He was a major at that time,
and the only Indian officer stationed in Kashmir. Kashmir's Hindu king
had been vacillating over the question of joining the newly independent
nation, and the general believed that swift and decisive action against the
Pakistani infiltrators had saved the day. Later, he was appointed secretary
to the United Nations' delegation on Kashmir. There had been political

tumult ever since the Partition in 1947, but a full-blown separatist movement had erupted only in 1987, after the government in power in New Delhi had rigged the state elections and thrown opposition leaders in jail. In the 1990s terror brought life to a standstill in Kashmir. And now? The governor said, "The problem can only be contained. We are holding Kashmir together only because of the army."

Mist from the rain spread from the ramparts of the governor's palace and covered the red roofs of the houses on the distant hills. It was peaceful in Jammu. The governor had reminded me that here the population was largely Hindu. But to the north, in the Kashmir Valley, he said "The Muslim population offers latent support to the militants." The governor was a soldier and a scholar—he had studied in Patna where I grew up, and in our home his name was mentioned with great respect—and he spoke equally on matters ranging from imperial history to the protocols connected with his office. But he folded his hands together and wrinkled his brow when I asked him about Pakistan. He said, slowly, that General Musharraf had carried on a long campaign of sending terrorists across the border, and "the call for a diplomatic solution was an attempt by Pakistan to enter Kashmir through the back door."

Back at the hotel, there was news of a mudslide on the highway to Srinagar. At the nearby Vaishno Devi shrine, four pilgrims had died from the cold. That explained the presence of the large crowd in the hotel's dingy lobby, pilgrims or tourists with nowhere to go. We were all waiting. The cafe in the hotel was named Reputations and I sipped milky tea, small globules of fat floating on the surface, releasing the full aroma of the plains of Punjab. A waiter brought the news from the hotel desk that the flight to Srinagar that day had instead returned to Delhi. I was reading Rajiv Chandrasekaran's *Imperial Life in the Emerald City*, a report from inside Baghdad's Green Zone, and thought distractedly about the piece of statistic that the occupying army in Kashmir was several times larger than the one in Iraq. It was not only the numbers that were disturbing—one armed soldier for every fifteen civilians, making Kashmir reportedly the most militarized zone in the world—but the kind of abuses that were linked to the armed forces. Just a few days earlier, in the first week of March 2007, I had read a story filed from Srinagar by my friend Shujaat Bukhari about the bodies that had been exhumed from graves around the nearby town of Sumbal. The DNA reports that had come from the Central Forensic Laboratory in Chandigarh had confirmed what everybody already knew: the five corpses that the police had claimed were of foreign Islamic militants shot in armed encounters were actually of local peasants and a carpenter. A dead militant means a cash reward, and the police and the paramilitary units were suspected of acting out of murderous, mercenary zeal.

The newspaper available in the hotel lobby, with badly reproduced government notices, offered little news. I went up to my room and turned on the television. The same footage of snow falling on a Srinagar street that I had watched earlier was being shown again and again. On another channel, the report being broadcast was called "Daughters of Desperation." It discussed how women in Andhra, widows of the farmers who had committed suicide, had been driven into prostitution. A woman stood alone in the middle of an empty stretch of highway, plastic bottle of water in hand, and a truck stopped and picked her up. On the History channel, a film about the Holocaust was being broadcast with Hindi dubbing. I changed channels and listened listlessly to the reports on the cricket World Cup match between India and Sri Lanka that was going to be played the next day. A young man in Bihar had said that he would sell his kidney to buy tickets to the tournament.

There was more depressing news for me the next day. I had woken before dawn and called the airline office in Delhi. All flights to Srinagar had been cancelled for the next four days. In mid-conversation with the official, the phone went dead. The amount of rain predicted for that day equaled what usually fell over a whole month. I discovered that there was no hot water in the bath. The taxi I had ordered didn't show up either, but it didn't matter because the flight back to Delhi was delayed.

The following week I finally reached Srinagar when flights resumed, but my luck failed a second time. The reason I had come to Kashmir was to meet Tabassum Guru, the wife of Mohammad Afzal Guru, who is on death row for his role in the attack on the Indian Parliament. However, when I reached her in Sopore, north of Srinagar, she waved me away saying she had no desire to meet with journalists.

Mohammad Afzal Guru was the man accused in the attack on the Parliament. While two of his co-accused, S. A. R. Geelani and Afsan Guru, had been acquitted, Afzal was sentenced to death by hanging in 2004. A fourth accused, Afsan Guru's husband, Shaukat Hussain, was sentenced to ten years in prison. The hanging was scheduled for October 20, 2006, but it was stayed after a mercy petition was filed with the president. In its judgment on his appeal, the Supreme Court recognized that the evidence against Afzal was only circumstantial and that legal procedures had not been followed by the police. Nevertheless, the judgment stated that the attack on the Indian Parliament had "shaken the entire nation and the collective conscience of the society will only be satisfied if capital punishment is awarded to the offender." In response, a group of Kashmiri leaders passed a resolution that read, in part, "We the people of Kashmir ask why the collective conscience of the Indians is not shaken by the fact that a Kashmiri has been sentenced to death without a fair trial, without a chance to represent himself?"

Afzal's family could not afford a lawyer. He was provided a court-appointed lawyer, but the lawyer never appeared. Then, a second lawyer was appointed, but she didn't take instructions from her client and agreed to admission of documents without proof. Afzal submitted four names of senior advocates to the court, but they refused to represent him too. The lawyer who was now chosen by the court stated that he did not want to appear for Afzal, and Afzal expressed a lack of confidence in the advocate. Nevertheless, under the court's insistence, this was the choice that both lawyer and client had to stay with. That is why, in the Srinagar resolution mentioned above, the Kashmiri leaders asked whether it was Afzal's fault that Indian lawyers thought it "more patriotic" to allow a Kashmiri to die than to ensure that he received a fair trial.

Such questions were raised from a sense of great helplessness. Only the naïve assume that the conflict in Kashmir is between fanatical militants and valiant soldiers. The real picture is much more complicated. In this system the conventional economic nodes no longer function, and all resource lines intersect at some level with the security state. There is a sense of enormous, often inescapable, dependency on those who are clearly seen as oppressors. This has bred complex schizophrenia in the society. Arundhati Roy has written, "Kashmir is a valley awash with militants, renegades, security forces, double-crossers, informers, spooks, blackmailers, blackmailees, extortionists, spies, both Indian and Pakistani intelligence agencies, human rights activists, NGOs and unimaginable amounts of unaccounted-for money and weapons. There are not always clear lines that demarcate the boundaries between all these things and people, it's not easy to tell who is working for whom."

It is this murky landscape that is so clearly illuminated by the night-flare that was Tabassum Guru's statement published in *Kashmir Times* in October 2004. Entitled "A Wife's Appeal for Justice," it is a unique statement, anguished and unafraid. It tells the story of the way in which the police and the armed forces have turned Kashmiris into collaborators, and, although the statement is no more than fifteen hundred words long, it demonstrates more starkly than most documents about Kashmir the brutal cost of military occupation.

In 1990, like thousands of other Kashmiri youths, Afzal had joined the movement for liberation. He had been studying to be a doctor, but instead went to Pakistan to receive training. He returned in three months, not having finished his training, because he was disillusioned. Upon his return he surrendered to the Border Security Force and was given a certificate stating that he was a surrendered militant. His dream of becoming a doctor was now lost; he started a small business dealing in medical supplies and surgical instruments. The following year, in 1997, he got married. Afzal was twenty-eight, and Tabassum eighteen.

After his surrender, Afzal wasn't free of harassment. He was always being asked to spy on other Kashmiris who were suspected of being militants. (This is Sartre, writing more than fifty years ago: "The purpose of torture is not only to make a person talk, but to make him betray others. The victim must turn himself by his screams and by his submission into a lower animal, in the eyes of all and in his own eyes.") One night, members of a counterinsurgency unit, the Special Task Force or STF, took Afzal away. He was tortured at an STF camp. Afzal was asked by his torturers to pay one lakh rupees and because there was no such money available Tabassum had to sell everything she had, including the little gold she had received on her marriage.

And, as at other points in her appeal, her own particular suffering is interpreted in the light of what other Kashmiris have experienced: "You will think that Afzal must be involved in some militant activities and that is why the security forces were torturing him to extract information. But you must understand the situation in Kashmir, every man, woman and child has some information on the movement even if they are not involved.

By making people into informers they turn brother against brother, wife against husband and children against parents."

One of the officers mentioned in Tabassum's appeal, Dravinder Singh, has been frank about the necessity of torture in his line of work. He has stated that torture is the only deterrent to terrorism. In fact, Singh has told a journalist in a recorded interview about having questioned Afzal: "I did interrogate and torture him at my camp. And we never recorded his arrest in the books anywhere. His description of torture at my camp is true. That was the procedure those days and we did pour petrol in his arse and gave him electric shocks. But I could not break him. He did not reveal anything to me despite our hardest possible interrogation."

After his release from the camp, Afzal had needed medical treatment. Six months later, he moved to Delhi. He had decided that he would soon bring Tabassum and their little son, Ghalib, to a place he had rented. But while in Delhi, Afzal received a call from Dravinder Singh,. Singh said that he needed Afzal to do a small job for him. He was to take a man named Mohammad from Kashmir to Delhi, which he did, and he accompanied the same Mohammad to a shop where he bought a used Ambassador car. The car was used in the attack on the Parliament, and Mohammad was identified as one of the attackers. Afzal was waiting at a bus stop in Srinagar for a bus to Sopore when he was arrested and taken to the STF headquarters and then to Delhi. Afzal identified the slain terrorist Mohammad as someone he knew. This part of his statement was accepted by the court but not the part where he said that he had acted under direction from the STF. Tabassum wrote, "In the High Court one human rights lawyer offered to represent Afzal and my husband accepted. But instead of defending Afzal the lawyer began by asking the court not to hang Afzal but to kill him by a lethal injection. My husband never expressed any desire to die. He has maintained that he has been entrapped by the STF."

There had been a lot of soldiers in Srinagar, but it was different in Sopore. They stood with guns on the streets and on rooftops. We had left behind leafless apple trees and neat rows of poplar. And painted roadside signs put up by the army and paramilitary units with messages like "Kashmir to Kanyakumari India Is One." In this town, there were only small, often half-finished, houses and grimy stores. My driver, Shafi, and I entered Sopore and then asked for the hospital run by Dr. Ibrahim Guru. That was where Tabassum Guru worked.

I found her easily enough. She was at the cashier's desk in the Inpatient Block. But she told me she didn't want to talk to me. I came outside to make calls to friends in Srinagar and found out that just a week or two earlier two journalists from Delhi had done a sting. Afzal's brothers had been collecting money for his defense but using the cash to buy property instead. The journalists had brought a spy camera and asked Tabassum if she felt that she had been betrayed by the Kashmiri leadership.

I decided to wait. I had come too far. There was a line of patients who kept walking up to the entrance of the hospital. A pony cart came by and dropped off a sick woman. Shafi, having learned that I was visiting from New York, wanted to know where in America the World Wrestling Federation's matches were held. We talked for a while, and then went inside the hospital again. There was a large crowd waiting in the area marked Outpatient Block. Most people were standing in the corridor, jostling against each other with a feverish energy that required good health. The few chairs were occupied and those who were sitting had adopted postures that suggested they had been waiting for days. There was a sign on the wall that said "Utilize Your Waiting Time Effectively — Plan Things to Do — Meditate — Do Breathing Exercises — Chant a Holy Name — Read Books." I studied that sign for a while, but I was greatly agitated. I decided to go back to Tabassum and tell her that I was leaving. She nodded and half-smiled, and then said goodbye.

From the road outside the hospital, lined with walnut and willow trees, I could see the snow-covered mountains. It was bitterly cold. Shafi was full of ideas about what I could have said to Tabassum to persuade her to talk to me, but none of them seemed to excite any optimism in my heart. I thought I was getting a headache and when I suggested lunch Shafi drove us to a cheap restaurant nearby. While we were eating the steaming plate of rice and the largely inedible meat, Shafi began to tell me that I should have persuaded Tabassum that what I wrote would have helped her husband. But I would have been genuinely reluctant to attempt that. I had seen pictures of mobs in Delhi and elsewhere burning effigies of Mohammad Afzal; activists for the right-wing Bharatiya Janata Party had exploded firecrackers on the streets outside the courthouse when Afzal was sentenced to death; the print and television media had repeatedly condemned him as a terrorist mastermind. How could I have assured Tabassum that what I wrote would be of help? There was another reason for my reluctance. When being interviewed about Afzal's brothers, Tabassum had said that she had never asked anyone for money to help in her husband's legal case. She had said, "Mera zamir nahin kehta" (My conscience doesn't allow it). There was great pride and dignity in that statement. And I was reminded of that again when, in Delhi a week later, I sat watching Sanjay Kak's powerful film *Jashn-e-Azadi* (How We Celebrate Freedom), which documents the cost of violence in Kashmir: an indigent woman in a hamlet is asked whether she has received the promised financial compensation from the armed forces for the wrongful death of her son, and the woman, her hands beating her breast, replies, "The heavens haven't fallen on this earth as yet that we should accept money from these pigs. I'll sell his share of the land. If I don't have enough for my child, I'll do that but not take money from them. . . . We don't want to accept anything from them because they snatched him away from my bosom. He was no *mujahid*, he was not guilty."

✳

For against this drabness, an overwhelming
impression of muddiness, of black and grey
and brown, color stood out and was enticing:
the colors of sweets, yellow and glistening green,
however fly-infested.
—V. S. Naipaul, *An Area of Darkness*

Soon after my return from India, I was reading Orhan Pamuk's memoir, *Istanbul*, for a class I was teaching on writing about cities. In his youth, Pamuk wanted to be a painter and he still saw his city with the eyes of an artist. Pamuk had written of Istanbul, "To see the city in black and white, to see the haze that sits over it and breathe in the melancholy its inhabitants have embraced as their common fate, you need only to fly in from a rich western city and head straight to the crowded streets; if it's winter, every man on the Galata bridge will be wearing the same pale, drab, shadowy clothes." Reading those words, I thought not of Istanbul, but of Srinagar. As it happened, I had flown in from "a rich western city." Everything in the city bore a drab look, draped in a dirty military green. Every house that was new looked either gaudy and vulgar or curiously incomplete; many structures were shuttered, or burned black, or simply falling down due to disrepair. Writing about a different city, Pamuk had thought that those who lived there now shunned color because they were grieving for a city whose past aura had been tarnished by more than 150 years of decline. I believe Pamuk was also describing plain poverty. And it was true of Srinagar too, both the grief and the wretchedness of poverty.

I thought about the film *Jashn-e-Azadi*, which had shown me another Srinagar. The film's richness lay in the space it had created, in the viewer's mind, despite the violence that was represented, for thought and for color. The filmmaker had discovered again and again in the drabness of the melancholy the gleam of memory: the memory of blood on the ground, of the beauty of the hills and red poppies, of keening voices of mothers, of the painted faces of the village performers. The memory of the numbers of the dead, of falling snow, of new graves everywhere, and always the shining faces crying for freedom. In a travelogue written more than four decades ago, V. S. Naipaul had described how out of the "cramped yards, glimpsed through filth-runnelled alleyways, came bright colors in glorious patterns on rugs and carpets and soft shawls, patterns and colors derived from Persia, in Kashmir grown automatic, even in all their rightness and variety." In Kak's film, riotous color is glimpsed only when we see tourists donning traditional Kashmiri costumes for photographs, holding in their hands flowerpots filled with plastic flowers.

When I think of the melancholy of Afzal and Tabassum Guru, it isn't color that I seek, but a narrative to give sustenance to their own lives. That is what was powerful about the story that Tabassum had told, giving coherence to what had been their experience and the ways in which it resonated with the experiences of other young Kashmiri couples. As with Pamuk's *Istanbul*, I found traces of Srinagar in a story about another distant place—Palestine. The film I was watching was *Paradise Now*. Directed by Hany Abu-Assad, it tells the story of two friends on the West Bank, Said and Khaled, who are recruited to carry out a terrorist attack in Tel Aviv. The two young men are disguised as settlers going for a wedding. But the would-be bombers get separated at the border, and the plan is called off, instigating some reflection and doubt on Khaled's part. But Said is determined. We learn about his motivation when, in the company of Suha, a young woman who has just returned to Palestine, he goes into a watch shop, and Suha notices that videos are also available at the shop. These are videos showing the execution of collaborators. Suha is shocked. She asks, "Do you think it's normal that those videos are for sale?" Said replies, "What is normal around here?" And then he tells Suha, quietly, that his father was a collaborator. He was executed.

In Nablus, cars keep breaking down. That is what gives Said and Khaled jobs. They have been working as mechanics. Nothing works. The houses look either bombed or unfinished. There are no cinemas because the cinema has been burned down. In all of this, Nablus resembles Srinagar. But more than any of this, Nablus is like Srinagar in the ways in which its children are scarred by the violence. I'm thinking of someone like young Ghalib, Afzal and Tabassum's son, and thousands of other Kashmiris. It is horrifying but not difficult to imagine that many of them will find words, to offer as testimony, that are similar to what Said, sitting in an empty room, speaks to the camera just before he leaves on his suicide mission:

> The crimes of occupation are endless. The worst crime of all is to exploit the people's weaknesses and turn them into collaborators. By doing that, they not only kill the resistance, they also ruin their families, ruin their dignity and ruin an entire people. When my father was executed, I was ten years old. He was a good person. But he grew weak. For that, I hold the occupation responsible. They must understand that if they recruit collaborators they must pay the price for it. A life without dignity is worthless. Especially when it reminds you day after day of humiliation and weakness. And the world watches, cowardly and indifferent.

7 ✳ A Night in an Army Camp

Ravi later said, as a matter of fact, that the boy had been
tortured—he used the passive voice—and provided
low-grade intelligence of anecdotal character. The boy's
ghostly figure haunted the room, proxy for all the
thousands of Kashmiri boys beaten and killed in custody
by the Indian armed forces since 1990.
—James Buchan, "Kashmir"

Colonel Prakash was lonely and he was very sick. When I had called him
from Delhi, he said that he would like me to see what the life of a soldier
was like in Kashmir. He added that it would do him good if I visited him
and stayed with him. The camp was in a volatile part of downtown Srinagar, and he told me that he would wait for me at a hotel. We could then
go to the camp together. I got there at eleven in the morning and noticed
immediately the puffiness around his eyes. He had grown thinner since I
had last seen him, and his gait was unsteady and even uncertain. I realized
that in fact his whole face was swollen. There was a dried yellow clot on
his lower lip. I suspected that he had already been drinking for some time,
but he assured me that he had only just woken up.

There were two iron gates at the entrance to the camp with guards looking down from concrete towers. Nets were draped over the towers to dis-

courage anyone on the street from tossing a grenade inside. Wires, drawn over the tall fence, carried a 10,000-watt electric current. Inside the camp, there was a long one-story structure on the left. On the yellow wall above the first door it said in big painted letters OICS LIVING. The letters OIC stood for "Officer in Charge" and that was what Prakash was. He had a one-room living quarter with an attached bathroom. Next there was a tiny office with a desk but Prakash never used it. His personal orderly sat there sometimes, waiting for his officer to call him. The next room in the row was for the officer who accompanied the military convoy that rested for a night there. Then came a room that had a couple of Hindi newspapers in it. On the wall outside, it mysteriously said MOTIVATION HALL. Another tiny room beyond that had the pay phone. The room beside it was the largest. Painted on the wall were the words WET CANTEEN and a soldier could buy beverages, or a pair of boots, or batteries, or a packet of chips. Three-egg omelets that cost ten rupees were quickly cooked over a paraffin stove and wrapped in a piece of old newspaper. There was another room adjoining the canteen, where a soldier sat in front of a telephone that didn't have a dial on it. Then were the dining halls, called "langars," and beyond, set at a perpendicular angle to the row of rooms described above, the building that served as the dormitory for the troops. The large piece of land that the two structures overlooked was paved with round, flat stones. It was used as a parking lot for the green Shaktiman army trucks. In the evening, a fat, middle-aged sergeant stood in the middle of the yard and gave short, sharp blasts in quick succession on his whistle, directing traffic with one hand in a lyrical way. As each truck, its engines roaring on low gear, eased into place, troops jumped out from the back.

Colonel Prakash is my father's second cousin. His father left his village in Bihar when he was only a teenager, and he had joined the air force, which at that time was still in British hands. He came back from the war changed. He smoked cigarettes instead of cheap bidis and drank whiskey in place of country liquor. This made him different from my father's other relatives. He had traveled outside India as a part of a British squadron. And Prakash too, growing up in different cities of the north where the air force bases were, had appeared modern to us. When I was a teenager growing up in Patna, he had stayed at my parents' home briefly, en route to a posting in the northeastern hills. He was a young officer, a captain, and he was a bachelor. He bought me alcohol, which was taboo in our home, and impressed me with his stories. It didn't take much to impress me, I'm sure, but his stories were unusual in that he seemed to have endless opportunities for having sex. He must have been the first person I met who had slept with prostitutes.

But that was nearly thirty years ago. We were now in the camp, sitting in his small, dark room, which reeked of kerosene because of the heater. Much of the space in the room was taken by the bed, covered with a Kashmiri bedsheet decorated with a print of pink flowers blooming on a green-leafed vine. There were more flowers on the curtains, sunflowers in a vertical pattern against a background of red. Prakash, whom I addressed as Chacha, sat on an easy chair, chain-smoking. On the wall, his military uniform hung from an inch-wide strip of metal with hooks. The shirt of his uniform appeared especially thin, as if it had been made for a schoolboy, and it had multicolored strips pinned to the chest. Prakash told me, one by one, what those strips represented: "Artillery Corps," "Service in High Altitude," "Service in Mizoram," and so forth.

Tea was brought for me by his "personal bearer," who put a glass of rum mixed with water beside Prakash. The bearer belonged to a tribe in Assam, and Prakash called him by the Assamese word for brother, "bhaiti." I began to regret having come to see Prakash. I had hoped that I would witness with his help what the Indian armed forces did in their attempt to suppress militancy in Kashmir. Instead, what I was faced with was a man who had trouble even getting out of bed.

Basharat Peer, a Kashmiri journalist and writer, has recorded the words of a man tortured at Papa-2, the infamous interrogation center in Srinagar: "They tied copper wire around your arms and gave high-voltage shocks. Every hair on your body stood up. But the worst was when they inserted the copper wire into my penis, deep into the urinary canal, and gave electric shocks. They did it with most boys. It destroyed many lives; many could not marry after that." Peer calls Papa-2 "the most notorious torture chamber in all of Kashmir." And he adds, "Hundreds who went there did not come back. Those who returned are wrecks."

It was becoming clear to me, as I sat with Prakash, that we could never have a coherent conversation about what was happening in Kashmir. I don't know exactly how to say this, but Prakash too, in his own way, was a wreck. I wasn't going to get anywhere with him. But he had his own ideas about what, as a tourist, I needed to see in Srinagar.

After I had finished my tea, he announced loudly that we were going to visit the famous Chashmashahi Gardens. Soon, Brother returned with a hip flask for Prakash and we were on our way. The gardens had been laid out for the seventeenth-century Mughal emperor Shah Jahan, who is famous for having built the Taj Mahal in Agra. The driver of our Jeep pointed out, along the way, sites that he thought would be of interest to me. A dilapidated building—corrugated sheets for a roof, boarded-up walls—was where Sheikh Abdullah once used to live. Now it was a hostel for a unit of the paramilitary outfit, the CRPF. Black ducks were swimming on the waters of the Dal. When the gardens came closer, the old driver began to name the trees we were passing, almond trees with small pink flowers, and apple, and tall deodar and pine trees. The entrance ticket cost only five rupees, but Prakash thought it beneath our dignity to buy them. There was a blue painted sign with black lettering that said

Entry By Ticket Only
NO PERSON INCLUDING
MILITARY/PARAMILITARY &
POLICE PERSONAL IS
ALLOWED TO ENTER THE
GARDEN WITHOUT TICKET
By Order
GOVT. OF JAMMU & KASHMIR

When we had climbed the steps, and the young Kashmiri at the top asked for our tickets, Prakash, still breathing hard from the climb, said in his theatrical baritone, "Hum fauji hain" (I'm an army man). The young man looked away, saying nothing. There wasn't any anger in his look, or helplessness or despair—it was just a quick turning away, eyes searching another horizon.

Five Marathi advocates were having their photographs taken, dressed in *pheran* and *topi*, traditional Kashmiri costumes. The young men offering this service held out for them a hookah and an unheated *kangri*. Above us were the terraced gardens and a fountain at the base of which lay fat white worms. Prakash was saying that the freezing water was very healthy and helped in digestion. He pointed to a few bungalows on the hill to our right and, with a touch of the old Prakash of my youth, said with a swagger, "Those houses are used by ministers when they screw women. All

kinds, even film stars. That is why no video photography is allowed here."
The air was cold and bracing, but I was beginning to feel depressed.

The name of the driver of the Jeep was Mir Sahib. When we were driving
back to the camp, Prakash said to Mir Sahib that he was to come early the
next day to take me to the airport. The driver nodded his head and then
suggested that if Prakash called the officer who was in charge of hiring
vehicles, all the paperwork would be in order. But Prakash said that he
wouldn't do any such thing. It was the driver's responsibility. This time
Mir Sahib's head stayed motionless. Prakash had been drinking from the
flask all this while and, taking my hand in his, he said that it was very nice
that I had come to see him. He began to talk about the letters I had written
to him when I was fourteen. He praised my English. When we reached the
metal gates of the camp, he said, "I had fallen in love with your sister. But
I didn't mention it to your parents."

I didn't say anything, but Mir Sahib spoke up again. I could see only his
eyes in the rearview mirror, small black eyes set in folds of wrinkled skin.
I heard him say, "Sir, will you please call them from your room?" Prakash
didn't reply. He was distracted. He asked me if I wanted warm soup. We
went to the hotel close to the camp, where Prakash had waited for me
in the morning. Instead of going to the restaurant inside, which wasn't
heated during the day for the lack of customers, we sat in the hotel's office.
The Kashmiri owner, a former bureaucrat, was wearing a jacket and kept
his large, hairy hands spread over the heater beside his desk. Next to him,
at another, smaller desk, two young women sat in front of a computer
screen. Prakash pointed at the owner and said loudly that he was a nice
man, but he had recently had a fall and hurt his ankle. Then he said that
the hotel business was failing and that is why the man had started a travel
agency. The women in the corner were his nieces, working on someone's
air ticket. I was introduced as someone who was writing about terrorism.
Prakash was slurring a lot, but he didn't stop speaking. He got up and
walked close to the heater and put his palms up in the air, as if he were
preventing a wall from falling.

The young women had their heads covered by hijabs, but they were
lively and looked at Prakash with curiosity. I had the feeling that he had
been there before and was tolerated as an amusing annoyance. But now he
said to the women, "Tell him whatever you feel about the terrorists. Will
the tourists come if they have a run of this beautiful valley? Tell him the

truth." The women weren't looking up anymore. Prakash appeared to be about to pat one on the head, gently, but he stopped. He said, "Don't be afraid. Tell him whatever you genuinely feel."

Both the women seemed to have discovered something compelling on their screens. Prakash said, "Tell him. Don't be afraid. Go ahead." Our host, a heavy man, shifted in his chair. Then he leaned forward and said, "Please sit down." But Prakash kept appealing to the women, until the hotel owner, the bad ankle giving him trouble, rose from his chair and, coming between Prakash and his nieces, said, "Mr. Prakash, I'm asking you as my guest. Please sit down."

Someone was knocking on the door. I had been taking a nap and when I opened my eyes, I saw Mir Sahib enter the room. Prakash was sitting on his easy chair, reading the newspaper. Mir Sahib said, "Sir, before I left, if you could speak to . . ."

Prakash said, "Do you have your key? Give it to me."

When Mir Sahib handed him the Jeep's keys, Prakash said, "Now you can go home. Your Jeep will remain here. You come here at seven in the morning and take my nephew to the airport."

Mir Sahib's shoulders were bent forward. He nodded and said nothing for a moment. Then he said, "You don't need to get angry. I will do as you say. I just need his order to come again tomorrow."

Prakash pointed to the door. When Mir Sahib had left, he picked up the phone and demanded that the Jeep be sent again the following day. Then he shouted, "Bhaiti!" When the bearer came in, Prakash gave him his glass and said, "Bring me another drink. And tea for him. And see if the driver is still outside." Mir Sahib stepped in a moment later. Prakash handed back the keys and, a finger raised in front of his face, said, "Hum jo kehte hain woh hukum hota hai" (Whatever I say is an order). I came out of the room and said goodbye to Mir Sahib before he drove off. I told him that Prakash had spoken to the officer and matters would be straightened out very soon. Mir Sahib had been quiet all day. He now screwed up his small eyes and raised his hands heavenward. He was chuckling.

There were shouts and somebody blowing on a whistle. Prakash said to me that the convoy was about to return. Within moments, the trucks were making their way through the gates, their machinery straining as if they were still climbing mountains. It was a quick and efficient entry. Prakash sent word to the convoy commander that the soldiers were to gather in the yard.

The evening was very chilly. I put on a coat, but Prakash had only flung on a thin shawl over his shoulders. His teeth began to chatter as soon as we had stepped out. The convoy commander was a young major, a short, stocky man in fatigues and a stylish, wide-brimmed military hat.

He saluted Prakash and said, "Sir, the men are tired."

Prakash said, "It is okay. My nephew wants to talk to them for a minute about how these brave men fight terrorists."

The major glanced at me as I stood, awkwardly clutching my notebook in my hand. He said, still rigid, "Sir, protocol doesn't permit it. Not without clearance."

Prakash laid his hand on his junior colleague's shoulder. With his teeth clenched, not because he was angry but because he was cold, Prakash said, "Don't worry. I'm the one responsible. I'll talk to Mathur."

I liked very much the major's direct manner. I felt that I was in the wrong and, in the face of his objection, I suddenly found that I couldn't think of the right question to put to the soldiers. But Prakash was adamant. He said, "Go ahead. Ask them."

I looked at the major and said, "It's quite alright. I just wanted to meet the troops."

Prakash said, "No problem. Meet them. Talk to them."

In Hindi, I began telling the assembled men that I was a writer living in the United States, and that while in Kashmir I wanted to see for myself the conditions under which the troops lived. "You make sacrifices," I said, "living away from your homes." The faces in front of me remained blank. "There are among you people from all over India. You must all belong to different faiths," I added, beginning to ramble. I asked myself what question the major would deem appropriate. He was standing by my side, looking down at the ground, his arms crossed behind his back. I stopped in mid-sentence. Prakash took over from me. He didn't have any questions for the troops either. Instead, he became their voice. Joining their ranks, and turning to face me, he began to speak in a loud, declamatory manner, "We are proud warriors. We follow orders. We are severely tested each day, but we are equal to every challenge. We have no home, the battlefield is our home. We have been trained in the highest traditions of the Indian army. We are ready to lay down our lives for the nation. Jai Hind."

Although the cold made his body shake, and his hands were bunched inside his pockets, he had pulled his shoulders back to stand at attention. At the end of the peroration, there was an answering shout from the troops. They were dismissed for the day and Prakash, lighting another cigarette, invited the major to his quarters for a drink. The young man gave me his hand to shake before he turned to his superior to say that he was leaving very early the next morning and he was going to bed. So we drank for a while without the major. Then the phone rang. There was someone called Wasim at the gate and the guards wanted permission to let him in.

I had heard about Wasim from Prakash. On the wall close to the side of the bed on which Prakash slept, there was a large mirror into whose frame he had inserted half a dozen photographs. These were images of his two daughters, and of his wife, who was visiting their elder child in New Jersey. But among those photographs there was a picture of a young Kashmiri man. He was wearing a brightly colored cardigan and standing in front of what might be his house. Prakash had said to me, "He's a poor, young Kashmiri. Very nice boy. I have adopted him."

Wasim appeared at the door. Prakash began to rail at him for not answering his phone all day. The youth said that his brother had taken his phone and gone to another town. Wasim was smartly turned out and his face had an elegant cast to it. When I was introduced, he took my hand in both his hands and said that he had been waiting to meet me.

"How did you like Kashmir?" he asked.

I told him that I had been coming regularly as a reporter over the past decade and a half. I didn't come as a tourist. As soon as I said that, I felt that I was trying too hard.

But Wasim smiled politely, not appearing to notice.

I asked him how he had met Prakash.

Wasim drove a scooter-rickshaw and once he had Prakash and his wife as his passengers. During the ride, Prakash had discovered that he had forgotten his wallet at home. Wasim had told him not to worry. He could always collect the fare later. Prakash had given him the address of the camp, and that is how Wasim had found out that his passenger was an army officer. Since then, whenever Prakash's wife was in Srinagar, Wasim took her around on his rickshaw.

I had assumed that Wasim had come to have dinner with us. I was feeling hungry, but Prakash apparently didn't eat at all. I asked Wasim if he had eaten, and he said yes. Bhaiti brought food for me prepared in the Wet Canteen: thick *parathas*, pickles, and chicken curry in a cracked china bowl. When I started eating, Bhaiti put a steel bowl in front of Prakash. It had in it *sattu* made from ground chickpeas, and Prakash mixed the powder with water, turning it into a fine paste. Then, he formed a ball in his long fingers and asked me to open my mouth. When I protested, Prakash said that he always gave food to Wasim and Bhaiti before he himself ate. And that's how it was that night too, the three of us getting a taste of the spicy *sattu*, before our host helped himself to a bit of food and then got up to wash his hands.

Prakash said to Wasim, "The reason I called you is that you have to come here at seven tomorrow morning. A Jeep will be here. You have to accompany my nephew to the airport." Wasim nodded thoughtfully. Prakash said to me, "These Kashmiris are bastards. They don't have any concept of time. They are also lazy. That is the main reason the army is here."

Wasim smiled at him, and then at me. When he left, I started to bustle about, trying to prepare for sleep. The small room was full of cigarette smoke and several times during the evening I had gone into the cold bathroom to blow my nose and get a breath of clean air. When I lay down on the bed, I put my face under the blanket. But it was no use. I still had the same air in my nostrils, the same bright light in my eyes, the same voice in my ear. I was coming down with a cold. I was filled with self-pity and rage. Still, I must have fallen asleep because I woke up to the sound of Prakash talking to me in the dark. It took me a moment to realize that he was speaking to someone on the phone. It was the middle of the night. Then, I realized that he was speaking to his wife in New Jersey. He was saying, "Haan, haan, he is sleeping here, right next to me. Baby, not May end. You must come back earlier. I miss you. Come soon . . . No, I won't lie to you. I haven't reduced. I can't do it like that. I will need nerve injections. Not alone. No. I will go there when you are back."

Bhaiti brought me tea at six in the morning. I hadn't slept well, but I felt refreshed and healthy; perhaps I was just relieved that I was leaving. Prakash slept through the noise of the convoy exiting the compound. The troops shouted in unison "Durga Mata . . . ki jai . . . ki jai . . . ki jai." I heard the barking of the army dogs that were taken out each morning to detect bombs on the road outside the gates. And then the engines roared again and the convoy was gone. When I was almost ready, Prakash opened his eyes and asked if Wasim had come. I went outside and saw him in the office next door. When I came back, Prakash wanted me to go out again and check if the contractor had sent Mir Sahib. I had seen that it was a different vehicle as well as driver, but I lied and said that everything was in order. Satisfied with the answers, Prakash said goodbye and asked me to come for a longer visit next time.

There was little traffic on the roads. Only the soldiers were everywhere, quiet men in khaki uniforms and white winter boots, guns in their hands. (Again, Basharat Peer: "The frisking, providing proof of identity, the rude questions—all were routine now, like brushing your teeth.") We had hardly gone a mile when Wasim, in a voice parodying Prakash, began to warn me theatrically about traveling in Srinagar. I began to laugh because he was genuinely funny, but also because I was a bit giddy at this show of rebellion. He was biting the hand that fed him. As soon as I had formed that thought in my head, I couldn't but recall the scene from the previous night. Prakash feeding us, with ridiculous affection, little balls of *sattu*. I laughed more uncertainly now. It made me uneasy, this mocking sense of independence. Hadn't Prakash said that he had adopted Wasim? In the mirror of the young man's behavior, I saw my own offensive lack of gratitude. Prakash had never said an unkind word to me. But I knew that it was different with Wasim, and he was no doubt aware of it. It is even possible that the defiance he was showing me was an attempt to distance himself from an image of being an agent of the army. Did he resent Prakash having turned him to some extent into a collaborator? The truth was that despite what Wasim was showing me of himself, he still had expectations from the enemy. Before long, he began to tell me how some months ago Prakash had offered to find him a job away from Kashmir, maybe in a peaceful place like Delhi or Chandigarh, but nothing had really happened. Had Prakash not done anything at all? Wasim conceded that Prakash had spoken to his wife's brother-in-law, a businessman, but that fellow had not been willing to hire a Kashmiri.

I asked him if he had felt bad about what Prakash had said about Kashmiris being bastards. Wasim smiled and said that by now he was used to it. He wanted me to know that whatever Prakash said couldn't compare to what happened in the police stations or the army's interrogation units. Once the Special Task Force men had picked him up because they found loose wires in the back of his scooter-rickshaw. It had looked suspicious to them. He was taken to a room where they told him that they knew he was transporting militants. He had cried in front of them. But nothing that he would say convinced his interrogators. The Deputy Superintendent of Police slammed him against the wall, and then four of his men worked him over. This went on for a week. After each beating, when Wasim had returned to the communal cell, it was two militants who consoled him and rubbed Iodex on his limbs. Which side was he to support, Wasim asked me, when he was released?

The talk had turned serious and Wasim returned to the point where we had started. Once again, he began making fun of Prakash and I saw how necessary it was for him to do it. He couldn't make fun of the hardened interrogators who could break him, but it was still possible to mock the warm but also pathetic Colonel Prakash. The talk of torture had had a cathartic effect on Wasim, and his laughter this time was more infectious. Even the driver was smiling now.

Wasim said, "He only knows how to drink and smoke. He is hollow inside. I really mean that. Everything has become rotten. I'm surprised he is still alive. The other day he said his back was hurting. I thought I would give him a massage. But when I pushed him on his side, I heard a crack and he began to scream aahhh, aahhh. . . ."

Now Wasim too was holding his side with both hands and he had half-slipped off the seat.

He said, "The military doctor told him the next day that he had broken a rib. My wife said to me, be careful what you do to that fellow, if you kill him by mistake, the sin will be on our heads."

8 ✳ Tourist-Theorist-Terrorist

Well aware of the 1960's communalism, and directly
influenced by collectives from the AIDS movement
—Act Up, Gran Fury, Group Material—Critical Art
Ensemble operates as a combination of scientific
investigative unit, anticapitalist guerilla cell, public
service agency and multimedia art studio.
—Holland Cotter, "The Collective Conscious"

The first draft of Critical Art Ensemble's book *Marching Plague* was
seized by the FBI, in May 2004, under Section 175 of the U.S. Biological
Weapons Anti-Terrorism Act expanded by the Patriot Act. Steve Kurtz, a
founding member of the art group, was arrested for suspected bioterrorism and then released. Although the files, notes, and books pertaining
to the project have still not been returned to the authors, the book was
finally published in 2006. The argument made in its pages is that after the
attacks of September 11 fear has served an authoritarian regime and its
profit-hungry counterparts. In the case of germ warfare and bioterrorism,
the book argues, all talk of preparedness is actually a cover for a profitable
militarization of the public sphere. Further, "If there is any real threat to
our bodies and health, it is not coming from weaponized germs, but from
the institutions that benefit from this weaponization." (Indeed, a report
in NewScientist, in July 2007, confirmed that deadly germs "may be more

likely to be spread due to a biodefence lab accident than a biological attack by terrorists." In the last five years, the American public has had near misses with accidents involving germs for plague, anthrax, Rocky Mountain spotted fever, and other diseases.)

The logic underlying the argument presented by *Marching Plague* is that even under ideal conditions, "germs are relatively useless as a tactical weapon." Not only is their efficiency questionable; they are dependent on unstable conditions such as the weather. The authors state flatly that germs "are not very effective field weapons compared to other WMDS (nuclear, chemical, and poison), so they offer no specialized function that any other WMD couldn't provide with more desirable results." For this and other reasons, funneling more and more funds into germ warfare research and the accompanying hype about overpreparedness is a terrible waste of public funds. *Marching Plague* argues for a shift in spending to aid the battles being waged against malaria and HIV that do, in fact, kill millions of people each year: "Much as during the Cold War, this moment of hypercapital expenditure in favor of expanding the war machine is as difficult to intervene in as it is to effectively support robust public health and health care for all." A security state cannot forever be allowed to replace a democratic state that genuinely protects the health of its citizens.

Critical Art Ensemble, or CAE, released *Marching Plague* as a sixteen-minute documentary, which received its American premiere in the 2006 Whitney Biennial. The documentary begins with a brief history lesson. At first we watch archival, black-and-white documentary footage from Japan: while scenes of the mobilization of the Japanese imperial army play in the background, the text that scrolls up on the screen is about Ishii Shiro, a professor of epidemiology for the Tokyo Army Medical School, who, in 1931, sold his superiors the idea that Japan needed a biological weapons program. Ishii's argument was that the Russians were spreading anthrax in Manchuria and that the Chinese were poisoning wells with cholera germs. These reports were never proven. But Ishii got what he wanted in terms of resources. He never developed a biological weapon and all his tests were either inconclusive or failures. (In its book, the CAE says, "From the present-day perspective, Ishii's brilliance was not his idea for germ warfare, but his recognition of the opportunity to create wealth and power for himself by capitalizing on the fear of germs and their destructive power.") Japan wasn't alone in investing in a germ warfare program (which it closed in 1943) based on misleading information and leading to unproductive re-search. In the documentary we are informed that the same pattern of dubi-ous assumptions and bad results occurred in the United States (1949–68) and in the United Kingdom (1940–64). The viewer is treated to archival footage from "Operation Cauldron," during which the British navy con-ducted tests to explore the use of plague as a tactical ship-to-ship weapon. The tests had begun with the navy using a harmless plague substitute, *Bacillus subtilis*, and the goal was to pump a mixture containing the bac-teria from the rear of a boat into the air, targeting a distant pontoon of guinea pigs. The final tests used actual plague. None of these tests yielded any useful results. Millions of pounds had been wasted.

The footage shows the naval men in uniform and protective rain gear carrying out their operations off the Isle of Lewis, Scotland, in 1952. There is a cut and then we are at the same place in 2005, with a boat motoring out under the overhanging, rain-threatening clouds. The text tells us that the Critical Art Ensemble has arrived to reenact "Operation Cauldron." What follows is part scientific experiment, part art, and part performance. The CAE uses *Bacillus subtilis* in an attempt to spray a pontoon full of guinea pigs from a mile away. Steve Kurtz appears in front of the bay to explain the ensuing process on camera. The CAE members, happily identified as amateurs, are shown creating bacteria: they're wearing rubber gloves and using pipettes to prepare the "broth" containing *Bacillus subtilis*. During this process, as well as later, the evidence of the CAE performing opera-tions is spliced with the archival footage showing the parallel, faithfully documented actions of the British navy team. At the conclusion of the experiment, when the swabs are taken from the guinea pigs as well as their human handler, it is clear that the exposure rate was very poor. This means that infection rate would be poor or zero because, like the harmless *Bacillus subtilis*, bubonic plague cannot be passed from person to person. So, like the results of the British navy's experiments, the CAE's findings are inconclusive.

Steve Kurtz appears on camera again, for one last time, standing with his back to the bay. He says, "Well, you saw it . . . We got out there and from a mile away we attempted to hit a pontoon boat full of guinea pigs. If it seemed a little absurd that we would do such a thing, and come all this way, well, you're right. This indeed is the very metaphor of a germ warfare program in general: it's absolutely crazy, it's useless, it's absurd, it's an exercise in stupidity . . . And I can't imagine why anyone would either expand an existing germ warfare program or create a new one. Who would do it?"

In response to that question, an announcer's voice exults, "The president of the United States." The smiling face of George W. Bush, sitting in an SUV, appears on the screen, and then we hear his voice in the background, "America will act . . . with the world's greatest military." His words are drowned by the sounds of recurrent applause and the screen gets filled with slow-moving figures in hazmat suits and gas masks. We have come to the film's end. The scenes of the federal workers carrying out germ warfare exercises are accompanied by the following words scrolling up in slow progression:

> In October 2001, anthrax spores are mailed to a select number of politicians and journalists. Of the thousands of people potentially exposed to the anthrax, five die. The anthrax spores used were eventually traced to U.S. Army stocks of bacteria. The government and military are quick to exploit the fear generated. The budget for germ warfare is increased from millions to billions. Assets once used to fight emerging infectious diseases that kill millions each year are being redirected to a useless and absurd germ warfare program.

✳

In the collage of images that end the documentary there is one piece of footage from an NBC station's news broadcast showing men in hazmat suits entering the doorway of a house, their guns drawn. Although we are not told this in the film, that house belongs to Steve Kurtz of the Critical Art Ensemble.

Kurtz is an art professor at the State University of New York at Buffalo. On May 11, 2004, his wife of twenty years, Hope, died of heart failure. When Kurtz called 911, one of the paramedics who came to the house noticed the petri dishes and sophisticated scientific equipment. The police called the FBI. Kurtz explained that the equipment and the microbes were going to be a part of an art exhibit about genetically altered food at the Massachusetts Museum of Contemporary Art. Over the past decade, the CAE has used harmless bacteria in participatory theater events to help the general public understand biotechnology and the many issues surrounding it. But nothing that Kurtz said allayed the suspicions that the petri dishes had incited. When he was on his way to the funeral home the next day Kurtz was illegally detained by agents from the FBI and the Joint Terrorism Task Force. Kurtz was told that he was being investigated for bioterrorism. His cat, computers, equipment, manuscripts, books, and even his wife's body were seized. The Erie County Health Department declared his house a possible health risk.

Kurtz was detained for twenty-two hours and it was not until a week later that he was allowed to return home and recover his wife's body. The Erie County Health Department declared the bacteria harmless and determined that Hope Kurtz had died of natural causes. The materials that had been confiscated from Kurtz's home have still not been returned to him. The following month, on June 29, 2004, a federal grand jury rejected the bioterrorism charges but handed down two indictments relating to mail fraud and wire fraud, charges arising from technicalities about how Kurtz received $256.00 of harmless, legally obtained bacteria from a scientist at the University of Pittsburgh. According to a story in the *L.A. Weekly*, the grand jury indictment might be proof that Kurtz's lawyer, Paul Cambria, knew of what he spoke "when he paraphrased former New York Chief Judge Saul Wachtler: 'The D.A. could get the grand jury to indict a ham sandwich.'" The prosecution kept grinding on, despite wide protests. In late April 2008, when the case came up in court, the federal judge dismissed it. The government found that it had no basis to appeal the dismissal.

If you go to the Critical Art Ensemble's website you learn that the CAE is "a collective of five artists of various specializations dedicated to exploring the intersections between art, technology, racial politics and critical theory." When I interviewed Kurtz over a period of several days during the July 4 holiday in 2007, I asked why his group had chosen to do the project on germ warfare. Kurtz's reply was both simple and direct: "We realized that the neocons would keep us in an unending war. Cultural resistance was going to take the form of anti-war work." It is arguable that the government had built a case against Kurtz precisely because of his anti-war work, which, under the logic prevailing at a time of national hysteria, is considered in some quarters to be both unpatriotic and even terrorism. It is fairly easy to see that there is very little substance or basis for prosecution, and this actually suggests that innocence or guilt is quite immaterial anyway. The main point is to introduce into our homes, with the help of an often compliant media, the armed and ready figure in the hazmat suit. It is an exercise that has the effect of saying to us that this is not an exercise. It is an act of war. At some fatal moment, we are expected to declare whether we are for or against the forces waging this war; but this isn't true for the most part because we aren't interlocutors in a debate as much as we are agents conscripted into an army of information. Which is to say, through the media footage of the figure in the hazmat suit holding a silent gun in his hand as he enters an artist's home, we stand informed of the armed and ready might of the state.

In the days following the indictment of Steve Kurtz, as well as Robert Ferrell (the scientist at the University of Pittsburgh from whom he had received the harmless bacteria), a defense fund was established by the friends and supporters of the CAE. At various fundraisers that were held, a brief film called *Evidence* would be screened. Only a few minutes long, *Evidence* takes a forensic look at the actions of the FBI in Steve Kurtz's home. In the first minute, we are offered a collage of media coverage of the search. (The television news bulletins had titles like "Art Cause for Alarm?" and "Bioterror Blunder?") Then, we are indoors. The camera maintains steady focus over sections of rooms examined by the investigators. There is no commentary, only a hum or a buzzing sound accompanying the words that appear at the bottom of the screen. These are explanatory captions, which scroll out as if typed in real time. It becomes clear that the filmmakers are also gathering evidence. The purpose here is to reveal the selective "method" adopted by the FBI, which took away books or materials that fitted a profile but disregarded the academic as well as artistic evidence that provided a context for the seized materials. Next we see a strip of insulation torn from the wood to which it was attached. The caption says: "Evidence of Bean the cat, trying to escape conditions of imprisonment for unknown number of days without food, water or company." (The cat, Kurtz says with a laugh on camera, is now in Canada. It is safe there; the FBI cannot get to it.) The evidence gets more serious. We see how sloppy the FBI's search was, or at least how slovenly. There is evidence on the floor of the test samples bagged and abandoned. Outside the house, there are bags upon bags of rubbish left by the investigators. Also, empty boxes of pizza and Gatorade bottles; sample jars and a waste disposal bucket; and even notes taken by the FBI during the search and their test kits. The gloved hands that have rummaged through the rubbish for the camera belong to the investigating artists. (Later, the trash left by the FBI itself became a part of an art exhibit; it was displayed at an exhibition, "Democracy in America: The National Campaign," in New York City focusing on freedom of speech.) The film ends with an artist friend of Kurtz's, Claire Pentecost, getting subpoenaed by the FBI. On her way to the door, she has picked up her camera and, while accepting the subpoena from the two agents in suits, she addresses them through her viewfinder. She too is collecting evidence.

One night during my visit to Buffalo, I was with Kurtz in a bar in his neighborhood (the sticker behind the bartender says "War Is Terrorism with a Bigger Budget"), and he began to tell me that he is always aware of the "impossibility of being." He meant that the struggle can never be won, and that is why his wife had died. I hadn't heard this note of pessimism before; in fact, earlier that day, he had repeated to me how his friends had rallied around him and helped him in his fight. There had been fundraisers in galleries, many letters of protest had been written, he had a lawyer with a great track record. More than anything else, I thought of works like *Evidence*, which showed artists responding, at the very moment in which they are being framed by the law, with a gesture that alters the picture through a reframing.

The same gesture is repeated in a more recent, feature-length, documentary film that has been made about the case, *Strange Culture*. Directed by Lynn Hershman Leeson, the film is a collage of interviews and enactments, aimed at presenting what happened to Kurtz and at explaining why the Department of Justice persisted with the case. The cultural critic Greg Bordowitz, who was interviewed on camera for the film, says that at the beginning he had thought that there would be "a learning curve" for the FBI. They had been unexposed to the sort of art that the CAE produced, therefore there had been some fear on the part of the authorities, but that once they had realized that Kurtz was not a terrorist, the case would go away. But that didn't happen, and Bordowitz was forced to revise his opinion. He says in the film, "I think the government, the FBI, the DA saw an opportunity to establish precedent in a way that they could extend the government's powers into the university system, into academia, into the art world. They saw an opportunity, and they ran with it." And still later, toward the film's end, Bordowitz adds, "The body of Steve's work is a growing body of evidence against the ways that the government, the military, science, and industry often collude against the public good, and this is primarily why he is being focused on, this is why he is seen as a good target."

The actors in *Strange Culture*, Thomas Jay Ryan playing Kurtz and Tilda Swinton as Hope, enact episodes that took place in their home or in Kurtz's classroom. But, in a Brechtian gesture, the actors also play themselves, discussing and making sense of genetic modification and transgenic technology, which were going to be the subjects of the CAE's presentation at the Massachusetts Museum of Contemporary Art exhibition until interrupted by Kurtz's arrest. (It is this formal technique that made one reviewer of *Strange Culture* write: "The director not only breaks the fourth wall, she reduces it to plaster dust.") In this sense, the film adopts what has been a practice of the CAE "tactical media" interventions, a more interactive dynamic that allows for more open, public-minded, activist art. For instance, in the gallery performance of "Free Range Grain," the project that had been scheduled to open at the Massachusetts Museum of Contemporary Art, the artists in white lab coats would ask the visitors, "Are you worried about your food being genetically modified?" and this would be followed by a period of discussion and even experimental lab work. Kurtz told me that he was interested in museum visitors having an experience that was essentially demystifying: over and over again, sitting down with individuals or groups, he would speak about the global food market, its consequences for food laws and barriers, and the danger of food supply being concentrated in the hands of a few multinational traders.

Kurtz's doctoral degree is in interdisciplinary humanities. He is a professor of art. How did he learn to separate DNA and speak to museum visitors about gels and reagents? Kurtz says that one afternoon during the fall semester of 2003 he had gone over to the molecular biology department and stuck flyers in the graduate student boxes, flyers asking for assistance in learning testing techniques, with money and travel provided. The collaborator Kurtz chose was an advanced doctoral student from Hong Kong. For the next five months, while Kurtz read everything about transgenic technology that he could lay his hands on, he also made a daily trek to a lab to do tests. "It was a pain in the ass," he told me, "A rough Buffalo winter." And here, in this story of an amateur's entry into an elite system of knowledge like biotechnology or genetics, particularly with an intention to throw it open to the public gaze, we get another clue to the reasons behind the government's overzealous prosecution. Kurtz is a disciplinary terrorist. As a CAE statement after Kurtz's indictment put it, "A biology club can talk about cells, but if it goes beyond the institutionalized boundaries of the life sciences, look out for the feds." In other words, by breaching disciplinary boundaries, and by, in effect, questioning the property rights to knowledge and the profits that accompany patentable research, Kurtz has conformed to the old trusted adage of crime fiction—he is in the wrong place at the wrong time. In the eyes of the law this puts him in the same category as a group of young Muslim men whose homes are only a few minutes away from Kurtz's house, in the old steel mill town of Lackawanna. It doesn't help matters either when the men responsible for the arrest of the "Lackawanna Six"—and awarded "the Attorney General's Award for Exceptional Service" by John Ashcroft—were part of the team marshalling the case against Kurtz. In fact, at a public meeting in New York City that I attended, Kurtz said that the Buffalo Joint Terrorism Task Force, rewarded with promotions and pay hikes after the conviction of the Lackawanna Six, had probably seen his own case and decided that a "cash cow" was staring them in the face.

※

No defense lawyer has seized the spotlight.
No intimate has insistently cried out, This is my son,
my brother, my husband, my friend; these are his loves,
his foibles, the neat and messy stuff of his complicated
human life. It is all perfectly understandable, and perfectly
opportune for police agents and prosecutors. Americans
are busy people; who can keep track of so many
disembodied, dehistoricized "detainees," "enemy
combatants," "American Taliban," and "terror suspects."
—JoAnn Wypijewski, "Living in an Age of Fire"

Sahim Alwan, Faysal H. Galab, Yasein A. Taher, Mukhtar al-Bakri, Shafal A. Mosed, Yahya A. Goba, who collectively came to be known as the Lackawanna Six, were all sentenced to six and a half to nine years in prison. Theirs was the first federal case involving suspected terrorist cells in the United States after the attacks of September 11. Each of the men had been convicted of having provided material support to al Qaeda. During the trial, the defendants' lawyers spoke against the implicit threat from the prosecutors that the government could toss their clients into a secret military prison without trial and, in the end, all the young men chose to accept guilt rather than risk being jailed in a place like Guantánamo. The attorney Patrick J. Brown, who defended one of the accused, told the *Washington Post*, "We had to worry about the defendants being whisked out of the courtroom and declared enemy combatants if the case started going well for us. So we just ran up the white flag and folded. Most of us wish we'd never been associated with the case."

Out of Lackawanna's total population, which is close to twenty thousand, the Yemeni-American community has around three thousand members. It is mostly working class, made up of the families of the migrants who first began to arrive, in the 1940s and 1950s, to labor in the town's now mostly abandoned steel mills. It was thought that the Yemenis would better withstand the fierce heat of the furnace because they were accustomed to life in the desert. Most of the Yemeni families, traditionally called "Arabians" by their fellow residents, live in a short stretch of the poorest section of town, within easy distance of the giant husks of mills that look like the stranded wrecks of tall ships in a place where the tide has run out. It was from this small place that, in the spring of 2001, the group of young American men traveled to Afghanistan, where they were put through what was essentially a terrorist boot camp, culminating in a meeting with Osama bin Laden, who told them that in the fight with America there were brothers "willing to carry their souls in their hands."

According to the *New York Times*, in the summer of 2001, an unsigned, handwritten letter arrived at the FBI building in downtown Buffalo. "Two terrorist came to Lackawanna . . . for recruiting the Yemenite youth," the letter reported. It named eight men who had gone to a bin Laden camp in Afghanistan; the writer, identified only as an Arab American, had written, "I can not give you my name because I fear for my life." The youths themselves had never spoken about their experience with anyone in the community. As one of the six, Sahim Alwan, would later explain, he didn't have any plans or any hatred of America, and when he left the camp early, having realized that he didn't belong there, he had left al Qaeda behind. The trip to Afghanistan had been the result of "a lot of curiosity" and a mistake. The letter that the FBI had received didn't touch on any of these ambiguities. In any case, nothing much was done by the authorities about the letter until, a few months later, the world seemed to change with the attacks on the World Trade Center. In the months that followed, the two recruiters who had taken the Lackawanna youth to Afghanistan came under the scanner (one of them as a prisoner in Guantánamo) and, from then on, it was only a matter of time before the six youths were hauled in. In the weeks before the first anniversary of the attacks of September 11, the FBI arrested one of the Lackawanna men in Bahrain on the night of his wedding. And soon thereafter, federal agents drove their cars to the Yemen Soccer Field in Lackawanna and arrested more of the men, carting away boxes of tapes, computers, and books from their homes. "One by one," President Bush announced, "we're hunting the killers down."

Later, at the State of the Union address in January 2003, the president said, "We've broken al Qaeda cells in Hamburg, London, Paris, as well as Buffalo, N.Y." But such assertions invited rational skepticism. After all, after coming back from Afghanistan, the Lackawanna men had all returned to their former lives. Nothing recovered from their homes or elsewhere suggested that they were involved in any conspiracy. The magistrate judge hearing the case, H. Kenneth Schroeder, asked the prosecutor, "What is it that these defendants were planning?" In response, the government attorney said, "It's a difficult question because the defendants by themselves have put the court in this box." By hiding the fact that they had been at an al Qaeda camp, according to the prosecutor, the defendants were "now throwing themselves on the court, in essence, and saying that you figure out what we're going to do." And what exactly did the government figure out?

More than a year after the Lackawanna arrests, after many months of "debriefings" or secret interrogation meetings, a law enforcement official admitted that the interviews had yielded "nothing earth-shattering." There were differences of opinion even among the government agencies. When the CIA described the Lackawanna Six as the most dangerous terrorist group in the United States, FBI officials tried to downplay the rhetoric. One FBI official said, "To say that they were 'the most dangerous terrorist group in the United States,' I wouldn't necessarily approve of that, because I have seen enough to know that they probably didn't have the means or the capabilities at that point to do something." And yet, the FBI too, despite this show of caution, could not erase the uncertainty from its claims, as was evident from the following assessment: "We were looking to prevent something. And we did. Obviously nothing happened. So we all did our job." But this is self-serving, circular reasoning. The government's claims are wrapped around an emptiness that is greater than the fact of a missing crime. What is really missing in this story about punitive action is a true sense of justice. This point was well made by the artist and writer Claire Pentecost when, in an article devoted to the trial of Steve Kurtz and the CAE, she wrote: "As the 9/11 report attests, in spring 2001 Ashcroft had taken terrorism off the list of funding priorities and Condoleezza Rice didn't have the time of day for the State Department terrorism experts. Although people at the top level of government have not been held to account for being unable or unwilling to heed mounting evidence that al Qaeda would become the number one U.S. threat, six young men from Lackawanna should have known that they risked 25-year prison sentences by exploring the promises of radical forms of their religion."

One of the Lackawanna Six, Sahim Alwan, was interviewed in prison, in July 2003, for a PBS *Frontline* documentary. In the course of that conversation he said that his trip to Afghanistan had been truly eye-opening. In the camp, bin Laden had come and said that he had men ready to die for their religion. Alwan told his interviewer that he had of course heard of extremism before his visit to the camp but learning about it firsthand made for a completely different and alienating experience: "At that point, I was like, I knew I was in shit. Excuse my language. But, you know, and I was like, wow, you know, this is, you know, it's real, it's real stuff." Alwan was the first to quit the camp, not having completed even his weapons training. Talking about one of his fellow Lackawanna men, one who has not been heard from since, Alwan recalled, "Elabaneh was standing there. You know, he was like, where are you going? I said, yo, I said, I'm getting the fuck outta here. I said, you know, I'm leaving. And, I left."

There is such clarity there. It's not that John Ashcroft ought to have given Sahim Alwan a medal for having learned his lesson. The real point is that the long and harsh punishment meted out to the Lackawanna Six in no way acknowledges the curiosity and perhaps even courage shown by the young men. More seriously, by having responded with overwhelming force, the federal government has not only failed to ask why the young men went to Afghanistan in the first place, it has put on a small immigrant community a burden of collective guilt and repression that builds on a new stereotype of a "foreigner" carrying in the crook of his arm a tiny bomb.

The brother of one of the convicted men told a reporter, "Everybody of ethnic background wants to know, 'Who the hell am I?'" The young men from Lackawanna had been born to working-class parents who were for the most part uneducated, unschooled in their own traditions as well as the new customs that they encountered in their adopted nation. Religion provided one of the answers. Dina Temple-Raston, in *Jihad Next Door*, writes about Lackawanna: "The young men there were unable to break free of the miseries that accompanied a town in decline, while at the same time they were unable to feel connected to a distant country and strict religion that nagged at them and worried their consciences wherever they went. The push and pull sapped all vitality from their lives. They found themselves looking for a way out: something—anything—to hold onto." Another Yemeni American from that area, a community leader who defended the actions of the youths despite what he believed was their naïveté, told another journalist, "A lot of people wrestle with this question of identity. I think these individuals wanted to know more about what it meant to be a true Muslim in a non-Muslim society." Once they reached the camps, most of the Lackawanna youths seemed to have realized that the plural identities that made them who they were (including, for good or bad, their identity as First World citizens, unused to the demands of a stay in a desolate part of Afghanistan) couldn't be limited to the al Qaeda doctrine of what it meant to be a Muslim. In other settings, this would have been considered a valuable lesson. But in the case of these young men it was allowed to work only as trauma and unspeakable guilt. As Sahim Alwan said during his *Frontline* interview, "We already knew we made a mistake. But I'm gonna be honest with you. We didn't talk about it. We didn't. I tried to forget the whole thing so bad that I had, after, when I was arrested, I had to remember things over, and over, and over. Even 'til now. I just, it's, it's a part of my life that's, I told you if I want to change it, I really, I really wish I can change it. And you try to do that. I don't know if that's psychological. But you try to forget. You force yourself to forget it."

Yasein Taher was one of the Lackawanna Six. He had been voted "friendliest" in the Lackawanna High School class of 1996; he was the soccer team co-captain and had dated and married a cheerleader named Nicole Frick. In early 2001 he underwent a change. He began going to the mosque each night and stopped watching television or listening to the radio. Nicole Frick told a journalist that her husband wanted no pictures on the walls and he avoided family events for fear of contact with women. But even Taher couldn't stand the camp in Afghanistan—he was more of a tourist than a terrorist. According to the interviews conducted by JoAnn Wypijewski for *Mother Jones*, Taher came back and told Abdulsalam Noman, his soccer coach, "Uncle, I appreciate this country more than any other time." At the camp, they had slept on dirty mattresses and eaten bad food. Taher told Noman, "It was a waste of time; we didn't learn anything."

It is not better weapons but better hotels that are going to win the war against al Qaeda. That is what the champions of free markets will say. But a different argument needs to be made much more urgently. In the years following the attacks of September 11, writes Ashis Nandy, "there has been a narrowing of cognitive and emotional range all around." The tactics of shock and awe used by the U.S. government against even its native population have only strengthened the hand of militant proselytizers. The absolute logic of condemnation does nothing but promote despair and abandonment among its victims. After the arrest of the Lackawanna youths, the Yemeni Americans of the first ward woke up to find that the police had taken occupation in their lives: police cars were parked on their streets, their houses were searched and they themselves were interrogated, there were surveillance cameras watching them from their perch on utility poles. A report in July 2009 revealed that senior Bush administration officials had debated testing the U.S. Constitution by sending American troops to arrest the Lackawanna Six; Vice-President Cheney and others were in favor of the president's power being used to direct the military to pick up the offenders and declare them enemy combatants. The use of the military to make arrests on native soil has few precedents, and even though President Bush ultimately decided to send the FBI to make the arrests, the language of the prosecution cast the Yemeni American youths as outsiders and enemies. In its case against the Lackawanna Six, the government argued that the youths had failed to demonstrate their "ties to the American community, let alone their allegiance to the American community." But there are more ways to express allegiance than understood by those patrolling the borders of identity. The active expression of dissent would be one of them. But that fundamental right, at this moment in time, seems such a distant horizon. Liberation from imprisonment in a stereotype would be a modest start. Is it something likely to happen any time soon?

Even before the legal case against the Lackawanna Six had been decided, government officials from President Bush down had started calling them "America's first homegrown sleeper cell." The lawyer for one of the youths asked in disbelief, "Bush still calls them a sleeper cell and for the life of me, I don't understand why. Don't cells plan things? Case targets?" The situation was perhaps best explained by Yassein Taher's uncle and former soccer coach, Abdul Noman, who told a journalist, "We're living in a time of fire. We Muslims now have to be extra careful of everything we do, and everything we say. It isn't safe to be a Muslim in America anymore. Nine-eleven has changed it all for us."

In August 2007, the New York Police Department released a ninety-page public report entitled "Radicalization in the West: The Homegrown Threat." Based on the study of eleven Islamic terror plots in the United Kingdom and the United States, its major assertion is that the participants in these plots followed a distinct psychological path, from being unremarkable, ordinary citizens to violent jihadists. The report even lays out a four-stage development cycle for each terrorist, a process that it claims is common to all the plots under scrutiny: pre-radicalization, self-identification, indoctrination, and jihadization. But do crude generalizations about stages of terrorism and the behavior of whole communities work for any sustained period of time?

In an article commenting on the profiling of Muslims since September 11, Bernard Harcourt of the University of Chicago Law School pointed out that "there are no empirical studies on racial profiling in the terrorism context." Harcourt cited another review that discovered "an almost complete absence of evaluation research on counter-terrorism strategies. From over 20,000 studies we located on terrorism, we found only seven which contained moderately rigorous evaluations of counter-terrorism programs." When law enforcement agencies profile members of a higher-offending group, Harcourt wrote, "they are essentially sampling *more* from that *higher-offending* group." To make matters more complicated, in the longer run "substitution effects" come into play; offenders recruit outside the profiled groups, or switch profiles, in order to escape detection, or they change tracks to other forms of crime. Thus, in both short-term and long-term contexts, racial profiling is suspect.

The New York Police Department's report on "homegrown terrorism" comes with a prefatory note by Raymond Kelly, the police commissioner, who writes that it is crucial to understand "the radicalization process in the West that drives 'unremarkable' people to become terrorists" and that his department's report is evidence that "the NYPD places a priority on understanding what drives and defines the radicalization process." But this is the same person who just over a year earlier had told Malcolm Gladwell, a writer for the *New Yorker*, that racial profiling of terrorists was "just nuts." Kelly had said: "We have a policy against racial profiling. . . . It's the wrong thing to do, and it's also ineffective. If you look at the London bombings, you have three British citizens of Pakistani descent. You have Germaine Lindsay, who is Jamaican. You have the next crew, on July 21st, who are East African. You have a Chechen woman in Moscow in early 2004 who blows herself up in the subway station. So whom do you profile? Look at New York City. Forty percent of New Yorkers are born outside the country. Look at the diversity here. Who am I supposed to profile?"

But now Kelly's police department has profiled, if not persons, then the process through which it thinks terrorists are made. The main examples it considers include the Lackawanna Six and Shahawar Matin Siraj, and its portrayals have as little specificity as the peeling "wanted" posters put up by the police on Delhi's walls. In the section on Siraj we are told that New York City's "Muslim communities have been permeated by extremists who have and continue to sow the seeds of radicalization." There is not a word there about the police informant who was the only one who came close to being a mentor to the young Siraj. There is nothing, too, about Abu Ghraib, the invasion of Afghanistan, or the war in Iraq. There is no acknowledgment of the special registration requirements for Muslims in the United States after September 11, 2001, or the bias attacks on those who are Muslims, or simply perceived to be Muslims. How exactly are the roots of disaffection going to be explained if, even before analysis begins, some of the more visible roots have been cut off?

In the *New Yorker* article in which Kelly had been quoted speaking against racial profiling, the ostensible argument was about the profiling of pit-bulls as killer dogs. The author showed that the kinds of dogs that killed people changed over time, that the problem didn't have to do with pit-bulls per se. If there were more problems with pit-bulls, it wasn't because they were more dangerous, it was just that they were more numerous. The ban on pit-bulls, as has happened in parts of Canada, was easy but misguided. It wouldn't necessarily save lives against dog attacks because whichever breed was perceived to be more aggressive would be bred in greater numbers in place of pit-bulls. Instead of the generalization that pit-bulls are killer dogs, there is need for a better generalization, "based not on breed but on the known and meaningful connection between dangerous dogs and negligent owners."

I have a generalization of my own, which is every bit as reductive as the New York Police Department's. According to the testimony of an undercover police officer during the Siraj trial, Matin Siraj had punched and beaten an Egyptian man who had insulted the young man by saying that all Pakistanis are terrorists. At another moment in the same trial, the police informant Osama Eldawoody, also an Egyptian, had testified that the FBI had first come to his home after a neighbor noticed many suspicious-looking packages in the doorway. The packages only contained clothing bought online. But during that conversation with the FBI, Eldawoody had said that his duty was to improve the reputation of Muslims and he wanted to help. A young man who behaved criminally and along with him the unemployed police informant who helped entrap him in a bombing conspiracy had one thing in common: in a narrative that was much larger than them, and far beyond their real control, they were being defined as terrorists. So, here's my generalization: a stereotype scripts the story of people's lives in a thousand defeating ways, and we owe it to all our social selves to produce new stories, with many exits, U-turns, detours, and destinations.

✳ We Are the World

We don't get it. We truly can't imagine what it was like.
We can't imagine how dreadful, how terrifying war is;
and how normal it becomes. — Susan Sontag,
Regarding the Pain of Others

The money, said the man in the witness box, was to be "used for shooting
and killing of innocent people" in the north Indian province of Punjab.
Harjit Singh, who was a government witness, could understand English
but spoke in Punjabi, his words translated by the interpreter standing
next to him. Singh was in his mid-thirties, tall and gaunt, a clean-shaven
Sikh with a receding hairline. The interpreter, a short and pudgy bespec-
tacled Pakistani man in his forties who was a former actor, wore a jet-black
toupee.

Singh had signed a cooperation agreement with the FBI's Joint Terrorism Task Force. He had been arrested for credit card fraud but was hoping
for a reduced sentence because he wore a wire to record conversations with
the man who was sharing his cell in a Brooklyn detention facility. That
man, a Pakistani called Khalid Awan, was the defendant. He too had been
convicted for defrauding credit card companies, to the tune of $2.5 mil-
lion, but, thanks to Singh's work, he was now on trial for providing material aid to terrorists. He was accused of sending money to the Khalistan

Commando Force, an Indian separatist group whose leader was hiding in Pakistan.

The trial was winding to a close. In another ten days, it would be Christmas. I had been taking the train in the morning to New York City. Every day, I looked at the broken ice on the Hudson and the sea gulls wheeling in the frozen air. From Grand Central Station, it was a short subway ride to the Federal Courthouse in Brooklyn. It was odd to come in from the cold and step into the quiet, wood-paneled room, filled for the most part with white faces, and to hear a detailed conversation about a bomb blast in rural Punjab. I would put my coat on the wooden bench and watch the American lawyer struggling to pronounce names like Paramjit Singh Panjwar. It reminded me a bit of a motorcyclist swerving around orange cones on a highway.

The defendant sat on the left with his two lawyers and a female interpreter from India. Each day Awan wore the same dark blue sweater. He used to be rich and his wife was a Pakistani television star. Awan had gray hair above his forehead, and there were dark circles around his eyes. All through the trial, he looked calm and didn't speak much.

Next in the witness box was John Ross, a detective and investigator working with the Joint Terrorism Task Force. He was stocky and well-built, looking slightly cramped in his green-colored suit. His head was clean-shaven. In reply to the prosecutor's questions, Ross laid down the history of the case. Harjit Singh had come to the authorities in prison and told them that Awan had confided that he had sent over $800,000 to Panjwar, a Punjabi terrorist living in Pakistan. Panjwar was a former bank clerk who had become the commander of the KCF, the military wing of the Khalistan movement. Ross described how Panjwar first fled to Nepal and then, after being involved in the deaths of several Indian paramilitary soldiers, went to Lahore, where he is still living under the care of the Pakistani intelligence agency, the Inter-Services Intelligence or the ISI.

The defendant, Awan, had come in contact with Panjwar in 1996, and had become friends with him. When Awan's sister got married, Panjwar was among the invited guests. Three or four times a month, the defendant and Panjwar spoke to each other on the phone. Supporters of the Khalistan cause in the United States, two of whom had testified earlier during the trial, would visit Awan and give him money meant for Panjwar.

When questioned by Ross in prison, after the tapes of the conversations between him and Singh in the cell had been played back to him, Awan admitted to having sent Panjwar only around $60,000 or $70,000. The money would be used, Awan had told Ross, "for bad things" in India. From his base in Pakistan, Ross said, Panjwar had been responsible for at least 250 deaths and hundreds of bomb blasts across the border. As I sat listening to this testimony, I experienced a strange emotion of dislocation. The killings in Punjab are seen, at least in India, as a matter of the past. While this courtroom conversation was taking place in late 2006, it returned me to the memories of my youth, when I was living in Delhi more than twenty years ago. I was an undergraduate student in 1984 when the Indian Army attacked the Golden Temple in Amritsar where Sikh terrorists had taken refuge; later that year, Prime Minister Indira Gandhi was gunned down in revenge by her Sikh bodyguards. In the days that followed, there were many more deaths as Hindu mobs in Delhi and other cities massacred thousands of Sikhs. The most tangible memory of those years for me is of bloodshed and shame, and it was painful to be returned to the past. But there was something more disorienting in the stale trial's sense of anachronism, its focus on Punjab rather than a place like Kashmir where ongoing terrorism exacts a daily toll in human lives.

It was rather remarkable that I was sitting in an American courtroom where the government prosecutor, in front of a federal judge, was openly recognizing the role of Pakistan's ISI in the spread of terrorism in India. One of the defense lawyers, during a sidebar conversation with the judge, had tried to point out that Pakistan was an ally of the United States. He said, "We are the ones arming these guys." He wanted the government lawyer to stop talking about the ISI, but the judge didn't accept the objection. After the attacks of September 11, it would appear that there was less squeamishness in talking about terrorism, at least the terrorism practiced by another state.

The truth was that Khalid Awan would not be in prison had it not been for the attacks of September 11. A routine check on Muslim immigrants in the New York area had led, in his case and in many other cases, to the discovery of credit card fraud. And the sting operation in the Brooklyn prison that led to his trial for providing material support to terrorists probably reflected law enforcement's search for bigger fish. This was the opinion of Awan's lawyers when I interviewed them later, and this too was a part of the disorientation I felt. Not only was Punjab no longer a theater of terror, it was also that Awan was very small fish.

But at least he was guilty. It could easily have been worse.

According to a report in the *Washington Post*, most individuals arrested on charges of crimes related to national security since September 11, 2001 had been "convicted of relatively minor crimes such as making false statements and violating immigration law—and had nothing to do with terrorism." Only a small number of those arrested were found to have any relationship with terrorism, much less with an organized group like al Qaeda or its leader Osama bin Laden. The *Post* found that contrary to President Bush's claim that half of the four hundred charged had been convicted of terrorism, the actual number was thirty-nine. The same report stated that "a large number of people appear to have been swept into U.S. counterterrorism investigations by chance—through anonymous tips, suspicious circumstances or bad luck—and have remained classified as terrorism defendants years after being cleared of connections to extremist groups." Juliette Kayyem, the head of the national security program at Harvard University's John F. Kennedy School of Government was quoted in the report as saying that "we have no accurate assessment of whether the war on terror is actually working."

The findings of a study done by Transactional Records Access Clearinghouse (TRAC) at Syracuse University, which based its analysis on the Justice Department's figures, were even more disheartening. In the five years since the attacks of September 11, the U.S. government caught 6,472 individuals in the anti-terrorism dragnet, but decided not to prosecute 64 percent of those charged. Even out of those prosecutions that were pursued, 9 percent of the cases were dismissed and thrown out of court. Only 27 percent of the individuals were convicted of any crime. No more than 1 percent received a substantial sentence of twenty years or more. According to the TRAC report, "of the 1,329 who were sentenced, 704 received no prison time and an additional 327 received sentences ranging from one day to less than a year." Thus, the report concluded, "the median or typical prison sentence for them all was zero because the majority received no time at all in prison."

In the case of Khalid Awan, the jury returned a guilty verdict on all counts, and later, in September 2007, the judge sentenced Awan to fourteen years in prison. A few weeks later, I went to the offices of the U.S.

attorneys who had prosecuted Awan. Near the desk of Assistant U.S. Attorney Kelly Currie was a picture of his office-mates in a *gurdwara* when they had gone to investigate the situation in Punjab. In the photograph, the Americans were sitting in the *langar* with their heads covered in the traditional Sikh manner. Detective Ross, wearing a small gun strapped to his ankle—"Walter PPK 380, JR's gun, James Bond uses it"—but quite relaxed in his office, spoke of his experience wandering around Chandni Chowk market in Old Delhi. Then Ross showed me a Punjabi newspaper he had brought back with him from Chandigarh because it had a photo of Saddam Hussein in it. On his bookshelf there were books on Sikhism. He also had a copy there of the Holy Qu'ran. We could believe that the world that the *9/11 Commission Report* had wanted to call into being had finally arrived—when in the fight against terrorism "the whole planet was the American homeland." And, if you wanted to go further you could say that terrorism, as we have come to understand it in the last few years, has ensured that U.S. law enforcement is becoming multicultural.

Three cheers for diversity.

This could be a cause for happiness in a sorry scenario where, as the TRAC report notes, the Justice Department's lead charge for one "international terrorist" was "26 USC 7203, the willful failure to file a return" and the lead charge for five other "international terrorists" was "42 USC 0408, a violation of the federal old age, survivors and disability insurance law." So while the facts in the war on terror tell a grim story, we can say that now, at least, the law-enforcement agents know the Prophet Muhammad from Mickey Mouse. We could all be satisfied about this and begin to feel optimistic about the world. The people I had met and interviewed in the U.S. attorney's office in Brooklyn were all decent men displaying no malice toward any group or nation—except that everything that the U.S. government has done since September 11 reminds us of the even deeper divisions being created between people and their knowledge of each other.

Let me recount a story told by a photographer for Getty Images in a book called *Reporting Iraq*. The photographer, Chris Hondros, had accompanied a U.S. combat unit, in January 2005, to Tal Afar in the north of Iraq. One night after the curfew, the unit was out on a patrol when a car turned onto the darkened boulevard and came toward them. Hondros said,

I had a feeling the situation was going to end up badly. So I moved over to the side, because I feared some warning shots would be fired. The car kept coming. It was dark. Sure enough, somebody fired some warning shots, the car kept coming. And then they fired into the car. And it limped into the intersection, clearly no longer under its own power, just on momentum, and gently came to rest on a curb. I was kind of paralyzed, and then slowly walked to the car and, sure enough, I hear children's voices inside the car, and I knew it was a family. The doors opened; the back doors opened, and kids just tumble out of the car, one after one after one—six in all. One was shot to the abdomen, though we didn't realize he was shot at the time, though he was bleeding profusely and as soon as he dropped, there was blood in the street. The soldiers realized it was a civilian car. They ran and grabbed all the kids and ran them to the sidewalk. In the front seat, what ended up being the parents were killed, riddled with bullets, instantly dead. The children in the back were, incredibly enough, okay, except for the one kid who was winged in the abdomen.

This is difficult to read, but it needs to be read because it is a story about the disaster of war. The shock of the shooting is experienced by the reader in slow motion. The epiphany I have on reading it, as if I were seeing it on a screen, on the grainy film the blurry movement of the car and the soldiers, hollows out the moment and makes it expand. My epiphany is that this is forever the truth of war: the grave injustice of any war. Even the war on terror is in its darkest, most dramatic form, the explosion of this tiny moment, because the fundamental inequality of power is a wall that cannot be breached without violence. That is what I think as I watch the scene unfold in the dark cave of my own mind, witnessing the numbing vaudeville of death, with the volume seemingly turned down because I can make out nothing of what anyone is saying or screaming.

Hondros goes on to tell us other things: the boy who had been shot in the stomach was flown to Boston for treatment; the boy told the Americans that the family had been out visiting and were trying to get home. And then, as if to chastise me for talking glibly about inevitable violence and for having mocked easy liberal pretensions about multiculturalism, there is in the photographer's testimony a little lesson in cultural awareness:

It was a little bit after the curfew, but time is never a precise thing to Iraqis—it's not like this German, iron-clad, six-to-one curfew. It's more like, all right, you're not supposed to be driving around at night. Generally speaking, you could be out on the roads after six o'clock and nothing would happen to you. They were just trying to hustle and get home, and they're driving along, and all of a sudden they hear shots. They don't see—it's dark—they don't see camouflaged soldiers in the dark in front of them. They just hear shots. Now, when you're in a car driving around in Iraq and you hear shots, your first instinct is to speed up, because either someone's shooting at you for some reason or somebody's about to get into a battle nearby. Either way, you don't want to be around there; you want to get out of there. And then, the headlight range—by the time they actually get into the region of your headlights, forget it, that's way too close, they're already engaging you by that point, shooting you up by that point. So that's why they didn't stop.

Such luck, such sorrow. In the end, this is what it comes down to: who will teach one to be modern, who will teach the other to be human? This is the central dilemma in the so-called clash of civilizations. Or, so it seems, in my dark despair. A car on a road at night with a man trying to drive close enough to be able to say "Sir, we are just a car with a family driving home." And on the other side a group of soldiers holding their guns as if to say "You're gonna die, motherfucker!" The soldiers wondering whether they too are going to die, and then finding the answer very close to them, on the little curve of metal under their tense fingers. It is often just that easy. Because this is what Hondros says:

Almost every soldier in Iraq has been involved in some sort of incident like that or another, I would say. Their attitude about it was grim, but it wasn't the end of their world. It was, "Well, kind of wished they'd stopped. We fired warning shots. Damn, I don't know why the hell they didn't stop. What're you doing later, you want to play Nintendo? Okay." Just a day's work for them. That stuff happens in Iraq a lot. That's why it's such a damn mess, because almost everybody's had something like that happen to them at the hands of U.S. soldiers. They hate them.

A picture that Hondros took that night shows a little girl sitting down on the sidewalk, crying, her tiny hands and her cheeks splattered with blood. She is wearing a gray dress with red and black flowers. The ground around her is spotted with drops of blood. A few drops of blood have also fallen on the dust-covered boot of a tall American soldier. We can see his fatigues and rifle and flashlight but not his face. In a radio interview, Hondros said that the picture of the blood-splattered little girl "is impossible to misinterpret" because it showed the child "essentially all alone in the world now." That is what the people all over had responded to. The interviewer can be heard agreeing with the photographer. She says that that is right, the child looks completely alone, she almost seems stranded "in the middle of nowhere."

I have quoted at length from Hondros's account of the incident at Tal Afar because I am held by the pathos of the images and the story of how they came to be. But I also intend to make a larger point about war in places like Iraq and the war against terror that the government is engaged in at home. I am not suggesting a weak analogy or parallel between the two different wars. Rather, the relationship between the two is more symbiotic. In some measure, we don't really see the images that Hondros is talking about, and we don't even fully experience their reality, because the spectacle of the war on terror screens that greater horror of the other war from our eyes. There is no crying girl in front of us, nor her dead parents, the father's skull collapsed because he has been shot so many times. Instead we watch the machinery of the state staging the war on terror. The SWAT teams making arrests ("Terror Plot Uncovered" "Sleeper Cell Discovered in Upstate New York"), prosecutors conducting trials ("Alleged Bomber Offers Testimony"), and judges sentencing the guilty ("Pakistani Gets Fourteen Years for Aiding Terrorism"). The slow, calm procedure of law hides from our view the brutality of the state and the horror of war. My argument is not even about those who are innocent and have been falsely charged for being involved in terrorism, although it would be perfectly justifiable to make that case too. Instead, the larger point is that the war on terror is obscuring from our sight the war in Iraq and its human cost. It is an elaborate and expensive distraction that hides from us the real crime.

✳ Notes

PROLOGUE A Missile in the Living Room

Donald Rumsfeld quote: Donald Rumsfeld, Department of Defense news briefing, Feb. 12, 2002.

Report in *Newsweek*: Evan Thomas and Michael Hirsh, "The Debate Over Torture," *Newsweek*, Nov. 21, 2005.

Stephen Grey quote: Stephen Grey, *Ghost Plane* (New York: St. Martin's Press, 2006), 42.

A report in the *Washington Post*: Peter Finn, "Detainee Who Gave False Iraq Data Dies In Prison in Libya," *The Washington Post*, May 12, 2009. Online at http://www.washingtonpost.com/wpdyn/content/article/2009/05/11/AR2009051103412.html.

Report in *New York Times*: Douglas Jehl, "Report Warned Bush Team about Intelligence Doubts," *New York Times*, Nov. 2005.

Colin Powell quotes: Transcript of Powell's speech to the U.N. on Iraq available at: http://www.cnn.com/2003/US/02/05/sprj.irq.powell.transcript.05/index.html; Steven Weisman, "Powell Calls His U.N. Speech a Lasting Blot on His Record," *New York Times*, September 9, 2005.

Mark Danner quote: Mark Danner, "Tales from Torture's Dark World," *New York Times*, March 14, 2009. See also Danner, "U.S. Torture: Voices from the Black Sites," *New York Review of Books*, April 9, 2009.

Barack Obama campaign statement: Barack Obama, "Renewing American Leadership," *Foreign Affairs*, 86.4 (July–August 2007), 14.

Obama after swearing-in: Mark Mazetti and William Glaberson, "Obama to Close Foreign Prisons and Guantánamo," *New York Times*, January 22, 2009.

Interrogation Memos: Mark Mazetti and Scott Shane, "Interrogation Memos Detail Harsh Tactics by the C.I.A.," *New York Times*, April 16, 2009.

But how real is the promise of change?: David Johnston, "U.S. Says Rendition to Continue, but With More Oversight," *New York Times*, August 24, 2009; Charlie Savage, "To Critics, Obama's Terror Policy Looks a Lot Like Bush's," *New York Times*, July 2, 2009, A14; Sam Stein, "Civil Libertarian Rips Obama's Speech: All Bells And Whistles," *The Huffington Post*, May 21, 2009. Online at http://www.huffingtonpost.com/2009/05/21/civil-libertarian-rips-ob_n_206343.html; Luke Mitchell, "We Still Torture," *Harper's Magazine*, July 2009, 49–55.

Release of the secret CIA report: ACLU Press release, "ACLU Obtains Detailed Official Record of CIA Torture Program," August 24, 2009. Online at http://aclu.org/safefree/torture/40838prs20090824.html; Glenn Greenwald, "What every American should be made to learn about the IG torture report," *Salon.com*, August 24, 2009. Online at http://www.salon.com/opinion/greenwald/2009/08/24/ig_report/

Prosecutor to investigate CIA abuse: Mark Mazetti and Scott Shane, "Investigation Is Ordered into C.I.A. Abuse Charges," *New York Times*, August 25, 2009.

President "wants to look forward, not back": "'Inhumane' CIA Terror Tactics Spur Criminal Probe," *The Huffington Post*, August 24, 2009. Online at http://www.huffingtonpost.com/2009/08/24/holder-to-appoint-special_n_267385.html

Abu Zubaydah: Jane Mayer, *The Dark Side* (New York: Doubleday, 2008), 154–57.

Fort Dix Six: Amanda Ripley, "The Fort Dix Conspiracy," *Time*, Dec 6, 2007. Online at http://www.time.com/time/nation/article/0,8599,1691609,00.html. Also see Carly Goldstone, "The Ft. Dix. Fix Was In," *The Daily Beast*, December 22, 2008. Online at http://www.thedailybeast.com/blogs-and-stories/2008-12-22/the-ft-dix-fix-was-in/2/

INTRODUCTION Have You Seen This Man?

The Mumbai gunmen: Somini Sengupta, "Dossier Gives Details of Mumbai attacks," *New York Times*, January 6, 2009. Online at http://www.nytimes.com/2009/01/07/world/asia/07india.html.

Channel Four documentary: *Dispatches: Terror in Mumbai*, Channel Four, directed by Dan Reed, first aired on June 30, 2009.

Shuddhabrata Sengupta quote: Shuddhabrata Sengupta, "Media Trials and Courtroom Tribulations," in *13 December: A Reader* (New Delhi: Penguin Books India, 2006), 38.

Book by S. Hussain Zaidi: S. Hussain Zaidi, *Black Friday: The True Story of the Bombay Bomb Blasts* (New Delhi: Penguin Books India, 2002).

Ashish Khetan on Mumbai attacks: Ashish Khetan, "Karachi to Mumbai: Terror, Step by Step," in *26/11 Mumbai Attacked*, ed. Harinder Baweja (New Delhi: Roli Books, 2009). I have quoted from emails sent to me by Khetan on July 11 and July 14, 2009.

"Most well-documented terrorist attack": Vikas Bajaj and Lydia Polgreen, "Suspect Stirs Mumbai Court by Confessing," *New York Times*, July 20, 2009. Online at http://www.nytimes.com/2009/07/21/world/asia/21india.html.

Arundhati Roy quote: Arundhati Roy, "Who Pulled the Trigger . . . Didn't We All?," *Outlook*, February 28, 2005.

Talal Asad quote: Talal Asad, *On Suicide Bombing* (New York: Columbia University Press, 2007), 30.

Report in *India Today*: Sayantan Chakravarty, "The Day India Was Targeted," *India Today*, December 24, 2001.

Charles Taylor and Robert Mugabe quotes: Joseph Margulies, *Guantánamo and the Abuse of Presidential Power* (New York: Simon and Schuster, 2006), 143. I also interviewed Joseph Margulies on June 2, 2007 in Fairfax, Virginia.

Report on Guantánamo detainees by Seton Hall Law School: Online at http://law. shu.edu/ProgramsCenters/PublicIntGovServ/CSJ/Guantanamo-Reports .cfm. Click on "Report on Guantánamo Detainees: A Profile of 517 Detainees through Analysis of Department of Defense Data."

Testimony of Mark Denbeaux: Same as above. Click on "14 Myths of Guantánamo: Senate Armed Services Committee Statement of Mark P. Denbeaux." Testimony was presented on April 26, 2007.

CHAPTER ONE Birth of a Salesman

Arjun Appadurai quote: Arjun Appadurai, *Fear of Small Numbers* (Durham, N.C.: Duke University Press, 2006).

Reports on the Lakhani trial: The reports filed by John P. Martin for the New Jersey newspaper, *The Star Ledger*, provide a perfect archive of the Lakhani trial. Martin's reportorial work, in my opinion, contributed to a trial that questioned the government's prepackaged indictment of a "terrorist." A lengthy report about Lakhani was presented on Chicago Public Radio's *This American Life* on July 7, 2005, under the title "The Arms Trader." This report, while drawing almost wholly on the analysis presented by the defense lawyer during the trial, has the great virtue of being not only persuasive but also engaging. My report relies primarily on interviews and court transcripts.

A plot to bomb New York City synagogues: Al Baker and Javier C. Hernandez, "4 Accused of Bombing Plot at Bronx Synagogues," *New York Times*, May 21, 2009; Michael Wilson, "In Bronx Bomb Case, Missteps Caught on Tape," *New York Times*, May 22, 2009; William Rashbaum and Kareem Fahim, "Informer's Role in Bombing Plot," *New York Times*, May 23, 2009.

A writer for the *Village Voice*: Graham Rayman, "F.B.I. Agent on Synagogue Case Has Questionable Record," May 21, 2009. Online at http://blogs .villagevoice.com/runninscared/archives/2009/05/the_fbi_agent_w.php.

Sherman v. United States: 356 U.S. 369, 372, 78 S.Ct. 819, 820, 2 L.Ed. 2d 848 (1958).

U.S. Court of Appeals decision in the Hollingsworth and Pickard case: *United States of America v. Arnold L. Hollingsworth, Jr. and William A. Pickard, III*, nos. 92–2399, 92–2483, 92–2694, and 92–2695, 27 F.3d 1196.

Death of a Salesman: Arthur Miller, *Death of a Salesman* (New York: Viking Penguin, 1949).

Orhan Pamuk quotes: Orhan Pamuk, "The Anger of the Damned," translated by Mary Isin, *New York Review of Books*, November 15, 2001.

CHAPTER TWO The Late Career of the Sting Operation

Trial transcript quotes: United States of America v. Hemant Lakhani. In the United States Court of Appeals for the Third Circuit. In the United States District Court for the District of New Jersey. Newark, New Jersey. Docket No. 05-4276. Ralph F. Florio, Official Court Reporter.

Operation West End and other stings: Detailed report available at the Tehelka website: http://www.tehelka.com/channels/Investigation/investigation1.htm. Also see Luke Harding, "Sting on a shoestring," *Guardian*, March 21, 2001; Alexander Zaitchik, "Aniruddha Bahal: The King of Sting," *The Independent*, July 16, 2007. I interviewed Aniruddha Bahal on July 28–29, 2006. Thanks to Tarun Tejpal for providing the recordings made during Operation West End.

Bribes to raise questions in the Parliament: See the report on Operation Duryodhana on Bahal's Cobrapost website: http://www.cobrapost.com/ documents/one.htm.

Aniruddha Bahal quotes: Aniruddha Bahal, "The Lens With Bite," *Outlook*, October 16, 2006.

CHAPTER THREE The Art of Surveillance

Graham Greene's novel: Graham Greene, *The Power and the Glory* ([1940] New York: Penguin, 2003), 131.

Okwui Enwezor quotes: Okwui Enwezor, "The Unhomely: Phantom Scenes in Global Society," Biennial of Seville (BIACS); catalog statement available at http://www.the-artists.org/artistsblog/posts/st_content_001.cfm?id=1612.

Paul Chan video: Paul Chan, untitled video, available for download at http://www.nationalphilistine.com.

Trevor Paglen quotes: Online at http://www.paglen.com/. The description of al-Masri's condition in the "Salt Pit" appears in Trevor Paglen and A.C. Thompson, *Torture-Taxi: On the Trail of the CIA's Rendition Flights* (Hoboken, N.J.: Melville House Publishing, 2006), 127. For the "missing persons," see also the following interview: "Secret CIA Prisons in Your Backyard," Omnesha Roychoudhuri, in conversation with Trevor Paglen and A.C. Thompson. Posted on September 22, 2006. Interview available at http://www.alternet.org/story/41923.

Book by Coco Fusco: Coco Fusco, *A Field Guide for Female Interrogators* (New York: Seven Stories Press, 2008).

Book by Jill Magid: Jill Magid, *Lincoln Ocean Victor Eddy*, 2007. Online at www.lincoln-ocean-victor-eddy.net.

Review of Magid's exhibition: Magid's exhibition *With Full Consent* was reviewed by Roberta Smith in the *New York Times*, July 26, 2007.

Gourevitch and Morris: Philip Gourevitch and Errol Morris, *Standard Operating Procedure* (New York: Penguin, 2008), 277–78.

Graner called ringleader: Christian Davenport and Michael Amon, "3 to be Arraigned in Prison Abuse," *Washington Post*, May 19, 2004, A1.

Gourevitch op-ed: Philip Gourevitch, "The Abu Ghraib We Cannot See," *New York Times*, May 24, 2009.

Course at the California Institute of the Arts: Course ID 517: Special Topics in Arts and Politics: "A Not So Simple Case for Torture." Instructors: Nancy Buchanan and Sam Durant. The work from the class is forthcoming as an anthology from One Star Press.

Description of Paul Shambroom's photographs: Jerry Saltz, "You There! Welcome to Donald Rumsfeld's War Machine," *Village Voice*, April 7, 2006.

Michael Levin quote: Michael Levin, "The Case for Torture," *Newsweek*, June 7, 1982.

Quotes from book by Jonathan Raban: Jonathan Raban, *Surveillance* (New York: Pantheon Books, 2006.), 3–7.

Report in the *New York Times*: Deborah Sontag, "Videotape Offers a Window into a Terror Suspect's Isolation," *New York Times*, December 4, 2006.

Graham Bader quotes: Graham Bader, "The Body Politic," *Artforum*, January 2007.

CHAPTER FOUR The Terror and the Pity

Play by David Hare: David Hare, *Stuff Happens* (London: Faber, 2004), 93.

Quotes from Martin Amis, Jay McInerney, and Ian McEwan about the literary consequences of the attacks of September 11, 2001: Pankaj Mishra, "The End of Innocence," *The Guardian*, May 19, 2007.

Quotes from *The 9/11 Commission Report*: *The 9/11 Commission Report: Final Report of the National Commission on Terrorist Attacks upon the United States* (New York: W. W. Norton and Company, 2004), 1, 340, 344, 347, 362, 52.

Book review by Ben Yagoda: Ben Yagoda, "*The 9/11 Commission Report*: How a Government Committee Made a Piece of Literature," *Slate*, Nov. 8, 2004. Online at http://www.slate.com/id/2109277/.

Essay by Arundhati Roy: Arundhati Roy, "The Algebra of Infinite Justice," *The Guardian*, September 29, 2001.

Leon Wieseltier quote: Leon Wieseltier, "The Catastrophist," *New York Times Book Review*, April 27, 2008.

Book by Ahmed Rashid: Ahmed Rashid, *Taliban* (New Haven, Conn.: Yale University Press, 2001).

Article and quotes by John Sifton: John Sifton, "Temporal Vertigo," *New York Times Sunday Magazine*, September 30, 2001.

Judith Butler quote: Judith Butler, *Precarious Life* (New York: Verso, 2004), 5.

Book by Mohsin Hamid: Mohsin Hamid, *The Reluctant Fundamentalist* (New York: Harcourt, 2007).

Article by Michael Wood: Michael Wood, "At the Movies," *London Review of Books*, Jan. 25, 2007.

Book and quotes by Anthony Swofford: Anthony Swofford, *Jarhead* (New York: Scribner, 2003), 5–7, 233.

Book and quotes by Michael Herr: Michael Herr, *Dispatches* (New York: Knopf, 1977), 20, 64.

Article by Andre O'Hagan: Andrew O'Hagan, "Iraq, 2 May 2005," *London Review of Books*, March 6, 2008.

Death of Lance Cpl. José Antonio Gutierrez: *The Short Life of José Antonio*

Gutierrez, a film by Heidi Specogna, released in North America by Atopia Distribution (2006).

Quote from Amnesty International: Richard Norton-Taylor, "Guantánamo Is Gulag of Our Time, Says Amnesty," *The Guardian*, May 26, 2005.

Moazzam Begg quotes: Moazzam Begg, *Enemy Combatant: My Imprisonment at Guantánamo, Bagram, and Kandahar* (New York: New Press, 2006), 2. The quote about the poem written by Begg's daughter comes from *Poems from Guantánamo: The Detainees Speak*, ed. Marc Falkoff (Iowa City: University of Iowa Press, 2007), 29.

"Torture memo": Assistant Attorney General Jay S. Bybee, "Memorandum for Alberto R. Gonzales, Counsel to the President, re Standards of Conduct for Interrogation under 18 U.S.C. 2340–2340A," August 1, 2002, reprinted in *The Torture Papers: The Road to Abu Ghraib*, ed. Karen J. Greenberg and Joshua L. Dratel (New York: Cambridge University Press, 2005), 172–73, 175.

Quote by Gourevitch and Morris: Philip Gourevitch and Errol Morris, "Exposure," *The New Yorker*, March 24, 2008. See also their *Standard Operating Procedure* (New York: Penguin, 2008), esp. 268–71.

Book and quotes by Saar and Novak: Erik Saar and Viveca Novak, *Inside the Wire* (New York: Penguin, 2005), 228–29. See also the testimony about his experiences at Guantánamo that Spc. Brandon Neely offered to the Center for the Study of Human Rights in the Americas, University of California, Davis, on December 4, 2008. Neely's testimony is important for confirming the story of the abuse of the Holy Qu'ran in the prison, and it can be accessed at http://humanrights.ucdavis.edu/projects/the-guantanamo-testimonials-project/testimonies/testimonies-of-military-guards/testimony-of-brandon-neely.

Report by Associated Press: "Ex-G.I. Writes about Use of Sex in Guantánamo Interrogations," *New York Times*, Jan. 25, 2005. See also the note above, Saar and Novak.

Time report of interrogation log: "Interrogation Log Detainee 063," available at http://ccrjustice.org/files/Publication_AlQahtaniLog.pdf. See also Adam Zagorin and Michael Duffy, "Inside the Interrogation of Detainee 063," *Time*, June 12, 2005. For a more detailed description of the torture practiced at Guantánamo and other places, see Mark Danner, "U.S. Torture: Voices from the Black Sites," *New York Review of Books*, April 9, 2009.

The writer named "C": J. M. Coetzee, *Diary of a Bad Year* (London: Harvill Secker, 2007), 126.

Book by Henri Alleg: Henri Alleg, *The Question* ([1958] Lincoln: University of Nebraska Press, 2006), ix.

Alberto R. Gonzales quote: Department of Justice website http://www.usdoj
.gov/jttf/.

Court case against Shahawar Matin Siraj: United States District Court, Eastern
District of New York, United States of America against Shahawar matin Siraj,
05 CR 104 (S-1) (NG), United States Courthouse, Brooklyn, New York. Court
Reporter: Gene Rudolph. For the transcript of the video-recording of the
conversation from August 23, 2004, see *Harper's Magazine*, October, 2006,
20–23.

In a Le Carré thriller: John Le Carré, *A Most Wanted Man* (New York: Scribner,
2008), 3.

A report in *Newsweek*: Michael Isikoff, "Investigators: The FBI Says, Count the
Mosques," *Newsweek*, February 3, 2003. Online at http://www.newsweek
.com/id/62965.

Paper and quotes by Neil Vidmar: Neil Vidmar, "Trial by Jury Involving Persons
Accused of Terrorism or Supporting Terrorism," Duke Law School Legal
Studies, Research Paper Series, no. 129 (October 2006), available at http://
ssrn.com/abstract=934792. (I am grateful to Aziz Huq for this reference and
also for the Harcourt essay cited below.)

Quote by Martin Stolar: William K. Rashbaum, "Guilty Verdict in Plot to Bomb
Subway Station," *New York Times*, May 25, 2006.

Mohammad Azmath quote: George Iype, "Here in India, I get respect and peace
of mind," *India Abroad*, September 8, 2006.

Japanese internment during the Second World War: Jerry Kang, "Thinking
through Internment 12/7 and 9/11," *Amerasia Journal* 27, no. 3 (2001) and 28,
no. 1 (2002).

Quotes by Aziz Huq: Aziz Huq, "Policing Terror, Policing Islam: Federal
Criminal Law Enforcement, Counterterrorism and America's Muslim
Minority Communities," in *Liberty under Attack: Reclaiming Our Freedoms
in an Age of Terror*, ed. Richard C. Leone and Greg Anrig Jr. (New York:
PublicAffairs, 2007), 168, 171, 173.

Quote from Dr. Zakia Ahmed: Dan McDougall, "I Didn't Recognize the Person
on Fire. I Didn't Recognize Him as My Son," *The Observer*, July 8, 2007;
Afshan Yasmeen, "Please Pray for Us, says Kafeel's Mother," *The Hindu*,
July 6, 2007.

Documentary by Harun Farocki: Harun Farocki, *War at a Distance*, Video Data
Bank, 2003. (Released initially in Germany as *Erkennen und Verfolgen*, 2003.)

Frank Lindh: Karen Breslau and Colin Soloway, "He's a Really Good Boy,"
MSNBC, December 7, 2001. Online at http://www.msnbc.msn.com/.

id/3067393. See also Frank Lindh, "Taking the Stand," *Washington Lawyer*, May 2005. Online at http://www.dcbar.org/for_lawyers/resources/publications/washington_lawyer/may_2005/stand.cfm.

Colin Powell quote: Quoted in Frank Lindh, "Taking the Stand."

U.S. State Department fact sheet: Quoted in Frank Lindh, "Taking the Stand."

Book and quotes by Jane Mayer: Jane Mayer, *The Dark Side* (New York: Doubleday, 2008), 99.

CHAPTER SIX   A Collaborator in Kashmir

Verse from Amit Chaudhuri: Amit Chaudhuri, *St. Cyril Road and Other Poems* (New Delhi: Penguin India, 2005).

Protests: The protests over the sentencing of Mohammad Afzal Guru, as well as the demonstrations in support of it, were well documented in the Indian press. I have also relied heavily on *13 December: A Reader* (New Delhi: Penguin Books India, 2006); and Nirmalangshu Mukherji, *December 13: Terror over Democracy* (New Delhi: Promilla and Company and Bibliophile South Asia, 2005).

Quote by Arundhati Roy: Arundhati Roy, "And His Life Should Become Extinct," *13 December: A Reader* (New Delhi: Penguin Books India, 2006), 122.

Statement and quotes by Tabassum Guru: Tabassum Guru, "A Wife's Appeal for Justice," *Kashmir Times*, October 21, 2004.

Jean-Paul Sartre quote: Jean-Paul Sartre, preface to *The Question* by Henri Alleg ([1958] Lincoln: University of Nebraska Press, 2006).

V. S. Naipaul quotes: V. S. Naipaul, *An Area of Darkness* (New York: Vintage, 1964), 130–31.

Memoir by Orhan Pamuk: Orhan Pamuk, *Istanbul* (New York: Alfred A. Knopf, 2005), 40–41.

Film by Hany Abu-Assad: Hany Abu-Assad, *Paradise Now* (2005) Distributed by Warner Independent Pictures.

CHAPTER SEVEN   A Night in an Army Camp

James Buchan quote: James Buchan, "Kashmir," *Granta* 57 (spring 1997).

Basharat Peer quotes: Basharat Peer, "Papa-2," *n + 1*, no. 5 (winter 2007).

Holland Carter quote: Holland Cotter, "The Collective Conscious," *New York Times*, March 5, 2006.

Book and quotes by Critical Art Ensemble: Critical Art Ensemble, *Marching Plague: Germ Warfare and Global Public Health* (New York: Autonomedia, 2006), 20, 32, 31, 40, 47. (The documentary film under the same name is commissioned and produced by Arts Catalyst.)

Paul Cambria quote: Judith Lewis, "From Baghdad to Buffalo: The Saga of Steven Kurtz's Bacteria," *L.A. Weekly*, July 15, 2004.

Review of *Strange Culture*: John Anderson, "Strange Culture," *Variety*, January 19, 2007.

News story from July 2007: Debora MacKenzie, "Plague of Bioweapons Accidents Afflicts the U.S.," *NewScientist.com*, July 5, 2007.

JoAnn Wypijewski quotes: JoAnn Wypijewski, "Living in an Age of Fire," in *Mother Jones* (March/April 2003). Online at http://www.motherjones.com/politics/2003/03/living-age-fire.

Patrick J. Brown quote: Michael Powell, "No Choice but Guilty: Lackawanna Case Highlights Legal Tilt," *Washington Post*, July 29, 2003.

Article about "unsigned, handwritten letter": Matthew W. Purdy and Lowell Bergman, "Where the Trail Led: Between Evidence and Suspicion; Unclear Danger: Inside the Lackawanna Terror Case," *New York Times*, October 12, 2003.

President Bush quotes: Quoted in JoAnn Wypijewski, "Living in an Age of Fire."

Trial of the Lackawanna Six: Quoted in JoAnn Wypijewski, "Living in an Age of Fire."

Quote from law enforcement official: Dan Herbeck and Lou Michel, "An Information Gap: Months of Debriefings with the Men Who Spent Time with an Al-Qaida Training Camp Have Yielded 'Nothing Earth-Shattering' about Osama Bin Laden or His Organization," *Buffalo News*, October 15, 2003.

FBI quotes: Quoted in Matthew W. Purdy and Lowell Bergman, "Where the Trail Led: Between Evidence and Suspicion; Unclear Danger: Inside the Lackawanna Terror Case."

Clair Pentecost quote: Claire Pentecost, "Reflections on the Case by the U.S. Justice Department against Steven Kurtz and Robert Ferrell," in *Marching Plague: Germ Warfare and Global Public Health*, ed. Critical Art Ensemble (New York: Autonomedia, 2006), 131.

Frontline interview with the Lackawanna Six: Online at http://www.pbs.org/ wgbh/pages/frontline/shows/sleeper/interviews/alwan.html.

Brother of the Lackawanna Six: Matthew Purdy and Lowell Bergman, "Where the Trail Led: Between Evidence and Suspicion; Unclear Danger: Inside the Lackawanna Terror Case," *New York Times*, October 12, 2003.

Dina Temple-Raston quote: Dina Temple-Raston, *The Jihad Next Door* (New York: Public Affairs, 2007), 36. I am indebted to Vijay Prashad for bringing Temple-Raston's book to my attention.

Quote by community leader: Quoted in JoAnn Wypijewski, "Living in an Age of Fire."

Ashis Nandy quote: Ashis Nandy, "The Other 9/11," *Outlook*, September 18, 2006.

A report in July 2009: Mark Mazetti and David Johnston, "Bush Weighed Using Military in Arrests," *New York Times*, July 24, 2009.

Quote about "sleeper cells": Dina Temple-Raston, *The Jihad Next Door*, 205–6.

Abdul Noman quote: Dina Temple-Raston, *The Jihad Next Door*, 206.

New York Police Department report: Mitchell D. Silber and Arvin Bhatt, NYPD, "Radicalization in the West: The Homegrown Threat," August 2007.

Article and quotes by Bernard Harcourt: Bernard E. Harcourt, "Muslim Profiles Post 9/11: Is Racial Profiling an Effective Counterterrorist Measure and Does It Violate the Right to Be Free from Discrimination?," Public Law and Legal Theory Working Paper, no. 123, March 2006. Online at http://ssrn.com/ abstract=893905.

New Yorker article: Malcolm Gladwell, "Troublemakers: What Pit Bulls Can Teach Us about Profiling," *The New Yorker*, February 6, 2006. Online at http:// www.newyorker.com/archive/2006/02/06/060206fa_fact.

EPILOGUE We Are the World

Susan Sontag quote: Susan Sontag, *Regarding the Pain of Others* (New York: Picador, 2004), 125–26.

Report in the *Washington Post*: Dan Eggen and Julie Tate, "U.S. Campaign Produces Few Convictions on Terror Charges," *Washington Post*, June 12, 2005.

Juliette Kayyem quote: See Dan Eggen and Julie Tate, "U.S. Campaign Produces Few Convictions on Terror Charges," *Washington Post*, June 12, 2005.

TRAC report: TRAC, "Criminal Terrorism Enforcement Since the 9/11/01 Attacks," December 8, 2003. Online at http://trac.syr.edu/tracreports/terrorism/

report031208.html (updated September 4, 2006, http://trac.syr.edu/tracreports/terrorism/169/).

Quote "the whole planet": *The 9/11 Commission Report: Final Report of the National Commission on Terrorist Attacks upon the United States* (New York: W. W. Norton and Company, 2004), 362.

Quote from *Reporting Iraq*: Mike Hoyt, John Palattella, and the staff of the *Columbia Journalism Review*, *Reporting Iraq: An Oral History of the War by the Journalists Who Covered It* (Hoboken, N.J.: Melville House, 2007). Several photographs that Chris Hondros took at Tal Afar in 2005 can be seen on his website, www.chrishondros.com. Hondros was also interviewed about the Tal Afar incident on NPR by Renee Montagne on March 26, 2007. The interview can be heard at http://www.npr.org/templates/story/story.php?storyId=9118474.

✳ Bibliography

"ACLU Obtains Detailed Official Record of CIA Torture Program," ACLU press release, August 24, 2009. Online at http://aclu.org/safefree/torture/40838prs20090824.html.

Agamben, Giorgio. "No to Bio-Political Tattooing," *Le Monde*, January 10, 2004.

Alleg, Henri. *The Question* [1958]. Lincoln: University of Nebraska Press, 2006.

Amis, Martin. "The Last Days of Muhammad Atta," *The Observer*, September 3, 2006.

Anderson, John. "Strange Culture," *Variety*, January 19, 2007.

Anderson, Jon Lee. *The Fall of Baghdad*. New York: Penguin, 2004.

Appadurai, Arjun. *Fear of Small Numbers*. Durham, N.C.: Duke University Press, 2006.

Asad, Talal. *On Suicide Bombing*. New York: Columbia University Press, 2007.

Bader, Graham. "The Body Politic," *Artforum*, January 2007.

Bahal, Aniruddha. "The Lens with Bite," *Outlook*, October 16, 2006.

Bajaj, Vikas, and Lydia Polgreen. "Suspect Stirs Mumbai Court by Confessing," *New York Times*, July 20, 2009. Online at http://www.nytimes.com/2009/07/21/world/asia/21india.html.

Baker, Al, and Javier C. Hernandez. "4 Accused of Bombing Plot at Bronx Synagogues," *New York Times*, May 21, 2009.

Bayoumi, Moustafa. *How Does It Feel to be a Problem? Being Young and Arab in America*. New York: Penguin, 2008.

Begg, Moazzam. *Enemy Combatant: My Imprisonment at Guantánamo, Bagram, and Kandahar*. New York: New Press, 2006.

Breslau, Karen, and Colin Soloway. "He's a Really Good Boy," MSNBC, December 7, 2001. Online at http://www.msnbc.msn.com/id/3067393.

Buchan, James. "Kashmir." *Granta* 57 (spring 1997).

Butler, Judith. *Precarious Life*. New York: Verso, 2004.

Bybee, Jay S., Assistant Attorney General. "Memorandum for Alberto R. Gonzales, Counsel to the President, re: Standards of Conduct for Interrogation under 18 U.S.C. 2340–2340A," August 1, 2002. Reprinted in Karen J. Greenberg and Joshua L. Dratel, eds., *The Torture Papers: The Road to Abu Ghraib* (New York: Cambridge University Press, 2005).

Chakravarty, Sayantan. "The Day India Was Targeted," *India Today*, December 24, 2001.

Chan, Paul. Untitled video. Online at http://www.nationalphilistine.com.

Chandrasekaran, Rajiv. *Imperial Life in the Emerald City: Inside Iraq's Green Zone*. New York: Alfred A. Knopf, 2006.

Channel Four. *Dispatches: Terror in Mumbai*. Dan Reed, dir. First aired June 30, 2009.

Chaudhuri, Amit. *St. Cyril Road and Other Poems*. New Delhi: Penguin India, 2005.

Coetzee, J. M. *Diary of a Bad Year*. London: Harvill Secker, 2007.

Cotter, Holland. "The Collective Conscious," *New York Times*, May 5, 2006.

Critical Art Ensemble. *Marching Plague: Germ Warfare and Global Public Health*. New York: Autonomedia, 2006.

Danner, Mark. "Tales from Torture's Dark World," *New York Times*, March 14, 2009.

———. "U.S. Torture: Voices from the Black Sites," *New York Review of Books*, April 9, 2009.

DeLillo, Don. *Falling Man*. New York: Scribner, 2007.

Eggen, Dan, and Julie Tate. "U.S. Campaign Produces Few Convictions on Terror Charges." *Washington Post*, June 12, 2005.

Eisenman, Stephen F. *The Abu Ghraib Effect*. London: Reaktion Books, 2007.

Enwezor, Okwui. "The Unhomely: Phantom Scenes in Global Society." Biennial of Seville (BIACS). Catalog statement available at http://www.theartists.org/artistsblog/posts/st_content_001.cfm?id=1612.

"Ex-G.I. Writes about Use of Sex in Guantánamo Interrogations," Associated Press, *New York Times*, January 25, 2005.

Farocki, Harun. *War at a Distance*. Chicago: Video Data Bank, 2003.

Foer, Jonathan Safran. *Extremely Loud and Incredibly Close*. New York: Houghton Mifflin, 2005.

Fusco, Coco. *A Field Guide for Female Interrogators*. New York: Seven Stories Press, 2008.

Gilani, Iftikhar. *My Days in Prison*. New Delhi: Penguin Books, 2005.

Gladwell, Malcolm. "Troublemakers: What Pit Bulls Can Teach Us about Profiling," *The New Yorker*, February 6, 2006.

Goldstone, Carly. "The Ft. Dix Fix Was In," *The Daily Beast*, December 22, 2008. Online at http://www.thedailybeast.com/blogs-and-stories/2008-12-22/the-ft-dix-fix-was-in/2/.

Gourevitch, Philip, and Errol Morris. "Exposure," *The New Yorker*, March 24, 2008.

———. *Standard Operating Procedure*. New York: Penguin, 2008.

Greenwald, Glenn. "What Every American Should Be Made to Learn about the IG Torture Report," *Salon.com*, August 24, 2009. Online at http://www.salon.com/opinion/greenwald/2009/08/24/ig_report/.

Grey, Stephen. *Ghost Plane*. New York: St. Martin's Press, 2006.

Guru, Tabassum. "A Wife's Appeal for Justice," *Kashmir Times*, October 21, 2004.

Hamid, Mohsin. *The Reluctant Fundamentalist*. New York: Harcourt, 2007.

Hany Abu-Assad, dir. *Paradise Now*. Warner Independent Pictures, 2005.

Harcourt, Bernard E. "Muslim Profiles Post 9/11: Is Racial Profiling an Effective Counterterrorist Measure and Does It Violate the Right to Be Free from Discrimination?," Public Law and Legal Theory Working Paper, no. 123, March 2006. Online at http://ssrn.com/abstract=893905.

Harding, Luke. "Sting on a shoetring," *Guardian*, March 21, 2001.

Hare, David. *Stuff Happens*. London: Faber, 2004.

Herbeck, Dan, and Lou Michel. "An Information Gap: Months of Debriefings with the Men Who Spent Time with an Al-Qaida Training Camp Have Yielded 'Nothing Earth-Shattering' about Osama Bin Laden or His Organization," *Buffalo News*, October 15, 2003.

Herr, Michael. *Dispatches*. New York: Knopf, 1977.

Hoyt, Mike, John Palattella, and the staff of the *Columbia Journalism Review*. *Reporting Iraq: An Oral History of the War by the Journalists Who Covered It*. Hoboken, N.J.: Melville House, 2007.

Huq, Aziz. "Policing Terror, Policing Islam: Federal Criminal Law Enforcement, Counter-terrorism and America's Muslim Minority Communities." In *Liberty Under Attack: Reclaiming Our Freedoms in an Age of Terror*, ed. Richard C. Leone and Greg Anrig Jr. New York: Public Affairs, 2007.

"'Inhumane' CIA Terror Tactics Spur Criminal Probe," *The Huffington Post*, August 24, 2009. http://www.huffingtonpost.com/2009/08/24/holder-to-appoint-special_n_267385.html.

"Interrogation Log Detainee 063." Online at http://ccrjustice.org/files/Publication_AlQahtaniLog.pdf.

Isikoff, Michael. "Investigators: The FBI says, Count the Mosques," *Newsweek*, February 3, 2003. Online at http://www.newsweek.com/id/62965.

Iype, George, "Here in India, I get respect and peace of mind," *India Abroad*, September 8, 2006.

Jabès, Edmond. *A Foreigner Carrying in the Crook of His Arm a Tiny Book*. Translated by Rosemarie Waldrop. Hanover, N.H.: Wesleyan University Press, 1993.

Jehl, Douglas. "Report Warned Bush Team about Intelligence Doubts," *New York Times*, November 6, 2005.

Johnston, David. "U.S. Says Rendition to Continue, but with More Oversight," *New York Times*, August 24, 2009.

Kang, Jerry. "Thinking through Internment 12/7 and 9/11." *Amerasia Journal* 27, no. 3 (2001); 28, no. 1 (2002).

Khetan Ashish. "Karachi to Mumbai: Terror, Step by Step." In *26/11 Mumbai Attacked*, ed. Harinder Baweja. New Delhi: Roli Books, 2009.

Le Carré, John. *A Most Wanted Man*. New York: Scribner, 2008.

Levin, Michael. "The Case for Torture," *Newsweek*, June 7, 1982.

Lewis, Judith. "From Baghdad to Buffalo: The Saga of Steven Kurtz's Bacteria," *L.A. Weekly*, July 15, 2004.

Lindh, Frank. "Taking the Stand," *Washington Lawyer*, May 2005.

MacKenzie, Debora. "Plague of Bioweapons Accidents Afflicts the U.S." NewScientist.com news service, July 5, 2007.

Magid, Jill. *Lincoln Ocean Victor Eddy*, 2007. Online at http://www.lincoln-ocean-victor-eddy.net/.

Marc Falkoff, ed. *Poems from Guantánamo: The Detainees Speak*. Iowa City: University of Iowa Press, 2007.

Margulies, Joseph. *Guantánamo and the Abuse of Presidential Power*. New York: Simon and Schuster, 2006.

Mayer, Jane. *The Dark Side*. New York: Doubleday, 2008.

Mazetti, Mark, and David Johnston. "Bush Weighed Using Military in Arrests," *New York Times*, July 24, 2009.

Mazzetti, Mark, and Scott Shane. "Interrogation Memos Detail Harsh Tactics by the C.I.A.," *New York Times*, April 16, 2009.

———. "Investigation Is Ordered into C.I.A. Abuse Charges," *New York Times*, August 25, 2009.

McCoy, Alfred. *A Question of Torture*. New York: Metropolitan Books, 2006.

McDermott, Terry. *Perfect Soldiers*. New York: HarperCollins, 2005.

McDougall, Dan. "I Didn't Recognize the Person on Fire. I Didn't Recognize Him as My Son," *The Observer*, July 8, 2007.

McEwan, Ian. *Saturday*. New York: Doubleday, 2005.

Meet the Press. News program, September 16, 2001. Transcript available at http://www.washingtonpost.com/wp-srv/nation/attacked/transcripts/cheney091601.html.

Messud, Claire. *The Emperor's Children*. New York: Alfred A. Knopf, 2006.

Miller, Arthur. *Death of a Salesman*. New York: Viking Penguin, 1949.

Mishra, Pankaj. "The End of Innocence," *The Guardian*, May 19, 2007.

Mitchell, Luke. "We Still Torture," *Harper's Magazine*, July 2009, 49–55.

Mukherji, Nirmalangshu. *December 13: Terror over Democracy*. New Delhi: Promilla and Company and Bibliophile South Asia, 2005.

Naipaul, V. S. *An Area of Darkness*. New York: Vintage, 1964.

Nandy, Ashis. "The Other 9/11," *Outlook*, September 18, 2006.

The 9/11 Commission Report: Final Report of the National Commission on Terrorist Attacks upon the United States. New York: W. W. Norton and Company, 2004.

Norton-Taylor, Richard. "Guantánamo Is Gulag of Our Time, Says Amnesty," *The Guardian*, May 26, 2005.

Obama, Barack. "Renewing American Leadership." *Foreign Affairs* 86, no. 4 (July–August 2007): 2–26.

O'Hagan, Andrew. "Iraq, 2 May 2005," *London Review of Books*, March 6, 2008.

Operation Duryodhana. Online at http://www.cobrapost.com/documents/one .htm.

Operation West End. Online at http://www.tehelka.com/channels/Investigation/ investigation1.htm.

Paglen, Trevor, and A. C. Thompson. *Torture-Taxi: On the Trail of the CIA's Rendition Flights*. Hoboken, N.J.: Melville House Publishing, 2006.

Pamuk, Orhan. "The Anger of the Damned," *New York Review of Books*, November 15, 2001.

———. *Istanbul*. New York: Alfred A. Knopf, 2005.

Passaro, Vince. "Dangerous Don DeLillo," *New York Times*, May 19, 1991.

Peer, Basharat. "Papa-2," *n + 1*, no. 5 (winter 2007).

Pentecost, Claire. "Reflections on the Case by the U.S. Justice Department against Steven Kurtz and Robert Ferrell." In *Marching Plague: Germ Warfare and Global Public Health*, ed. Critical Art Ensemble. New York: Autonomedia, 2006.

Powell, Michael. "No Choice but Guilty: Lackawanna Case Highlights Legal Tilt," *Washington Post*, July 29, 2003.

Purdy, Matthew, and Lowell Bergman. "Where the Trail Led: Between Evidence and Suspicion; Unclear Danger: Inside the Lackawanna Terror Case," *New York Times*, October 12, 2003.

Raban, Jonathan. *Surveillance*. New York: Pantheon Books, 2006.

Rashbaum, William K. "Guilty Verdict in Plot to Bomb Subway Station," *New York Times*, May 25, 2006.

Rashbaum, William K., and Kareem Fahim. "Informer's Role in Bombing Plot," *New York Times*, May 23, 2009.

Rashid, Ahmed. *Taliban*. New Haven, Conn.: Yale University Press, 2001.

Rayman, Graham. "F.B.I. Agent on Synagogue Case Has Questionable Record," May 21, 2009. Online at http://blogs.villagevoice.com/runninscared/ archives/2009/05/the_fbi_agent_w.php.

Report on Guantánamo Detainees. Online at http://law.shu.edu/ ProgramsCenters/PublicIntGovServ/CSJ/Guantanamo-Reports.cfm.

Ripley, Amanda. "The Fort Dix Conspiracy," *Time*, Dec 6, 2007. Online at http://www.time.com/time/nation/article/0,8599,1691609,00.html.

Riverbend. *Baghdad Burning: Girl Blog from Iraq*. New York: Feminist Press at the City University of New York, 2005.

———. *Baghdad Burning II: Girl Blog from Iraq*. New York: Feminist Press at the City University of New York, 2006.

Rose, David. *Guantánamo: The War on Human Rights*. New York: New Press, 2005.

———. "Tortured Reasoning," *Vanity Fair*, December 16, 2008. Online at http://www.vanityfair.com/magazine/2008/12/torture200812.

Roy, Arundhati. "The Algebra of Infinite Justice." *The Guardian*, September 29, 2001.

———. "And His Life Should Become Extinct." In *13 December: A Reader*. New Delhi: Penguin Books India, 2006

———. Introduction to *13 December: A Reader*. New Delhi: Penguin Books India, 2006.

———. "Who Pulled the Trigger . . . Didn't We All?," *Outlook*, February 28, 2005.

Roychoudhuri, Omnesha. "Secret CIA Prisons in Your Backyard." Interview with Trevor Paglen and A. C. Thompson. Posted September 22, 2006. Online at http://www.alternet.org/story/41923.

Rumsfeld, Donald. Department of Defense news briefing, Feb. 12, 2002.

Saar, Erik, and Viveca Novak. *Inside the Wire: A Military Intelligence Soldier's Eyewitness Account of Life at Guantanamo*. New York: Penguin, 2005.

Saltz, Jerry. "You There! Welcome to Donald Rumsfeld's War Machine," *Village Voice*, April 7, 2006.

Sartre, Jean-Paul. Preface to *The Question* [1958] by Henri Alleg. Lincoln: University of Nebraska Press, 2006.

Savage, Charlie. "To Critics, Obama's Terror Policy Looks a Lot Like Bush's," *New York Times*, July 2, 2009, A14.

Scahill, Jeremy. *Blackwater: The Rise of the World's Most Powerful Mercenary Army*. New York: Nation Books, 2007.

Sengupta, Shuddhabrata. "Media Trials and Courtroom Tribulations." In *13 December: A Reader*. New Delhi: Penguin Books India, 2006.

Sengupta, Somini. "Dossier Gives Details of Mumbai attacks," *New York Times*, January 6, 2009. Online at http://www.nytimes.com/2009/01/07/world/asia/07india.html.

Sifton, John. "Temporal Vertigo." *New York Times Sunday Magazine*, September 30, 2001.

Silber, Mitchell D., and Arvin Bhatt. "Radicalization in the West: The Homegrown Threat." New York: NYPD Intelligence Division, August 2007.

Smith, Clive Stafford. *Bad Men*. London: Weidenfeld and Nicolson, 2007.

Sontag, Deborah. "Videotape Offers a Window into a Terror Suspect's Isolation," *New York Times*, December 4, 2006.

Sontag, Susan. *Regarding the Pain of Others*. New York: Picador, 2004.

Specogna, Heidi. *The Short Life of José Antonio Gutierrez*. Film released in North America by Atopia Distribution, 2006.

Stein, Sam. "Civil Libertarian Rips Obama's Speech: All Bells and Whistles," *The Huffington Post*, May 21, 2009. Online at http://www.huffingtonpost.com/2009/05/21/civil-libertarian-rips-ob_n_206343.html.

Swofford, Anthony. *Jarhead*. New York: Scribner, 2003.

Temple-Raston, Dina. *The Jihad Next Door*. New York: PublicAffairs, 2007.

Thomas, Evan, and Michael Hirsh. "The Debate Over Torture," *Newsweek*, November 21, 2005.

Transactional Records Access Clearinghouse (TRAC). "Criminal Terrorism Enforcement Since the 9/11/01 Attacks," December 8, 2003. Online at http://trac.syr.edu/tracreports/terrorism/report031208.html. Updated on September 4, 2006: http://trac.syr.edu/tracreports/terrorism/169/.

Updike, John. *Terrorist*. New York: Alfred A. Knopf, 2006.

Vidmar, Neil. "Trial by Jury Involving Persons Accused of Terrorism or Supporting Terrorism." Duke Law School Legal Studies, Research Paper Series, no. 129, October 2006. Online at http://ssrn.com/abstract=934792.

Wieseltier, Leon. "The Catastrophist," *New York Times Book Review*, April 27, 2008.

Wilson, Michael. "In Bronx Bomb Case, Missteps Caught on Tape," *New York Times*, May 22, 2009.

Wood, Michael. "At the Movies," *London Review of Books*, January 25, 2007.

Wright, Lawrence. *The Looming Tower: Al-Qaeda and the Road to 9/11*. New York: Alfred A. Knopf, 2006.

Wypijewski, JoAnn. "Living in an Age of Fire," *Mother Jones*, March/April 2003. Online at http://www.motherjones.com/politics/2003/03/living-age-fire.

Yagoda, Ben. "*The 9/11 Commission Report*: How a Government Committee Made a Piece of Literature," *Slate*, November 8, 2004. Online at http://www.slate.com/id/2109277/.

Yasmeen, Afshan. "Please Pray for Us, Says Kafeel's Mother," *The Hindu*, July 6, 2007.

Yee, James, and Aimee Molloy. *For God and Country: Faith and Patriotism Under Fire*. New York: PublicAffairs, 2005.

Zagorin, Adam, and Michael Duffy. "Inside the Interrogation of Detainee 063," *Time*, June 12, 2005.

Zaidi, S. Hussain. *Black Friday: The True Story of the Bombay Bomb Blasts*. New Delhi: Penguin Books India, 2002.

Zaitchik, Alexander. "Aniruddha Bahal: The King of Sting," *The Independent*, July 16, 2007.

✳ Index

Human Rights Watch, 6
Humiliation, 57, 103, 150
Huntington, Samuel, 96
Huq, Aziz, 132–33
Hussain, Shahed, 52
Hussain, Shaukat, 143–44

"Illegal combatants." *See* "Enemy combatants"
Imagination: hate as failure of, 66–67; need for Americans to use their, 94–95; of terrorists, 68
Imperial Life in the Emerald City (Chandrasekaran), 142
India, 37; anti-terrorism courts in, 1, 15; corruption in, 59–60, 63; and Kashmir, 141–61; Pakistan's relations with, 24; police in, 1–5, 15–25, 61; Right to Information Act in, 63; sting operations in, 60–64; terrorism in, xii–xiv, 1, 13–19, 24–25, 36, 97, 143–44, 146, 180–83; torture by, 3–5, 9, 20–23, 97, 142–43, 151, 153, 161; U.S. immigrants from, 11–12, 132; 1984 violence in, 181; War on Terror's effects on, 97–98. *See also* Channel Four; *Specific places in*
Indianapolis (Indiana), 53–54
Informants: creation of, by state officials, 141–50, 158–61; as criminals and victims, 10–11, 42–45, 52–53, 178, 179–80; as instigators of "terrorist" crimes, 11, 34–36, 40, 52, 54–55, 111–18, 122–26, 133–35, 177; payments to, 11, 38, 40, 41, 43–45, 52, 53, 70, 111, 124, 128, 130, 170; state narratives about, 18–19; suicides of, 53. *See also* Entrapment; *Specific informants*
Inside the Wire (Saar and Novak), 103–4
Intelligence. *See* CIA; FBI
Interrogations: by CIA, 6–7, 72; by FBI, 6, 28–29; at Guantánamo, 104–6; by Indian police, 3–5, 15, 18–24; Obama on, 8, 9; training for, 74–75. *See also* Torture
Inter-Services Intelligence (ISI-Pakistan), 62, 180, 181
Intimacy, 77–78
Iran, 95
"Iraq, 2 May 2005" (O'Hagan), 101
Iraq War, 107, 127, 130, 142; art about, 79–82; human cost of, as crime, 183–

86; motivations for, 6–7; Muslim revenge for, 111, 112, 177; as September 11, 2001 attacks consequence, 5, 89, 92–93, 95, 97
IRA terrorism, 87
Ishii Shiro, 163
ISI (Pakistani Inter-Services Intelligence), 62, 180, 181
Islam. *See* Muslim(s)
Islamic Books and Tapes (Bay Ridge book store), 112, 120–23
Isle of Lewis (Scotland), 164
Israel, 131, 149–50
Istanbul (Pamuk), 148–49
Ivory (stripper), 48–49

Jaal (film), 14
Jaish-e-Mohammed (terrorist group), 19
Jalal, Abu, 4–7, 10
Jamaica, 177
Jammu (Kashmir), 141–42
Japan, 163–64; U.S. immigrants from, 132
Jarhead (Swofford), 99–100, 103
Jashn-e-Azadi (film), 148, 149
Jews, 49, 51, 123; dressing like, 114, 115
Jihad Next Door (Temple-Raston), 174
Joint Terrorism Task Force, 166, 170, 179, 180
Journalism. *See* Media
Jury practices, 70, 126–30
Justice: courts as lacking competency to administer, xi; and jury practices, 70, 126–30; limitations of American system of, 10; Lindh's father on, 137; punitive action vs., 172–73; torture as destroying possibility of, 7–9. *See also* Arrests; Detention; Entrapment; Law; Lawyers; Military commissions; Payments; Terrorists
Justice Department (U.S.), 102, 111, 133, 138, 168, 182–83

Kaczynski, Theodore, 137
Kak, Sanjay, 148, 149
Kasab, Ajmal, 18–19
Kashmir, 59, 141–61, 181. *See also* Kashmir Valley
"Kashmir" (Buchan), 151
Kashmir Times, 145
Kashmir Valley, 21–23, 142
Kashyap, Anurag, 14

San Jose State University (California), 26
Santos, José Eduardo dos, 39
Sarfarosh (film), 14
Sartre, Jean Paul, 145
SAVAK, 95
Schroeder, H. Kenneth, 172
Scotland, 87, 89, 133, 164
Second Plane, The (Amis), 98–99
Second World War, 98, 132
Secrecy (as War on Terror aspect), 66, 67–68
Security Series (art exhibit), 83, 87
Senate Armed Forces Committee (U.S.), 26
Senegal, 28
Sengupta, Shuddhabrata, 14
September 11, 2001 attacks: global changes since, xi, 24–25, 64–65, 89, 172, 175–76, 181, 183; hijackers in, 53, 98–99, 104, 124; jury questions regarding, 127, 130; law enforcement's failures regarding, 53, 55; literature of, 4–5, 75–79, 83–89, 92–107; registration requirements for U.S. Muslims after, 177, 181; success of, from terrorists' point of view, 87, 89; "terrorist" cases after, xi, xii, 33–51, 54–58, 64, 89, 111–40, 162–78; and U.S. views of Taliban, 137–38. *See also* Fear; *9/11 Commission Report*; Surveillance state; War on Terror; World Trade Center
Seton Hall Law School, 25–26
Seville Biennial 2006, 67
Sexual abuse (of women), 60. *See also* Rape
Shafi (driver), 146–47
Shah, Mona, 120
Shah Jahan, 154
Shambroom, Paul, 83, 85–89
Sheikh, Ahmad Omar Saeed, 20
Sherman v. United States, 53
Shiv Sena (Hindu party), 2
Shnewer, Mohamed, 11
Shrivastava, Aditya, 16, 19
Sifton, John, xi, 96–97
Sikhs, 181
Simple Case for Torture, or How to Sleep at Night, A (film), 81–82
Singh, Dravinder, 146
Singh, Harjit, 179–81
Singh, Rajbir, 23

Siraj, Saniya, 120, 122, 135
Siraj, Shahawar Matin: as accidental terrorist, xii, 111–40, 177, 178; family of, 113, 116, 118–20, 122, 133–35; letters written by, 133–35
Slate, 93
Slim Shady (Eminem), 72
Smith, Jacqui, 89
Soldiers: and "collateral damage" of war, 183–86; depictions of, in art, 82–83; narratives of, 99–101, 103–4; as scapegoats, 78–79, 103
Somalia, 95
Sontag, Susan, 177
Sopore (Kashmir), 143, 146–48
Spann, Mike, 139
Special Task Force (STF), 145–46, 161
Springfield (Missouri), 46, 48–49
Srinagar (Kashmir), 141–44, 146, 149–61
Srivardhan (Indian), 2, 3
Standard Operating Procedure (Gourevitch and Morris), 78, 102–3
State Department (U.S.), 138, 173
Staten Island, 112, 123–25
Stereotypes, 13–29, 98–99, 128–29, 131–33, 171–78
Stewart, Jon, 139–40
Stewart, Lynne, 69–71
Stewart, Rory, 96
STF (Special Task Force), 145–46, 161
Sting operations, 58–65, 147, 179–82
Stolar, Martin, 116, 117, 130, 131
Strange Culture (film), 168–69
Stuff Happens (Hare), 92
Suicide bombings, 125, 130–31
Sumbal (Kashmir), 142–43
Supreme Court (India), 144
Supreme Court (U.S.), 26, 132
Surveillance (Raban), 83, 85, 87–89
Surveillance state (anti-terrorism state): artists and writers on, xi, 66–91, 167–69; bungling by, xii; and counter-terrorism evaluations, 176–77; as creating then punishing crimes allegedly associated with terrorism, 33–57, 111–40; difference between, and individuals, 81; fear's role in, 162–63, 165–69, 171, 175, 177; in Kashmir, 144–45, 160; protecting oneself from, 26–29; unconstitutional actions by, 7–10, 24, 63–65, 67–68,

whole world as homeland of, 183; world anger toward, 56–57, 94–95. *See also* Constitution; Detention; Payments; Rendition; Surveillance state; Terrorists; War on Terror; *Specific officials, departments, agencies, and wars of*

United States v. Arnold L. Hollingsworth Jr. and William A. Pickard III, 54

United States v. Hemant Lakhani, 33–58

University of California-Berkeley, 71

University of Pittsburgh, 166, 167

University of South Florida, 129

Up Airways, 47–48

Updike, John, 98

USA Today, 53, 56

Vidmar, Neil, 128–30

Vietnam War, 79, 95, 100

Village Voice, 52

Voir dire, 126–30

Wachtler, Saul, 166

Walavati (India), 1–4

Wallerstein, Immanuel, 83

War: as a disaster, 183–86; narratives about, 99, 100; need to banish, 107; opposition to, 166–67. *See also* Soldiers; *Specific wars, including* War on Terror

War at a Distance (film), 136

War on Terror, 127; all of us as participants in, 67, 75; artists and writers on, xi, 66–107; civil rights consequences of, 7–10, 12, 24, 63–65, 67–68, 175–76; as diverting attention from greater horror of Iraq War, 186; as diverting money from natural disaster relief, 86; families as collateral damage in, 3–4, 133–36, 143–50; fear's use in, 162–63, 165–69, 171, 175, 177; global effects of, 97–98; narratives about, 4–5, 11, 18–19, 24–25, 93–107; as permanent state, 24; question of efficacy of, 182; secrecy associated with, 66, 67–68; state's creating then punishing crimes

allegedly associated with, 33–57, 111–40. *See also* Afghanistan; Al Qaeda; Detention; "Enemy combatants"; Iraq War; September 11, 2001; Soldiers; Stereotypes; Surveillance state; Terrorists; Torture

Washington Lawyer, 137

Washington Post, 6, 182

Waterboarding, 7, 8, 10

Weapons of mass destruction: biological, 6–7, 162–70; fears about, 89, 162–63; and New York subway bombing "conspiracy," 111–15, 120–21, 135. *See also* Weapons sales

Weapons sales, 35–41, 49, 52, 54–55; sting operations regarding, 58–65; by United States, 181

Whitney Biennial, 163

Wieseltier, Leon, 96

"Wife's Appeal for Justice, A" (T. Guru), 145

Wing, Carlin, 82

Women: abuse of, 60, 61, 63; men's attitudes toward, 153, 154–56; use of, in torture, 73–76, 103. *See also* Rape

Wood, Michael, 99

World Trade Center, 35, 69–70, 102, 127, 172. *See also* September 11, 2001 attacks

Wypijewski, JoAnn, 170, 175

Yagoda, Ben, 93–94

Yamayoshi, Chie, 83–84

Yemen, 136, 171–76

Yoo, John, 10, 102

York College (City University of New York), 71

Yousef, Ramzi, 137

Yousry, Mohamed, 71

Yugoslavia, 95

Zachary, Tad, 85

Zaidi, S. Hussain, 17

Zimbabwe, 25

Zubaydah, Abu, 7, 10

Amitava Kumar is a professor of English at Vassar College.
He is the author of *Nobody Does the Right Thing* (2010), also
published by Duke University Press; *Home Products* (2007);
*Husband of a Fanatic: A Personal Journey through India,
Pakistan, Love and Hate* (2005); *Bombay—London—New
York* (2002); and *Passport Photos* (2000). He is the editor of
Away: The Indian Writer as Expatriate (2004); *World Bank
Literature* (2003); *The Humor and Pity: Essays on V. S. Naipaul*
(2002); *Poetics/Politics: Radical Aesthetics for the Classroom*
(1999); and *Class Issues: Pedagogy, Cultural Studies, and the
Public Sphere* (1997).

Library of Congress Cataloging-in-Publication Data
Kumar, Amitava, 1963–
A foreigner carrying in the crook of his arm a tiny bomb /
Amitava Kumar.
p. cm.
Includes bibliographical references and index.
ISBN 978-0-8223-4562-6 (cloth : alk. paper)
ISBN 978-0-8223-4578-7 (pbk. : alk. paper)
1. Terrorism. 2. Terrorists. 3. War on Terrorism, 2001–
I. Title.
HV6431.K84 2010
363.325—dc22   2009049958